D1441968

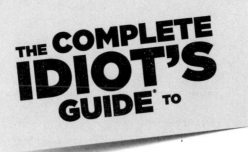

Swimming

by Mike Bottom and Nathan Jendrick

ALPHA

A member of Penguin Group (USA) Inc.

ALPHA BOOKS

Published by the Penguin Group

Penguin Group (USA) Inc., 375 Hudson Street, New York, New York 10014, USA

Penguin Group (Canada), 90 Eglinton Avenue East, Suite 700, Toronto, Ontario M4P 2Y3, Canada (a division of Pearson Penguin Canada Inc.)

Penguin Books Ltd., 80 Strand, London WC2R 0RL, England

Penguin Ireland, 25 St. Stephen's Green, Dublin 2, Ireland (a division of Penguin Books Ltd.)

Penguin Group (Australia), 250 Camberwell Road, Camberwell, Victoria 3124, Australia (a division of Pearson Australia Group Pty. Ltd.)

Penguin Books India Pvt. Ltd., 11 Community Centre, Panchsheel Park, New Delhi—110 017, India

Penguin Group (NZ), 67 Apollo Drive, Rosedale, North Shore, Auckland 1311, New Zealand (a division of Pearson New Zealand Ltd.)

Penguin Books (South Africa) (Pty.) Ltd., 24 Sturdee Avenue, Rosebank, Johannesburg 2196, South Africa

Penguin Books Ltd., Registered Offices: 80 Strand, London WC2R 0RL, England

Copyright © 2011 by Mike Bottom and Nathan Jendrick

International Standard Book Number: 978-159257-965-5
Library of Congress Catalog Card Number: 2010913760

13   12   11   8   7   6   5   4   3   2   1

Interpretation of the printing code: The rightmost number of the first series of numbers is the year of the book's printing; the rightmost number of the second series of numbers is the number of the book's printing. For example, a printing code of 11-1 shows that the first printing occurred in 2011.

Printed in the United States of America

Note: This publication contains the opinions and ideas of its authors. It is intended to provide helpful and informative material on the subject matter covered. It is sold with the understanding that the authors and publisher are not engaged in rendering professional services in the book. If the reader requires personal assistance or advice, a competent professional should be consulted.

The authors and publisher specifically disclaim any responsibility for any liability, loss, or risk, personal or otherwise, which is incurred as a consequence, directly or indirectly, of the use and application of any of the contents of this book.

Most Alpha books are available at special quantity discounts for bulk purchases for sales promotions, premiums, fund-raising, or educational use. Special books, or book excerpts, can also be created to fit specific needs.

For details, write: Special Markets, Alpha Books, 375 Hudson Street, New York, NY 10014.

Publisher: *Marie Butler-Knight*

Associate Publisher: *Mike Sanders*

Senior Managing Editor: *Billy Fields*

Senior Acquisitions Editor: *Paul Dinas*

Development Editor: *Lynn Northrup*

Senior Production Editor: *Janette Lynn*

Copy Editor: *Lisanne V. Jensen*

Cover Designer: *Rebecca Batchelor*

Book Designers: *William Thomas, Rebecca Batchelor*

Indexer: *Tonya Heard*

Layout: *Brian Massey*

Proofreader: *John Etchison*

To my mother, who has supported my swimming for over 45 years with the attitude that when I am happy about a race, this is good, and if not, a full plate of her spaghetti and meat sauce will always make me feel better; and to the late George Haines, whose innovative and caring coaching has motivated me to be a better man.

—Mike Bottom

Contents

Appendixes

Introduction

You may have heard the expression, "The best things in life are free." It may be hard to believe, but in some cases it really is true. You can flip through magazines or television channels and never run short of people trying to sell you something "guaranteed" to give you that happier, healthier life you've been searching for. And if you search the Internet, there's no shortage of people reviewing these very same products and telling you, "If it seems too good to be true, it probably is."

But here's a secret: you really *can* be happier, healthier, and live a longer life—for free. No three easy payments, no shipping and handling, and no five-step process or timeshare presentation required. You can do it just through your own efforts. It's called swimming. Whether you prefer a pool, a river, a lake, or even the ocean, you can use this practical, easy-to-learn skill to clear your mind, get the body you have always wanted, and maybe even one day save a life.

Mankind has always needed water for survival, but it wasn't until the last century or so that people started trying to master it with their bodies instead of with boats. Walking and running have remained largely the same over the course of history, but swimming as both a means of recreation as well as a sport has experienced significant changes as we learned and developed easier, faster ways to move through the water. And over that same period of time, doctors and health advocates learned that the act of swimming is one of the most beneficial things you can do for your body. In fact, more and more studies come out each year promoting how wonderful swimming is for good health. And these benefits aren't relegated to any particular age group or gender; they are there for the taking for anyone who wants them. Swimming is as beneficial for a first-grader as it is for a centenarian and can also be a beneficial addition to an athlete's training program, providing muscular stimulus not possible through other forms of exercise.

People of all activity levels can also benefit from swimming. That means whether you currently run marathons on a regular basis or haven't exercised in 30 years, you can still hop in the pool on this very day and start changing your life for the better. *Note, supervision of a lifeguard or lifeguard-certified coach is required when engaging in any and all training regimens mentioned in this book.*

Swimming is low-impact, gentle on the body, fun, and a great workout. It's also a lifesaving skill. According to USA Swimming's Make a Splash water-safety initiative, nine people drown every day in the United States. Imagine being able to better your life and potentially one day save someone else's through a single skill. We are here to help you achieve your goals physically and mentally through swimming. When you look good, you feel good—and when you feel good, all things are possible. So let's hit the pool!

How This Book Is Organized

The book contains 18 chapters organized under five parts. Use this book in the way that works best for you—you can read it through from the beginning, or pick and choose chapters you're particularly interested in. You'll also find three appendixes: a glossary of swimming terms, a helpful list of online resources, and brief bios for the swimming pros who contributed to this book.

Part 1, Get with the Wet Set, explains the many health benefits you'll receive from taking part in a regular swimming program. We'll explain the science that proves the benefits of what you're about to dive into, the atmosphere around pools and what all the different markings and notations mean, and how to pick the suit and accessories that fit you best.

Part 2, Taking the Plunge: The Basic Strokes, details the four primary swimming strokes: freestyle, backstroke, breaststroke, and butterfly. We'll break down each part of the stroke and show you the correct technique. You'll be swimming like a pro in no time!

Part 3, Starts and Turns, discusses the proper and quickest way to enter the water and the best way to move from one stroke to another, no matter which stroke you're swimming or which stroke you want to do next.

Part 4, Train Smart, covers a variety of training techniques, strength training, drills, and tools that will put you on the road toward quick results and further build your confidence and skills in the pool.

Part 5, What Else to Know, fills you in on all the "in-between" stuff, from the best methods to combat chlorine-damaged hair to the best way to fuel up for your next training session. And if you're interested in pursuing your passion and finding a Masters swim team, we'll tell you how to do that, too.

Extras

In addition to useful advice and information, you'll find four different types of sidebars sprinkled throughout these chapters:

SINK OR SWIM

These sidebars warn you of common mistakes, misconceptions, and dangers you might run into as you train. Pay attention to these boxes to prevent any dangerous or uncomfortable situations in the water.

FUN FACTS

These sidebars contain trivia, history, and other facts from the aquatic world!

THE PROS KNOW

Check these sidebars for tips from professional athletes, Olympic gold medalists, and other pros to make your learning fast, fun, and safe.

DEFINITION

Swimming is full of terms that are specific to the sport; these sidebars will tell you what certain words mean and make you feel like a veteran before you ever step into a pool.

Acknowledgments

I want to thank my wife Lauralyn for providing the supportive base that allows me the freedom to be creative and dedicated to fast swimming.

—Mike Bottom

Many thanks to everyone behind the scenes who have been supportive and helped make this book possible: Don Anderson, David Arluck, all of our athlete and professional contributors, Paul Dinas and the entire Alpha Books team, Lynn Northrup, and, of course, my wife and always my first editor, Megan Jendrick.

—Nathan Jendrick

Trademarks

All terms mentioned in this book that are known to be or are suspected of being trademarks or service marks have been appropriately capitalized. Alpha Books and Penguin Group (USA) Inc. cannot attest to the accuracy of this information. Use of a term in this book should not be regarded as affecting the validity of any trademark or service mark.

Get with the Wet Set

The health benefits you'll receive from taking part in a regular swimming program are numerous. You will begin to notice them quickly, both by looking in the mirror and in assessing how you feel every day. And these health benefits don't go away when you leave the pool—they stick with you everywhere you go. All it takes is some solid effort and basic knowledge to start unlocking the fortunes given by this wonderful form of exercise. This part will make you feel like a pro before you even take that first exciting step onto the pool deck. We'll explain the science that proves the benefits of what you're about to dive into, the atmosphere around pools and what all the different markings and notations mean, as well as how to pick the suit and accessories that fit you best. Anyone can learn to swim—and in this part, we'll show you how.

Learn to Swim at Any Age

In This Chapter

- How swimming benefits both body and mind
- Swimming as a social sport
- The importance of setting goals
- Letting go of your fears
- Finding lessons no matter your age
- How to find a suitable swim team

With people older than 100 still competing in organized competitions, age can never be used as an excuse to keep you from learning how to swim. Everyone has a first lesson—even swimming greats such as Olympians Michael Phelps and Ian Thorpe—and yours can be just days away. It's never too late to start, and it has also never been easier to do it.

The key to learning to swim, or improving your skills to a more comfortable level, is finding the right teacher. That teacher doesn't have to be someone else, though; you may be your own best instructor. With help from resources such as this book, you're already on track toward a happier, healthier future. But if you need additional assistance, don't be afraid to ask.

Adults asking for swim lessons are not unique or even rare occurrences. It happens every day, all over the world. Swimming is a fantastic method of exercise and a great life skill, and people of all ages are urged to get involved—and they're doing it every day. Swim schools, universities, community pools, and even individual instructors are offering their knowledge to help you learn. Like any skill, you have to take the initiative to get involved and get going—and once you do, you'll realize what a wonderful decision you made.

What the Experts Say

In case you need some extra incentive, science has proven that the sooner you start swimming, the better! Let's take a look at some studies:

- A 2009 study from the University of South Carolina, which was later published in the *International Journal of Aquatic Research and Education*, found that swimming can cut in half the risk of men dying as compared to competitors in other sports. Swimmers were shown to have a significantly lower rate of mortality and a significantly increased level of cardio-respiratory fitness.

- Research published by Wiley-Blackwell in 2009 showed that within just six weeks, children with asthma had reduced symptoms after taking a regular swimming program. The children in the study showed significant improvements in all kinds of clinical measures, including symptoms, doctor's office and hospital visits, and even school absenteeism.

- A study published in the *Journal of the American Academy of Orthopedic Surgeons* (JAAOS) in 2009 found that physicians should be encouraged to recommend moderate exercise to expecting mothers even if they've never exercised before. The study found pregnant patients benefited from activities such as swimming, which reduced back and muscle pain, lowered maternal blood pressure, improved mood, and reduced swelling. All these benefits came with no risk increases to the mother or unborn baby.

The amount of research that shows swimming as a beneficial activity to human health spans every race and gender, from young children to the elderly. Now that you know it's one of the best things you can do for your mind and body, let's start getting you the vital information and skills necessary to take advantage of these amazing benefits!

FUN FACTS

The oldest swimmer to ever win an Olympic swimming medal is Great Britain's William Henry, who did so in 1906 at age 47.

The Effects of Exercise on the Brain

We know exercise, especially swimming, is great for the body. The number of benefits, ranging from improved cardiovascular health to improved body composition, are just too numerous to name. But what is often overlooked is the effect that exercise has on the mind. These benefits are equally beneficial, if not more so, than the profound effects training has on the body.

Exercise has been proven to treat depression, improve memory, and give people an overall sense of well-being and happiness. Also, research shows us that these improvements are spread across the board to people of both genders, all races, and any age. Not only does exercise improve cognitive function, but it also helps repair that which has been lost by age. Studies have shown that sedentary people who begin aerobic exercise programs have quick improvements in functions, including planning, memory, scheduling, and more. Not bad just for breaking a sweat!

Let's look at some studies that will offer some concrete proof as to why you should be exercising for the sake of your body *and* mind:

- A study published in the February 2003 issue of the *Journal of Gerontology: Medical Sciences* stated that people who exercise have significant differences in the brain than those who do not. Researchers found, by using magnetic resonance imaging (MRI), that physically fit and active individuals had a much slower decline in brain density than sedentary people. The largest differences, researchers found, were in the areas of gray matter in the brain, which is the area involved in memory and learning skills.

- A 2001 study from the *Society for Neuroscience* showed that young people who exercised aerobically for a half hour just two to three times weekly over the course of three months had statistically significant improvements in cognitive tests. More telling, the study subjects' scores on those same types of cognitive tests actually fell when the aerobic exercise routines were ended.

- A 2007 study from the University of California, Irvine, *Institute for Brain Aging and Dementia*, showed that exercise provides broad effects on brain health—particularly those that include protection of the areas responsible for learning and memory—and helps prevent neurodegeneration as well as offering an easing of depression, especially in older populations.

The one thing all these studies have in common, despite their research spanning age ranges that differ by as much as 70 years, is that they all agree positive changes happen fast. Within just a few weeks, the brain—right along with the body—improves in myriad ways. The benefits of exercise are limitless, and swimming is a fantastic way to obtain them!

The Social Aspect

The reasons to swim go even beyond the health aspects that apply to your body and mind. Because it's an activity that people of all ages from all walks of life pursue, there are numerous other reasons to get to the pool nearest you as quickly as possible!

While you may think of swimmers as spending most of their time with their faces in the water, this isn't actually the case. Swimming, whether you're on a club team or just show up regularly at your local community pool, gym, or YMCA, is a very social sporting choice. Swimmers tend to be very dedicated to their fitness endeavors, and having these types of people around creates a very positive atmosphere to help you reach your own goals as well.

Further, if you are part of a club or team, many conduct regular functions outside the pool for team members and their families to get together. Not only does this make staying healthy a fun thing, but it's also a great way to meet people and get involved in your community if you haven't done so in the past or if you have recently moved to a new area and want to make new friends quickly.

FUN FACTS

It has been reported that the great philosopher Plato considered a man who didn't know how to swim "uneducated."

Goal-Setting

Swimming is one of the few sports where you can take a lot of what you do in the water with you once you're out of it. Unlike sports such as baseball or football, where your performance has to do with a lot of other factors, swimming gives you a chance to test yourself and see how far you have progressed in a linear, timed fashion.

In baseball, for instance, how far you can hit a ball is ever-changing. The pitch you're hitting, the speed of the throw, the bat you're using, the speed and direction of the wind … the list of factors that will affect your swing and hit distance is huge. In swimming, it's just you and the water. You can wear the same suit (or style of suit), and no matter where you go, a 25-yard pool is a 25-yard pool. Race away, test yourself, and see what happens.

So what are the advantages of that, you might ask? By wanting to get better, you're taking on something prolific without realizing it. You're setting goals, and goal-setting is the key to reaching great things in your life. All the Olympic champions you have ever seen, in any sport, reached their level of success because they set goals and laid out a plan to achieve them. By deciding to get fit by choosing to get in the pool and to improve your lifestyle, you're practicing a technique you can use in every aspect of your life.

There have been countless pages written by some of the greatest athletes and minds the world has ever seen on how to put goal-setting to work for you, but it's not a complicated process. Before we get into the techniques and programs that make up the majority of this book, let's take a quick look at how you can put them to your best use and how to set your own goals:

1. **Decide what you really want.** In the case of this book, we're guessing it's improving your body composition and cardiovascular health and/or learning to swim. Wherever you apply this goal-setting to your life, you have to be specific in what you're after. General phrasing such as "Look better" just won't cut it. What do you want to look better? Your abs? Bigger arms? Stronger legs? Let's make a decision and swim with it! For our examples here, we'll presume you are a new swimmer and want to teach yourself to swim.

2. **Set a time frame.** Obviously, learning to swim is an ongoing endeavor because you can always better your best, but you have to give yourself a realistic period of time to evaluate yourself. This allows you to judge your progress and take pride in what you have accomplished. Set short-term and long-term goals. For example:

   • Two weeks: be able to swim 25 yards (one length of the pool) with proper breathing technique without stopping.

   • One month: be able to swim 100 yards (four lengths of the pool) with proper technique and flip turns without stopping.

   • Two months: be able to swim 500 continuous yards (twenty lengths of the pool) with proper technique and flip turns.

3. Write the steps to accomplish each goal, such as the following:

    • Learn to float by the end of the first week of practice.

    • Practice kicking each day.

    • Practice pulling with a buoy each day.

    • Practice breathing when using a pull buoy each day.

You would do the same thing for your further-dated goals by building on your initial accomplishments.

If you stick with your schedule and work hard to achieve each step, the task as a whole doesn't seem as daunting. Focus on each step, one by one—and as you mark them off with success, you will find that your overall goal is much more attainable.

Conquering Your Fears

It isn't uncommon for people to be wary of entering the water for the first time. So if you're one of the many who are less than comfortable with water right now, you're not alone—and it's perfectly okay. Swimming is one of those things in life it's never too late to start with—and never too early. Babies are being introduced to water before they can even walk, and people well past the age of retirement are just learning to swim. You *can* do it. Millions of other people have done it before you, and millions more will do it after you.

The main component of learning to become comfortable in the water is simply to spend time there. You don't need to jump in head first and do laps just because you're in a pool. Hang out in the shallow end, walk around in the water, and float and relax in an area in which you can easily stand up. Getting your bearings in a depth that leaves you worry-free is the quickest path toward comfort.

If you have never tried to float in the past, give it a shot. Hold your breath and lie face down in the water, and let your body float on the surface. When you need to breathe, simply stand up. Try the same thing on your back. You'll find that in short order, you could float on your back all day if you wanted with just a little kicking motion with your feet.

Another method of getting accustomed to the water is to use a kickboard, which you can find free to use at most pools. Hold it out at arms' length in front of you and extend your body out, kicking your feet behind you. You may find at first that your kick is in need of some practice, so you aren't able to move very quickly or far—but that's not the point. You're learning that the water is calming and gentle, and somewhere you're going to have a lot of fun. (We discuss kickboards and other equipment in Chapter 2.)

Finding Lessons

An unfortunate truth about swimming pools, specifically in America, is that they are not money-making endeavors for their operators. Most pools are highly subsidized by taxpayers in the communities around the pools or paid for by schools or universities. While being invaluable resources—teaching lifesaving skills and promoting physical fitness—they are expensive to operate and maintain. Because of the cost, the majority of pools try to help offset this expense by renting out time to clubs and other organized teams. Signing up for one of these teams is a great option to get in the water. But if that's too much of a jump at one time, these same pools generally also offer individual or small group lessons, and they have these available for people of all ages.

SINK OR SWIM

Swimming isn't just a great workout; it's also a lifesaving skill. There are nearly 4,000 drowning deaths each year in the United States, with more than 1 in 4 being children 14 or younger. Learn to swim to improve and protect your life and the lives of others!

You can call local pools in your area to find out about their learn-to-swim programs, and you can also look up many pools on the Internet. One resource for finding swim lessons near you via the Internet is the search tool at www.swim.com, which allows you to enter your ZIP code and select whether you're interested in lessons for infant, child, or adult. Prices vary by instructor and pool, so check around and find something comfortable for your budget and schedule. Then make an appointment as soon as possible.

Additional places you may want to check are simply your local pools, whether they be at a high school or a community center. If you're a member of a gym or fitness club, including YMCAs, they may also offer additional options for you. Depending on the instructor, there are lessons available for everyone—ranging from practically newborns to seniors—so keep looking around until you find a place and price you're comfortable with.

What to Look for in an Instructor

When you find a database of potential swimming instructors, you shouldn't just pick one who has a fun name or looks like a nice person. You're going to be paying your hard-earned money to someone in exchange for a service, so you want to make sure you make the right choice.

On most database listings, you'll have some general information about the person, including any prior experience they may have, previous places they have coached or instructed, the age group they worked with, their availability, pricing, and any certifications they may have. Here are some things to consider when choosing an instructor:

- **How much experience does this person have?** There's nothing wrong with someone trying to get started in a new profession—it's a great thing, and they may be an absolutely terrific instructor. But is that a risk you want to take with your time and money? Many instructors have experience as assistant coaches of summer league or club teams or have taken courses on how to teach lessons. If the listing you're looking at does not include these things, you may want to continue on even if the person is relatively close to you or is offering a good deal. With things such as lessons, you often get what you pay for.

- **What age group has this person worked with?** Someone may have 10 years of coaching experience, but it's possible that it is all with extremely young children. If someone has only taught three- and four-year-olds how to swim, his or her years of experience may not be quite as beneficial to you. At those ages, instructors are often teaching kids how to be comfortable in the water and working on bubbles, focusing less on actual technique-based swimming you will use for fitness purposes.

  On the other hand, you may find someone with only two years of experience—but it has all been spent with people older than 18. In these cases, this person likely has a grasp on your particular individual goals.

- **Is the person certified?** Keep in mind that a certification does not necessarily mean a quality instructor. That said, though, there are a lot of benefits and some knowledge gained by seeing an instructor who has various certifications. If he or she is certified in CPR/First Aid/Water Safety, for instance, you will have a comfort level with that person and know he or she has a grasp on lifesaving skills and a high level of comfort with water.

If the instructor you're looking into is USA Swimming coaching certified, you will know he or she has all of these certifications as well as having gone through a background check, and the person will have also likely worked for an accredited USA Swimming club, either as an assistant or head coach. In fact, this instructor may very well be the coach of a team near you, as coaches often also work outside their normal jobs by teaching private swimming lessons.

- **What kind of learner are you?** You want to ask yourself how you learn best. Are you someone who needs more one-on-one attention from an instructor to learn a particular skill, or are you fine with learning among a group of people who are also looking to attain the same skill? You want to take a look at the types of lessons your instructor offers and double check before booking what you're getting. You don't want to expect a full half-hour or hour of an instructor's undivided attention, only to show up to the pool and discover it's a class that includes five other people.

- **What kind of schedule does he or she offer?** Scheduling is a big part of taking lessons. If you find an instructor who only works on Fridays from noon to 4 P.M., for example, and you just happen to have one particular Friday off but it isn't a regular thing for you, it's likely best to find someone with a more flexible schedule.

You certainly won't need to take swim lessons forever, but you will want to be consistent until your comfort level with your skills has improved by a significant margin. That can happen quickly, but what if you want a refresher? You don't want to have to wait months to get in with the same teacher you've enjoyed working with. Because everyone has his or her own teaching styles, if you have found one person who works for you, stick with him or her. But to do that, you'll need to make sure you can fit the lessons into your schedule. Remember, this person is working for you, and this is a fun activity you're taking on—so don't stress yourself out or go to any crazy lengths to fit your schedule with someone else's.

THE PROS KNOW

If you're unsure of which types of lessons you will respond best to, don't be afraid to try both types—group and individual—because you may find advantages to both. In group lessons, you may have less individualized time to ask questions and get critiqued, but you will get an opportunity to see and hear questions and concerns other people have that you may be able to take something positive away from. Depending on the levels of other people in the group, you may actually find that you're able to fix a problem in your technique before you ever have it!

Joining a Team

It's very common for people to be most motivated by learning or training in a group setting. There are multiple advantages to training with a team. The most obvious benefit is having a coach there to help you when he or she notices a flaw in your technique. It's important to remain patient in these situations, though, as you'll generally be training with a dozen or more fellow swimmers that the coach is trying to keep an eye on. Some coaches are more "hands-on" than others and openly offer advice while others are quiet and may need to be approached if you're after constant critiques.

We should note that most teams for older children and adults are not learn-to-swim programs. Generally, they do maintain groups of all skill sets, but a general knowledge and comfort in the water is usually required. After that, though, signing up may be the best and fastest way for you to improve your skills.

Depending on your age, the quickest resources at your disposal to find local teams are www.usswim.org (for age-group swimming) and www.usms.org (for Masters swimmers older than 18; see Chapter 18). You can also check out your local YMCA for an expansive network of swim teams around the country.

What to Ask Your New Coach

Before joining any team or club, you should inquire as to the cost and fees. This may not be a question for a coach, though, and many organizations will have this information on their websites. Do a search on the Internet first, and if you can't find what you need, be sure to ask. Fees associated with swimming are relatively small but do include registration fees and monthly dues, and when you compete, meets have a surcharge plus a modest fee per event you'd like to swim. Once you know it will be an affordable endeavor for you, jump right into the specifics.

To get the most from your time spent on a swim team or with a new club, you should speak with the coach (or coaches, in some cases) and let him or her know why you're there and also pose a few questions for your own knowledge and comfort.

Some coaches remain relatively quiet during a workout. This isn't because they don't care; rather, it's simply because their team may be made up of a wide variety of people who all maintain different goals. A lot of swimmers who are there for the fitness aspect don't like to be told each day what they can do to go faster. Speed, for some, really has no meaning as long as they're enjoying themselves and remaining fit.

If you're looking for specific technique tips or have certain goals, make sure you let your coach know at the outset of joining the team. By being aware of what you're trying to achieve, your coach will be in the proper position to help you.

THE PROS KNOW

If you're new to the sport, you will want to ask your coach how workouts are designed. Most coaches have specific routines they follow, and you want to be aware of what's coming. Ask about how lanes are divided so you don't end up as a new swimmer jumping in front of the fastest people on the team. You can also inquire about competition schedules and what meets the team attends and how often.

Working with Your Instructor

If you're joining a swim team, following the workout is going to be your best bet. If you're signing up for swim lessons, though, things are a bit different. In lessons, you're going to be in a much smaller group or even just one-on-one with your instructor. Make the most of your time and the money you're spending to learn such a great skill.

When learning to swim, don't be timid. You may be a little nervous because the entire activity is new to you, but assure yourself that you're in good hands. Relax and have fun with it, but at the same time—even though you're the student—take some control. An instructor will only try to teach you what he or she feels you need to know. He or she won't get too advanced too quickly, but will try to keep your skill set gradually advancing.

Swimming is one of those things, though, where it is very important to have a solid base of fundamentals before moving forward with something new. If you don't have a complete grasp on something your instructor has tried to teach you, tell him or her. Don't just "go with the flow," so to speak. A great number of things in swimming build off each other. Essential skills such as floating, sculling, the "streamline," and other motions are extremely common. But if you aren't sure how to do them well consistently, it will affect how you learn subsequent skills.

Your instructor wants you to learn to swim and wants you to enjoy it. Don't get overwhelmed, and let him or her know if you need to slow down or go over something again. Your instructor will be happy to help, and you will feel a great sense of accomplishment with each new skill you learn.

The Least You Need to Know

- Swimming is great for body and mind and is doctor recommended!
- Set goals for yourself and take the steps to reach them.
- Look into instructors thoroughly before booking.
- Take time to ask questions before joining a team.

All the Essentials Except Water

In This Chapter

- How to choose the right suit
- Swimsuit care tips
- All about goggles
- Picking the right type of cap
- Additional gear and accessories

Every activity has its own requirements when it comes to necessary clothing, optional accessories, or even just random cool stuff you may want to include because you're now involved with that particular endeavor. Swimming is no exception. There are lots of different options in everything you will use—from swimsuits to goggles to kickboards—and the choices can (and do) fill aisle after aisle at your local sporting goods store.

Here, we're going to make you a pro at understanding the differences among the various tools of the trade in swimming. When you hit the local store or the nearest swim shop, you'll know exactly what you're after and how to find the best gear for you.

The Basics of Swimwear

You can choose from numerous cuts and designs of swimsuits. We'll cover the basics, and you can decide which one you'd like to try in the pool first. If you find you aren't a fan of one style, don't be afraid to try others until you find the one that's most comfortable for your body. Be aware of several differences when choosing what suit you'll purchase.

Types of Material

Swimsuits are generally made from either polyester or Lycra spandex. Manufacturers have used some other materials to design certain garments, but the vast majority of suits you'll find are constructed of these two fabrics.

The main difference you'll notice is that the Lycra suits are smoother and perhaps more pleasing to the touch than the polyester suits. Lycra suits are generally very comfortable and easier to fit your particular form. They are also generally available in any design you could ever want. Their disadvantage is that they don't tend to last as long as polyester suits because they tend to stretch out more quickly. Polyester suits, as you might have guessed, kind of switch those advantages/disadvantages around. They last longer, but they're a bit stiffer and often not as "cool" looking if you're also after aesthetics in your swimwear.

FUN FACTS

A century ago, swimsuits were made from wool. While it became very heavy once wet, it was chosen for modesty purposes because it did not become semi-transparent in water.

Swimsuit Styling

As for the cut of the suit, when it comes to the traditional training suit—a one-piece creation—women generally only have a single, main choice with various options in the size of the shoulder straps and the directions in which they connect. There are countless two-piece suits out there that are designed for swimming, of course, but when it comes to actual training for fitness, these are far less commonly found.

For men's suits, there are actually three different basic types of suits available that—while not much different in actual size—provide varying amounts of coverage and comfort.

Briefs

Believe it or not, the small underwear-like suit you see is not called a "Speedo." That's actually just the name of a brand that has made swimsuits for many years. Briefs are the most basic and affordable swimsuit option for men. Some people prefer a suit that provides a bit more modesty, while others like that this suit type has no obstruction of the hips. It's basic, cheap, and gets the job done, and you can totally pretend you're a former cast member of *Baywatch* while wearing one.

Square-Leg Suits

A relatively new cut to find its way to the market, these are about the mid-thigh length of old 1970's runner's shorts but provide more coverage than briefs while avoiding the knee altogether. Some swimmers find that having a suit end close to the knee is a bit uncomfortable when kicking, thus making this cut of suit a great option. These suits are, quite literally, the in-between for briefs and Jammers.

Jammers

No one knows for sure the origin of the name "Jammer," but these popular waist-to-knee suits offer more coverage than the brief as well as additional advantages. In big meets, swimmers often shave their bodies to reduce drag from body hair. With Jammers, this is slightly less important. Additionally, when you pick a properly sized suit, it offers a bit of muscle compression that may help you feel more powerful when kicking in the water and reduce fatigue. On top of that, they provide the most coverage of suits available for men, and they're also the most popular cut of suit in competition.

Getting the Most from Your Suit

No matter which suit you choose, you want to make sure you get the longest possible life from it. Swimsuits can serve you well for a solid period of time if you treat them properly. And because they can be expensive, you will want to make sure you follow some basic advice as to how you can prolong their usefulness in your training.

- After every practice or competition, make sure you rinse out your suit. Don't just toss your suit into a corner when it's fresh from the pool. Chlorine is a very rough chemical when it comes to fabrics, so rinsing it well in fresh water will help keep the damage to a minimum. It doesn't take long: just rinse, wring it out, then rinse again, and wring it out. Afterward, you can put it on a hanger and allow it to dry or you can simply lay it over the edge of a shower rod or bathtub.

- Always allow your suit to dry completely before putting it away. Leave it out to dry, and make sure you don't set it in the sun. Not only can the sun do all kinds of crazy things to your swimsuit colors—it'll cause fading into various horrible shades—but it will also weaken the fabric and cause your suit to stretch and rip.

- Make sure you always store your swimsuit in a dry place. Don't allow it to dry and then store it near moisture (damp towels, for example).

SINK OR SWIM

Never wash your swimsuit in the washing machine or dry it in the dryer. It doesn't need either, and doing one or both will do irreparable damage in the form of discoloration, unwanted stretching, or tearing.

Goggles 101

Swim goggles aren't made anymore like they were in your parents' generation, and that's a good thing. While many people still remember the red-eyed days of swimming in chlorine back before goggles were even allowed in the pool, there are a tremendous and growing number of swimmers who wouldn't know what to do with their head underwater and no eye protection.

The 1976 Olympics were the first to allow goggles. Those were primitive by today's standards, but they were amazing for their time (and extremely basic). Plastic lenses with a rubber strap and foam padding between the lens and the face to prevent water from leaking in was the story of the day. The goggles, while somewhat effective, actually had a lot of flaws. The foam deteriorated quickly, the rubber strap stretched out often, and the lenses didn't have nearly the sophistication we have today.

Fast-forward a couple decades, and goggles have reached the equivalent of advancing from a motor car to space travel. Goggles today are form-fitted, hydrodynamic, gasket-sealed, and UV-protected works of art. And fortunately, because swimming is so popular, goggles aren't only sold at swim shops but also at sporting goods stores everywhere and at thousands of online retailers. If you can't find a pair of goggles that you think will look good and fit well on you, then the only explanation is that you must not really want goggles!

Choosing Your Eyewear

When selecting goggles, you'll want to find a pair that feels comfortable when fitting on your face. No matter what a manufacturer may tell you, there is no one-size-fits-all goggle. Some people love the gasket-sealed models while others have problems with them pinching. Some models have dense, hard rubber seals that may press too firmly over the eyes. But make sure before discounting one type or another that you adjust the width between the lenses. Goggles usually come with adjustable nose pieces, and there's no "factory default"—so definitely play around with them. You may find that right out of the package, a pair of goggles is extremely uncomfortable—perhaps the worst you've tried—but by extending the distance between the lenses, they could suddenly become your most favorite pair.

After you find a design you like, consider what kind of lenses work best for you. Many styles of goggles come with lens options to better suit your training. If you train outdoors, you may find metallic lenses extremely beneficial for deflecting the sun, especially when swimming the backstroke. For swimming indoors, clear goggles generally work well, but you can also get tints of all different colors that may better suit the lighting or atmosphere of your favorite pool. That said, if you really like, say, blue-lens goggles, you can get away with using them anywhere. Goggles are made in just about every color under the sun, and they're universally useful. Just because a reflective pair may work slightly better outside, that doesn't mean you can't use any pair of your choice. Find one that makes you happy.

THE PROS KNOW

Goggles are relatively affordable, so if you have various training sites and really can't decide which set of goggles to choose, it shouldn't be too much of a strain to buy more than one pair. Depending on the type, you can get a basic pair of goggles for as little as $5, or spend upward of $30 for fancier, racing-level goggles.

If you like the simplicity of your dad's old pair of goggles, look for a basic, single-strap, foam model. For those who want the ultimate in simplicity and affordability, you can try "Swedish goggles," which you put together by hand. They have no gaskets and seal by the nature of their design, and they cost about the same as a six-pack of soda.

The options you have in goggles are seemingly endless. Some manufacturers make 50 different styles. When you combine that with a couple dozen other companies that make many different options as well, you'll find that you are able to track down a pair very easily that will fit not just your budget but also your style.

An important thing to note with goggles is that more expensive does not necessarily mean better. In general, almost all goggles share the basic characteristics of being made of plastic and rubber, and the quality of those things varies relatively little. The most important facet of choosing a pair of goggles is comfort. Swedish goggles, for example, are certainly the most inexpensive eyewear option available. If they're comfortable for you, there's no reason to spend more on a fancier pair. On the other hand, if you can't stand them, it's certainly worth it to pay a few more dollars for a pair you enjoy wearing.

Goggle Accessories

You may have thought that it was enough to just have hundreds of options for the goggles themselves. And you may have thought that goggles themselves were an accessory. Well, they are, but you can also get some things that pair with your goggles to make them better, clearer, or more high-tech.

Anti-Fog Spray

Over time, goggles become more prone to fogging up while you swim. There's no set time period for this to happen, and in fact it can vary widely due to the chemical levels in the pools you swim in and how you take care of your goggles. Initially, you will find that your goggles go quite a while remaining crystal clear. Then you will notice they slowly start to fog up, and after a while, they may become a bit blurred only a few hundred meters into your workout.

Don't worry; it doesn't mean you need to get rid of your goggles. If the straps are sound and the seals are good—meaning no water leaks into your eyes—you have plenty of life left from your favorite pair. You can bring them back to life with some anti-fog spray, which several manufacturers make and is very inexpensive (usually only a couple dollars). Simply spray onto your lenses after you rinse them and allow to dry.

FUN FACTS

The S.S. *Olympic,* sister ship to the *Titanic,* was the first ocean liner with a swimming pool—an amenity that would become standard fare on luxury ships around the world. Its maiden voyage was in 1911.

Replacement Straps

Generally, when you pick a pair of goggles, you do so not just for the lenses but also because they provide an overall fit with which you're very comfortable. This includes the type of straps. You have options available of double straps for a more secure fit or single straps (see the following sidebar). These variations also come in a variety of thicknesses. If a goggle strap breaks, you may find you want to change them. There are a lot of options, so feel free to try something new:

- "Bungee" straps are more durable than the usual light rubber, but they aren't compatible with every type of goggle. If you want to go with these, just make sure you test them out first.

- "Split-strap" replacement options are one piece of rubber that splits off on both sides to attach to the upper and lower portions of your goggles. This makes for exceptionally easy adjustment.

THE PROS KNOW

Should you choose single or double straps? Most people go for double straps for the versatility in positioning on your head. They do require a little more adjustment to get right, but that can often pay off in comfort. On the flip side, the single straps are very easy to use and put on but may not be as secure as you'd like them. If you need a median answer because you like the single strap but don't like it moving around, try putting a cap on over your goggles. This can often help them stay in place much better.

Mp3 Player

In any gym, at the beach, on the sidewalk, or just about anywhere exercise activities are going on, you can find people listening to mp3 players. As of a few years ago, swimmers decided they didn't want to be left out anymore, and several companies began manufacturing waterproof music players that can attach to goggles.

One example is the "Aquabeat" waterproof mp3 player from Speedo. It, like others in the same category, is fully waterproof up to several meters in depth and has built-in rechargeable batteries. It attaches to your goggle strap and has waterproof earphones that go into your ears so you can hear your favorite songs even when churning out laps. If you love to swim but find yourself getting bored after a while, you may want to try one of these types of units and see whether they keep you more entertained while becoming more fit!

Latex or Silicone Cap, or No Cap at All?

It's extremely rare to see a woman swim without a cap, and it's also very common to see men wear them. Even if you have short hair, you may enjoy the streamlined and smooth feel a cap provides.

Caps come in two basic types: latex and silicone. You'll see caps in any color you could ever imagine, with more design options than you can count. You can get one with the flag of your country, with different animals, famous quotes, landmarks, or even a cap with your name. If you're really creative, you could even buy a blank cap and have your own personal design printed on it. The options are limitless. But regardless of what you want on the cap, there are still two materials you'll need to choose from:

Latex: These caps are the most common. They're cheaper than silicone and easier to adjust. The downside is that they're not very smooth, so they can pull hair more easily (which is uncomfortable for some people). They also are the less durable of the two and can stretch out over time significantly faster than silicone. That said, because of their price, you could get several latex caps for the price of one silicone cap, which would give you the options to have several different colors or designs available. The cost of a latex cap is generally just a couple of dollars.

Silicone: Offering a tighter fit and longer life, silicone caps are a solid but more expensive choice. These stretch very minimally and typically fit the head better than latex. They do cost more—upward of $10 to $12— but they will last longer and fit better, which just might make their price worth it to you.

Of course, there's the option of going without a cap at all. You may find over time that even if your hair is relatively short, you will feel your head being pulled around a bit from the water. It isn't necessarily an uncomfortable feeling, but you may or may not prefer it. The longer your hair is, the less we suggest going without a cap.

Additional Gear

You've probably noticed walking down the "water sports" aisles at your favorite sporting good stores that there's a lot more in those sections than goggles and caps. Swimming, like any other exercise, has a significant number of accessories you can add to enhance your time in the water. Some are designed to promote your training while others are designed to improve your level of comfort in the water, which is particularly useful if you are just learning how to swim.

Nose Plugs

People usually associate nose plugs with synchronized swimming, but they're a huge asset to lap swimming and racing as well. Some of the top swimmers in the world today choose to use these in the biggest meets of their lives because they aid them in focusing their breathing through their mouths. If you have trouble with water getting up your nose while swimming or even just during flip turns, give nose plugs a try.

Fins, Monofins, and Zoomers

Likely the most valuable tool a beginning swimmer can use, fins are perfect for easing the transition from being a lifelong land athlete to an aquatic superstar. Fins lengthen the body and help the swimmer kick a significant amount of additional water, which makes staying flat and afloat remarkably easy. By remaining high in the water, the hips don't sink enough to cause any difficulty in rotating the body to breathe and allow a beginner to learn proper technique in a short period of time.

THE PROS KNOW

Fins aren't just for beginners. They're also great for doing speed work as well as getting a great leg workout. You can do a variety of kick sets (we'll give you examples in Chapter 14) that allow you to build strength and endurance in your muscles, all without the stress on your knees you would experience if you were running or in the gym.

The monofin is a much more advanced fin, but one you may want to try someday. A company called Finis developed a fin unlike any other. Instead of having two independent fins, they created one large fin into which both feet can be inserted. The amount of water a swimmer wearing a monofin is able to kick behind is unbelievable. It makes for an amazing leg and core workout as well as providing a huge amount of fun due to the speeds a swimmer can reach when kicking with this device.

When used properly, a monofin can also be a great aid in developing ankle flexibility. Because the feet are together, the ankles get an equal stretch when kicking, and since you are able to control how hard you kick, it's easy to control the tension you feel.

Monofins are available online through the Finis website; see Appendix B.

Zoomers were created with fitness swimming in mind. They are shorter than your standard fin and angled so they encourage shorter kicking, which works your leg muscles more. They also channel water with their design and allow for the development of an extremely efficient kick.

You can find Zoomers online (see Appendix B) or in some chain sports stores.

Kickboards

Kickboards are great training tools because of the variety of abilities they offer you. As you may have guessed from the name, these are designed to allow you to stay afloat while working on your kick. You don't have to worry about your arms or turning your head to breathe.

A kickboard is like a mini-surfboard in that it floats and will let you float with ease. When you don't worry about sinking, it's much easier to relax and focus on learning. For kick sets and exercising your legs, these are also great tools that allow you to solely focus on working out your lower body and getting a great burn going. You can, of course, pair fins with a kickboard and do some really intense training that is sure to get your metabolism moving to burn fat and build muscle at the same time.

Pull Buoys

A pull buoy is another tool used for helping a swimmer float. Pull buoys are designed to fit between a swimmer's thighs and when extended out in the water will keep the hips afloat, preventing the need for a kick. In the opposite sense of a kickboard, this tool is also great for focusing on exercising just your upper-body muscles. Further, this is a great tool for practicing breathing because your hips won't sink and thus won't pull your chin down in the water.

Snorkels

One of the most overlooked training tools for both improving technique as well increasing your level of fitness through swimming is the snorkel. One of the main problems people have with learning to swim or with swimming long distances revolves around breathing. Whether it's technique-based or efficiency-based, breathing is often the culprit of delayed results.

In the sense of learning technique, the main portions of swimming have to do with properly moving the arms and legs, timed together to propel you forward. Breathing is really just a small part of the stroke, but it's integral. A snorkel solves problems associated with breathing because you don't have to rotate your head to get air. You can keep your head down, in line with the body as it is supposed to be (which we will discuss shortly), and focus on just moving your arms.

SINK OR SWIM

If you don't keep your head in alignment, no matter what stroke you are swimming, it will affect your spine. And from there, it's really a domino effect: the neck moves the spine, the spine moves the shoulders, and the shoulders affect overall body alignment, which alters the hips—and ultimately, it pushes your legs down, creating drag. That's a lot of side effects from just breathing!

Snorkels can help when it comes to endurance, too. The reason is because breathing incorrectly, even if it doesn't stop you in your tracks, can take a lot of extra effort. When you're overexerting yourself with inefficiency, you end up getting a much shorter workout than you otherwise could. Snorkels help by allowing you to work on proper technique without wasting energy on poor technique. And once you have your technique down, you can swim with or without the snorkel with much better efficiency.

Snorkels have two basic forms when used for the pool. There is the standard side-mounted snorkel, which looks more like a diver's snorkel and fits into your mouth and runs up the side of your head. This is a decent choice, and several companies make these types of snorkels, so they shouldn't be hard to find.

The second type you may see in the pool is made by a company called Finis and is the more preferable option for using a snorkel in the pool. The "swimmer's snorkel" mounts and runs up the center of your face so that it extends in front of you instead of to the side. The advantage is that as you're swimming, and as you get progressively faster, the snorkel doesn't try to pull itself away due to the resistance of the water. When it's right in the center, even when you're swimming fast it stays perfectly in place and allows you to breathe normally and focus on your technique instead of becoming distracted with timing your air intake and rotating your neck. These types of snorkels do cost a bit more than conventional snorkels, but it's likely you'll find the comfort and convenience worth the additional cost.

Hand Paddles

In just about every swimmer's gear bag, you'll find a pair of paddles that are usually either round or square, although you can find pairs in a variety of different shapes and sizes. Attached to these plastic pieces are usually straps of rubber tubing, strategically placed so a swimmer can place his or her hand inside. These paddles have a variety of benefits for the user; specifically, pulling more water, which entitles him or her to a better workout. On top of that, it's a great training tool for teaching proper arm position.

When the paddle is in its proper position—vertical—that means your arm is in the proper position. You quickly learn to feel the differences in positioning, which allows you to more quickly get into the habit of always using the proper technique.

Additional Exercise Equipment

Not everything you do in the pool requires you to be floating, pulling, or kicking your way down the pool. There are a lot of great ways to exercise in the water that you can do while standing up and a lot of tools you can use to add variety to your aquatic exercise program.

You can usually find a pretty good array of aquatic fitness items at your local sporting goods store. We'll take a look at a few, and if some sound entertaining to you, feel free to give them a go!

Aquatic Fitness Gloves

Fitness gloves are usually made from neoprene or another permeable material. They resemble a basic glove but generally have open fingers and are webbed between fingers. They share similarities with hard-plastic hand paddles in that they allow you to pull more water, which allows for an even better upper-body workout.

One additional advantage some gloves give you is the option for adding small weights on the backside of the hand. This allows for extra tension on the muscles of your forearms and shoulders to kick your workout into a higher gear.

Hydro Dumbbells

Hydro dumbbells are exactly what they sound like: weights for the water. They are designed to help you float while building upper-body strength as you move them through the water. They don't require swimming to be used, but they are much easier on your joints than if you were doing a curl or shoulder press on the gym's dry floor.

Hand Weights

Several companies make hand weights that you can take in the water and use for a variety of exercises. They're similar to dumbbells in that they are easy to hold, but these generally aren't meant to float, so you'll need to keep a hand on them. You can use them for training your upper body through the same motions you would use with weights on land, or you can keep them in hand while doing some water jogging for added resistance.

Jogging Belt

Jogging belts are made to be used in deeper water. You can place one around your waist, and it offers you back support while helping you stay up in the water. This offers you the ability to, as the name states, jog in the water and gain cardiovascular and muscular endurance benefits.

The Least You Need to Know

- Suits come in a variety of cuts and materials that affect their prices, so be sure to pick one that is both budget-friendly and comfortable.
- To get the longest possible life from your swimsuit, always rinse it with fresh water immediately after swimming and allow it to air dry.
- Goggles come in a variety of shapes and sizes and comfort can vary widely, but more expensive does not necessarily mean better.
- Most caps are made of either silicone or latex, with silicone generally being the more comfortable but also the more expensive of the two.
- Accessories like fins and pull buoys are great training tools available to new swimmers that can make the learning process much easier.

At Home in the Pool

In This Chapter

- The earliest pools
- A guided tour of the average pool
- Endless pools and natural pools
- Pool chemicals
- Understanding how we move through water
- Basic pool safety and etiquette issues

In the grand scheme of things, people haven't been playing around with water for all that long. Even the now very common practice of filling holes in the ground with water for recreation is a relatively fresh notion. As such, there are many things new swimmers can learn about pools and associated swimming venues and features. Ask anyone what a football field looks like, and they can probably describe it with general precision. But if you inquire about a pool, you may get a blank stare or an extremely simple answer.

After this chapter, you will not only be able to describe everything there is to know about a pool, but you'll also feel comfortable going to a pool and have detailed knowledge about all the intricacies and nuances to be found in and around that big body of chlorine (or a similar chemical).

A Brief History of Pools

Swimming pools are known or have been known by a variety of different names, including bath house, swimming bath, and wading pool. Further, the venues that house these bodies of water aren't just called pools. They are also called aquatics centers and natatoriums. This latter part is important to know for the simple fact that if you're trying to find a place to swim in the phone book, you may need to search outside the letter *P.*

While seen as important since the early Roman days for soldiers, swimming didn't really take off as an organized activity and fitness endeavor until the 1700s. The initial growth of the sport was largely focused in England, and with the revival of the modern Olympic Games in 1896 in Athens, Greece, the sport finally found international footing and grew exponentially.

The majority of early swimming venues were actually not even pools at all. While ancient baths had been built long ago, they were far too expensive to be built with any sort of regularity in the modern world. For decades, the courses swum were simply roped-off areas of lakes or oceans. Of course, this provided no recourse from the tide and waves and also prevented swimming all year long due to the weather.

In time, pools were built by affluent clubs and educated cities around the world. With technology eventually introduced that allowed the heating of pools more efficiently, swimming suddenly became a viable activity for women and children of all ages, in addition to the men who had previously braved the temperatures. Since that point, the development of pools—both standard and unique in features—has taken off, and many milestones for swimming have been reached over the last century:

- In 1907, the Racquet Club of Philadelphia built the world's first above-ground pool.

- By 1925, the city of San Francisco boasted about its Fleishhacker pool, which was the largest in the entire United States at 1,000 feet long and 150 feet in width— big enough to accommodate more than 10,000 swimmers at once.

- In 2004, Nemo 33 opened in Belgium, the deepest pool in the world at 33 meters (more than 108 feet).

- Not to be outdone, though, and certainly wanting in on swimming-related records, the country of Chile came through in 2008 with an epic body of water to call its own. Its pool, in Algarrobo on the southern coast of the country, is 1,000 yards long—the length of 40 college swimming pools put together!

As you can tell, swimming has always been a desired sport around the world. The issue had long been bringing the ability to get in the water to the majority of people. Thanks to today's technology, we are able to swim every day of the year in heated water to improve our health and happiness. And as technology continues to develop even further, who knows what the next great invention will be in the world of pools—or how big the next record setter may be!

A Guided Tour of the Pool

Basic comfort in the water comes from familiarity. When you're comfortable with your surroundings, water suddenly doesn't seem so daunting. And really, it shouldn't. You control how you move in it, you can float right on top of it, and it's really relaxing once you get over any fears you may have.

Pools are built in three basic distances. While there are a few well-documented cases of pools—particularly older ones—having been built at odd lengths, these are the ones you will run into just about anywhere:

- **25 yards (75 feet):** This is the length of the typical high school pool in America, and in fact, the United States is the only country to use this distance. This is why you won't hear of records in yards pools being notated as "world records." Instead, they are "American records" (or in the case of foreign swimmers breaking them, "U.S. Open records")—which just means the fastest swim ever in the United States. Community pools around the nation are also built to this standard, and it is also the distance the NCAA championships are competed over. In 100-distance races (in yards or short-course meters), you will make three turns before finishing.

- **25 meters (about 82 feet):** Meters are the method of measurement for pools in every other country around the world. Being slightly longer than yards, you end up adjusting your swimming to take a couple more strokes before turning—but like yards pools, you still have three turns in a 100-distance race.

- **50 meters (about 164 feet):** This is an Olympic-size pool. Every Olympic Games since their initial use of pools for swimming events in 1924 has been raced in this format. In these pools, it is possible to have races of a single lap (no turns).

Other Pool Types

On top of the standard distances you'll find in most pools, there are a variety of other options that can be found anywhere, from homes to national parks—each with their own advantages and disadvantages.

Endless Pools

Since the 1980's, people have had the opportunity to get their very own pool at home, even if they didn't have the space for a traditional training facility. "Endless pools," as they have come to be called, are tubs that resemble large baths. They are equipped with a motor or propeller that pushes water at a swimmer using varying speeds, allowing the swimmer to go through the exact same motions as in a traditional pool but while staying in place.

Endless pools have the following advantages:

- Fits into a small space

- Allows exercise from home

Here are some disadvantages, however:

- Very expensive (more than $20,000 for a basic system)

- Only fits one swimmer at a time

- No ability to practice turns

Natural Pools

Often found in some strange places, natural pools are unique and delightful wonders. These are pools like none other in that, just as the name implies, they are naturally derived. While these days they are often man-made, they are done so with nature's materials and contain no chemical additives—that means no chlorine or bromine—and no mechanical parts.

Natural pools are sanitized by the movement of the water through vegetation, the sun's ultraviolet (UV) rays, and the variety of life that calls the pool its home.

Here are some advantages:

- No chemicals means no drying effect on the skin, such as is found with chlorine

- Unique ambiance

- No harsh effect on swimsuits from the water

Natural pools have some disadvantages, though:

- Temperature dependent on Mother Nature

- Irregular sizes

- Not generally available year-round

FUN FACTS

Olympic pools weren't heated until the Los Angeles Olympic Games in 1932. This left the competitors at the mercy of Mother Nature for the water temperature which, during some Olympics, was reportedly in the 50-degree range.

What Goes into the Pool

Throughout the years, a number of different methods have been used to keep pool water clean. Some of these have caused concerns from people who don't understand them—because, after all, they are chemicals. Fortunately, the science behind maintaining hygienic pool water has also always included the ensured safety of swimmers. Still, there are several popular methods of filtering that the public should be aware of.

The necessity of using sanitizing chemicals is important to note, whether you're planning to fill up a pool at your home or are heading to your local gym facility. Large bodies of water are terrific breeding grounds for bacteria and other germs. When additional chemicals are introduced to the water through a swimmer's hair and skin, it can create an unhealthy environment. The use of the following basic chemicals in pools shouldn't pose any risk to you and are in fact required by health codes for any public facility.

Chlorine

By far the most commonly used product to keep pool water clean is chlorine. Chlorine is both bleach and a disinfectant, and aside from being used in swimming pools, is also used in municipal systems and water treatment plants to clean drinking water. As a gas, chlorine can be dangerous enough to irritate the respiratory system. When used at levels necessary for cleaning water, though, there is little cause for concern about health.

Bromine

A chemical used that is quite similar to chlorine is bromine. This chemical has many of the same characteristics of chlorine when it comes to cleaning and sanitizing water and may also be slightly less irritating to the eyes and skin. Bromine has a slightly better stability in warmer temperatures, so you may find this particular chemical being used more often in community pools that cater to a very young or older audience, as well as in hot tubs and spas.

Pool Components

One of the best things about swimming as exercise and sport is that you can feel at home anywhere in the world in a pool. Unlike biking or running, where you have to adjust to the terrain, you can put a standard pool in any country around the world and swimmers will feel comfortable training. You don't need signs in any particular language, because pools have their own dialect of sorts that transcends nationality. From flags to lane lines to the line on the bottom, there are standards that are maintained around the globe.

Flags

Flags are particularly important for backstroke swimming. They tell swimmers how far they are from each wall so that when swimming, they don't collide with it and injure themselves. In some pools, there may be distinctive markings on the ceiling or a big enough object to the left or right to notice from the corner of your eye, but those types of things just aren't reliable. And if you're swimming outdoors, you're really out of luck. So long ago, flags were introduced to fix the plight of backstroke swimmers everywhere.

The flags you see in pools will be the same distance from the walls in every similar-length course in the world. For 25-yard pools, the flags will be 15 feet from each end of the pool. In 25-meter and 50-meter pools, the flags will be 5 meters (about 16.4 feet) away from the wall, which is slightly farther than in yards pools.

Lane Lines

Lane lines weren't used in the Olympic Games until 1924, but today, every competition pool has them. The lines are separated by dividers that are most often made of plastic, although they can also be made of rope and buoys. For competition purposes, lane lines must be at least 7 feet apart from one another.

No matter what course the pool is set up for, 15 meters away from each wall you will see a strikingly different-colored marker on the lane line—most often yellow—that is used to mark distance. In competition, if a swimmer remains underwater past that marker, he or she is disqualified from the race.

Bottom Line

Every competition-ready pool has solid, dark-colored lines that run almost the entire length of the pool across the bottom center of each lane. The lines on the bottom of the pool allow you to turn without lifting your head and know exactly where you are in the lane at all times. This is particularly helpful when you are swimming in a counterclockwise motion with other people in the lane so that you don't collide. This line is regulated to a minimum of 10 inches wide and ends as a "T," with the last portion a width of 1 meter. The line ends 2 meters (6.7-feet) from each wall.

Blocks and Backstroke Grips

Starting *blocks* are only officially used during competitive swimming events. Many pools have rules against lap swimmers using them, so you will definitely want to check before stepping up onto them. If you're on a team of sorts, you will probably get ample opportunity to use these.

DEFINITION

Blocks are flat or angled platforms elevated above the surface of a pool to facilitate a dive into the water. They can, by rule, be elevated as high as 30 inches above the water level.

Starting blocks are often removable from pools, but when they're present, they have to follow exact specifications. In short-course yards pools, they can be no higher than 2 feet and 6 inches above the water's surface. In short- and long-course meter pools, the blocks can be no less than .5 meters (1 foot, 8 inches) and no more than .75 meters (2 feet, 5½ inches) from the surface of the water.

Slightly below the starting platform itself are handles or other types of grips that are used for backstroke starts. Swimmers hold on to them at the beginning of their races to put themselves in a position to push off and arch themselves into the water. These are placed between 1 and 2 feet above the surface of the water.

See Chapter 9 for full details on starts.

Pace Clock

Many pools have some sort of pace clock on deck at one end of the pool—an easily visible clock that counts out 1-minute intervals. Pace clocks come in a few different forms, such as digital and the old-fashioned dial type with a big needle that travels in circles. Most commonly, you will find a big, round pace clock hanging on the wall at one end of the pool or set up at the end of a lane. Pools with digital pace clocks usually have them hanging up on the wall on the side of a pool deck. Pace clocks are easy to read, and with just a little practice learning the terms used around a pool deck, you will be able to read the clocks with ease.

Here's an example set: *4×100 at 1:20*

For this set, you can start when the second hand on the pace clock is on the "00" second mark on a digital clock or the 60-second mark on a regular pace clock. You will swim the 100 yards, then leave for your next 100 when the second hand reaches the .20, which would notate that 1-minute, 20-seconds has passed. After pushing off once the 20 comes around and swimming another 100, you would then leave again on the .40. For the last 100 you'll leave again on the "00" (or 60, depending on the type of clock you're using).

The following terms are used with a pace clock:

- "On the top" means you will leave when the second hand is "on the top" of the clock, either at the 60-second mark or the "00" mark.

- "On the bottom" refers to the bottom of the clock. This would be the "30" on either style of pace clock.

What a Drag: Moving Through Water

Even with all our technological advancements, we are still learning how to be better swimmers. The main method is by reducing *drag*. We do our best to conquer this challenge by improving our technique to push more water behind us, thus propelling us forward, as well as improving the alignment of our body. There are various types of drag, such as form and frictional drag, and the focus is to reduce all of these to their bare minimums.

DEFINITION

Drag is the resistance of the water against your body. It is caused by the size of a swimmer's body, his or her swimwear, inefficient technique, and even body hair.

Form Drag

Form drag is caused by your body's shape. A perfect example is standing in a pool of water that reaches up to your neck and trying to run. It won't be a very fast way to cross the pool. But if you flatten your body out on top of the water, kick with your legs, and pull with your arms—which we call swimming—you can move much, much faster. You do this by reducing your drag, because when you're flat and long, you move through the water more like a boat.

Form drag can be overcome by improvements in technique as well as from simply slimming down the body, which is something you'll find swimming will help you do naturally. While it may sound like being of a bigger stature is a detraction from the ability to swim fast, it's not. That's because swimming is a measure of proportion and efficiency. If you are able to use proper technique—which we cover in upcoming chapters—that creates propulsion proportionate to your size, allowing you to move very quickly through the water.

Frictional Drag

Frictional drag is caused by the exterior of your body. Things such as swimwear and body hair create this type of drag and can be taken down to a minimum by wearing form-fitting suits—and, as many swimmers do for championships meets, shaving.

Water is significantly denser than air, which helps us understand why it is much more difficult to move through. Because of air and water being completely different mediums, passing through them shares few characteristics. Whereas air can be propelled through relatively well with force, simple force is extremely inefficient in the water.

Swimming is a graceful effort. Thrashing through the water is not only hard to watch, but it's also a very poor way to travel through it. Fast and effective swimming looks and feels easy.

In the pool, to move efficiently you need to, in theory, try to displace a greater amount of water behind you than you will encounter in front of you. This occurs by using your hands, arms, and feet in the same way you would use the oars of a boat while keeping yourself long and flat, and creating as little frictional drag as you can. That, of course, is why the undersides of boats are smooth—a smooth bottom creates fewer obstacles and allows a smoother passage through water. By the way, it's a misconception that all swimmers—men included—have to shave their legs. Sure, shaving is something that competitive swimmers do at championship meet time, but even then it isn't something *all* swimmers do. It's entirely optional, not necessary for learning how to swim, and not even necessary for swimming fast. So breathe easy and put the razor away—you don't need it!

Basic Water Safety

Much of staying safe around pools is common sense. Even with that said, though, we would be remiss if we didn't cover a few basic safety issues that will ensure your time spent at the pool is not only healthy but also safe.

You've heard it before but we will reiterate: Don't swim alone—either in a pool or in any body of water. Accidents happen, and if one should occur while you're in the water, make sure someone else is around. This isn't to say always go to the pool with a friend, but just make sure there are other gym-goers or team members there at the same time. If you're in the ocean, stay within sight of everyone else. In rivers, lakes, and the like, make sure someone on shore or in a boat knows you're in the water and can keep an eye out for you.

Make sure you never consume alcohol before getting in (or on) the water. It's a myth that there's any set time you need to wait after eating before swimming—you should only swim when you feel well enough to do so—but never, ever mix drinking with the pool or an open body of water.

SINK OR SWIM

Never jump or dive into water when you don't know its depth. This can cause serious injury if you jump into a pool or other body of water that is only a couple of feet deep, either to your legs if you go feet first, or to your head and neck if you dive in head first.

Basic Public Pool Etiquette

To ensure the enjoyment of every patron at a public pool, some basic rules of etiquette should strictly be followed. We'll get into more detail on in-water etiquette in later chapters, but as far as the facility and non-exercise parts go, here are some things to keep in mind:

- **Shower before entering the pool.** You will notice signs everywhere before entering that advise people to do this, and you'll notice a vast majority of people walking right past them. Please set an example and at least rinse quickly. This is for the safety of everyone. The sweat and chemicals on your body, from your cologne or deodorant to your hair spray or gel, will get into the water and react with the pool chemicals. If water is accidentally swallowed while swimming, digestive problems, respiratory illness, ear infections, and skin or eye irritation can result if the water is particularly unsanitary. So while you should make sure you never swallow pool water, practice good hygiene to help do your part in keeping the pool clean for everyone. If you bring young children, make sure they are wearing watertight diapers made for swimming.

- **Don't crowd the end of the lane with your things.** You absolutely should bring with you a water bottle and any additional accessories you want to use, such as a kickboard, but keep them neat at the end of the lane. Set them off to the side whenever possible and not directly in the center, where people will be climbing in and out of the water.

- **When you arrive, take a minute to watch the lanes.** Find the lane that will work best for you. If it's crowded, see which group you'll best blend in with. It isn't always the lane with the fewest number of people. You may see three people in a particular lane and four in another, yet the latter may be best for you if the first has people far exceeding your comfortable speed or technique.

- **Be flexible.** You may show up to the pool one day and decide you want to run in the pool for your cardiovascular exercise instead of swim. It's a great workout, but if you find the pool has people actually swimming in each lane, be flexible to the point you can swim until you find a free lane to do your running.

THE PROS KNOW

Look for "family swim" times on the pool schedule. The lane lines are generally removed during this period, and you can expect far fewer swimmers and more casual pool-goers.

Public Swimming Pool Fees

The economics of your particular area will generally affect how much it costs per swim at your local pool, but there are ways to save no matter the cost of admission.

A common price for pool entry is about $3 to $5 per person per lap-swimming session. These usually run two or three hours at a time, and you are able to enter the pool anytime during the session and stay until the end. Obviously, the closer to the start time you arrive, the more swimming you will be able to do if you so choose. Regardless, it's definitely cheaper than a matinee movie (which you might not even like) and so much better for your health.

There are a couple of options you may want to check to ensure you're getting the most for your swimming dollar:

- **Check into local gyms that have pools.** Even if you don't care to use the weights or other amenities available, the monthly membership fee may save you money depending on how often you want to swim. Gym fees can range from around $30 to $50 a month. If you currently pay $4 to go to open swim and swim more than 8 times a month, paying a monthly gym fee may be a more practical option (especially if one is located closer to your home). Additionally, the schedule for the pool may be more conducive to your own available timing, and if you are near a gym chain, your membership may include entry into more than one club that you can use.

- **Investigate local swim clubs.** If you're one of the countless recreational swimmers who like to train every single day, membership in a local club may be just right for you. Monthly dues to the club vary from team to team, but they generally offer flexible schedules as well as guaranteed pool time when you're there. On top of knowing you'll have a place to swim—and not show up to find a class going on, for example—you will also have the advantage of working with an experienced coach.

The Least You Need to Know

- Few pools are alike, so be cautious of things such as water temperature and depth; older pools tend to be more shallow for diving.
- Pools come in three main lengths: 25 yards, 25 meters, and 50 meters.
- Bodies of water such as endless and natural pools make it convenient to find a place to swim, but be aware they can be expensive or inaccessible at certain times of the year.
- Various types of chemicals are used to keep pools clean and safe, but be sure you or your children don't ingest pool water.
- Always swim with the goal of reducing as much drag as possible.
- Polite swimming is safe swimming at public pools, so be considerate as to where you put yourself and your equipment and be mindful of others around you.

Taking the Plunge: The Basic Strokes

One of the reasons why swimming is so popular is because it's just about impossible to get bored. With four strokes, three kicks, and countless drills at your disposal—a number of which we'll cover in this book—every day at the pool will be a unique experience. But on top of being enjoyable day in and day out, you'll find that you reach your health and wellness goals more quickly with swimming than with just about any other form of exercise. Consider swimming a wet "total gym." Whereas you might find certain exercises just don't feel right for your body in the gym, when it comes to swimming, you're sure to find a comfortable, challenging way to work all your muscle groups. You can isolate specific body parts, build strength, burn fat, and more—all without ever feeling like you're even sweating!

Freestyle

In This Chapter

- Understanding the basics of freestyle swimming
- The right way to kick and pull
- Learn the freestyle in six easy steps
- The three styles of freestyle
- Tips for avoiding common mistakes

The most commonly swum stroke in any body of water can go by several names but is most often referred to simply as "freestyle." You see it in the marquee events in the Olympic Games and in triathlons, and you see it being done by great-grandparents in your local pool. Whether it's for competition or strictly for fitness, if you're going to spend time in the water, it's the stroke to know. And fortunately, it's very simple.

What Is Freestyle?

The *freestyle* stroke is the fastest way to swim through the water. It has become so advanced that in 1905 the world record in 100 meters for men was just under 1 minute and 6 seconds. Today, that record sits under 47 seconds. For women, it started at 1 minute 35 seconds and is now at 52 seconds!

DEFINITION

Also known as the "crawl," **freestyle** is the most common stroke swum today; conducted by taking individual strokes with one arm at a time while maintaining an alternating up-down kicking pattern with the legs.

The freestyle has become so advanced that coaches today know that there isn't just one way to teach this stroke. We've evolved the stroke so that one method doesn't meet the needs of what's necessary to get the speed you want or are capable of. There are, instead, three styles of freestyle:

- **Hip-driven freestyle:** a distance-oriented stroke, generally seen at 200 meters and longer in competition; the standard fitness swimming stroke

- **Shoulder-driven freestyle:** a sprint-speed stroke, generally seen in competition at 50 and 100 meters, with the rare swimmer using it for distances up to 200 meters

- **Body-driven freestyle:** designed to get people to the end of the pool quickly, driving strong into the wall for the last few meters of a race

Each of these styles has a different *drive point:* that is, where the power, and thus speed, is derived from. In this chapter, we will explain where your speed is best generated with each type of stroke while teaching you the proper form for each. Once you've learned the techniques, we'll show you when to get the most benefit from the variety of options so you can put them into practice the next time you hit the pool.

DEFINITION

The **drive point** is the area of the body that is the catalyst for propelled motion.

Basic Techniques

While each swimming stroke might seem daunting to the beginner, you can rest assured that they are all actually very simple. The main techniques are standard throughout any "version" of the stroke. So unlike a new language you may learn to speak, where absolutely everything is different, in freestyle swimming you're only making small changes but for big gains. But before we focus on the stroke you will use, let's look at a few basics.

Body Position

Consistent body position is key to good swimming form. Most great swimmers have a flat backside, almost no arch in their backs, no bulge in their glutes, and heads that don't ride out of the water. This is the most efficient body position in the water, and it has a place in every stroke. Primarily, it is the foundation upon which good swimming is built. For freestyle, there is no point during swimming in which you will want to break this trend. Even when you rotate to take a stroke or breathe, you still stay as flat as possible and don't allow your back to arch.

Understand that any change in body position will interrupt the flow of the fluid around the body. As the body moves through the water, the backfill of the water into the space that the body moves out of is helping with propulsion. Any time you disrupt this flow, you're going to slow down.

To get a better idea of the position you're trying to maintain in the water, you can simply think about the most basic posture you know on land: standing up straight, eyes looking forward, head in line with the shoulders, and back straight. This proper posture wouldn't just make your mother proud—it will also help you swim fast and efficiently.

FUN FACTS

Don Schollander became the first swimmer to win four gold medals in one Olympics in 1964. Mark Spitz would go on to win seven in 1972—a record that would remain until 2008, when Michael Phelps won eight.

Thinking "Long"

You'll hear staying "long" often in swimming circles, and it's very much a literal term. When swimming, try to make yourself as long as possible and take each stroke accordingly. With each arm, whether you're swimming hip-, shoulder-, or body-driven freestyle, you want to extend your arm to full extension before entering the water with your hand and beginning your pull. The same is to be said about your toes: think long. Point them toward the end of the pool behind you. Most people will find this difficult to do at first, so you'll want to quickly add ankle stretching to your daily routine. Fortunately, the ankles are easy to stretch and can be worked often; see Chapter 10 for simple ankle stretches to do alone or with a partner.

Complete Each Cycle

A "cycle" is complete when you perform each movement involved in a stroke and return to your starting position. In freestyle, for example, you have your right-arm pull, your breath (when applicable), kick, and left-arm pull. Once you begin pulling again with your right arm, you've begun your next cycle.

Just Keep Kicking

Throughout the entire cycle of a stroke, it's important to keep a solid kick going. For the most part, the kick is a stabilizer. There are a few swimmers who have a strong enough kick that allow it to add to propulsion, but for most swimmers it simply stabilizes the hips. There's also an emphasis on the downward beat of the kick, because it helps bring the hip around for setting up the next stroke.

The kick of the freestyle stroke starts at the hips and goes all the way through the tips of the toes. Much like kicking a soccer ball, you're generating the power at the hip—and it increases in velocity as your move your leg downward. You can think of it, too, like a whip, where you're starting at the handle and increasing in speed until it snaps at its end.

When you're thinking about your kick, remember to always keep your legs going. Most of the great swimmers who use this style of freestyle—Peter Vanderkaay, Ian Thorpe, and Erik Vendt, to name a few—all have powerful six-beat kicks, meaning they kick six times per stroke cycle.

Streamline, Streamline, Streamline

A word you'll quickly learn to love is *streamline*. This word refers to a fully extended position, with both arms stretched above your head, biceps pressed behind your ears, hands on top of each other with your back straight, and—when you're in the water—your toes pointed behind you. This is the most efficient position you can assume in the water, and off each turn and start by far the fastest way to move down the pool.

Example of a streamline position with the body positioned flat and straight from fingertips to toes.

THE PROS KNOW

Many swimmers have a problem with getting water up their nose when they start. To avoid this, simply exhale slowly from your nose in between breaths. This also allows you to only have to breathe in when your mouth clears the water, while keeping you comfortable when your face is underwater.

Kicking Is Always Your Friend

Something you'll never stop doing in freestyle swimming is kicking. It's essentially the equivalent to using the pedals when riding a bike. It's also very similar when you're learning how to do it. Sure, you can watch someone else do it and get the general idea, but there are some things you should know to ensure it's done properly and most efficiently.

A proper freestyle kick, known as the "flutter" kick, starts from the hip and works its way down to the tips of your toes. One at a time, you kick your legs downward as if you were extending a whip. You start the motion at your hip and move down the leg until you snap at the end of your pointed foot. During the kick, you maintain just a slight, comfortable bend at the knee that allows for the whipping motion to complete.

A great way to practice this kick is to get into the pool and face the wall. Extend your arms out and grab the wall or gutter. From here, extend your body out into the water, facing down. While still holding onto the wall, practice your kick. When you're doing it properly, you'll feel your body stay high in the water and break the surface. If you feel yourself sink, here's a short list of things you may need to fix:

- **You could be arching your back.** When you're doing this type of practice, make sure your arms are fully extended after grabbing the wall and that your head is in line with the rest of your body. Point your eyes directly toward the bottom of the pool. If your chin is pushed forward, it will cause your spine to bend and push your hips down, which makes kicking a lot more difficult.

- **You may not be pointing your toes.** Think of your leg like the oar of a boat: if you're pointing it straight to the bottom and moving it up and down, you won't go anywhere. Work on your ankle flexibility, and point your toes as much as possible.

- **You could be bending too much in the knee.** You only want a slight bend in the legs—about as much as when you're standing in place on land.

The Freestyle Pull

Every coin has two sides, and there are essentially two sides to the freestyle stroke. You have your kick, which is controlled from the hips and manages the lower half of your body. Then you have your "pull," which is what we call the sequence of movements you carry out with your arms and core muscles.

The pull's main objective is to do exactly what you think: pull water. You grab water when your arm is extended, and then you pull it down the length of your body and push it behind you. This action moves you forward and through the water, just like an oar propels a boat.

You can best understand the basics of the pull by using an accessory called a pull buoy, which we introduced in Chapter 2. Generally, these are inexpensive and are not much more than molded pieces of foam that you place between your legs while you're in the water. If needed, you can also substitute a pull buoy with a kickboard, but that is slightly more difficult due to its smaller width.

Once you have your pull buoy in the water with you and in place, lengthen yourself out in the pool in the streamline position and float. First, take your right arm, while keeping it straight, and move so that it is lined up just outside your right shoulder. All you are doing is moving it from the streamline position a few inches toward the side of the pool.

Hand entry should take place just outside the shoulder on freestyle to ensure comfortable, efficient pull patterns.

From here, you bend at the elbow while keeping your elbow on the surface of the water, as if you were making an "L" shape out of your arm. Throughout this process, you keep your hand completely open with your fingers straight.

Once your arm is in that bent position, pull your arm back and down the length of your body, keeping your elbow up toward the surface and your fingertips pointing down.

The elbow stays up during the pull to provide the maximum amount of surface area with which to pull water.

After pulling down the distance of your body and fully extending your arm, bend at the elbow and lift it skyward, bringing your arm out of the water followed by your hand. This is called your *recovery*. Now you simply bring that hand back out in front of you by rolling your shoulder forward, placing it in the water in the same place you began your pull. Congratulations! You have completed your first full arm stroke!

To swim with both arms, you simply begin your other arm's pull—in the previous photo, the left arm—as your right arm begins its recovery.

FUN FACTS

On August 6, 1926, Gertrude Ederle became the first woman to swim the English Channel. Not only was she the first woman to accomplish that feat, but her time was also faster than that of any man who had completed the same swim up to that point. She would later win three Olympic medals.

Freestyle for Beginners in Six Easy Steps

Without a doubt, the easiest way to truly learn how to swim for beginners is by adding some equipment to the mix—most notably, a pair of fins and a front-facing snorkel (see Chapter 2). The fins provide great buoyancy and power even for beginning kickers, and the snorkel allows an individual to stay flat and not worry about rotating or risk-taking in water while breathing.

Here are six easy steps you can follow that will take you from "never-swam" to "new talent" faster than Michael Phelps can say "gold":

1. Put on your fins and a snorkel, and lie face down in the water. Keeping your back flat, your head down in line with your body, your eyes fixed on the bottom of the pool, and your hands down by your hips, begin to kick so you start moving through the water. The fins will propel you and make it easy to stay afloat.

2. Roll your body to the side, to the point where your mouth is just clear of the surface of the water. Breathe, then return to the face-down position. Practice breathing to your strong side within the movement of the body as you rotate, as opposed to lifting your head (which would cause the body to move out of alignment). (You can also try this after you take the snorkel off, but for now we're just getting you in the habit.)

3. Repeat the same steps, but instead of only breathing on one side, alternate rolling from side to side to a breathing position on both sides.

4. Roll to your side with your arm out, as if you were taking a stroke, and take the breath without disturbing the flow of water on your body balance. Extend your right arm (or whichever is your strong arm) forward (above your head), then roll to the right side, bringing your face up for a breath but keeping your arm out and shoulder down. Then kick, as you try to balance your body. Take a breath, bring your head back down, and repeat the process on the other side.

5. Keeping your left arm at your side, take a full stroke while keeping your right arm extended and maintaining your kick (this is the same thing we did when practicing the pull with the pull buoy; the only difference is that we are now kicking). Rotate the body fully to return to the starting position, which will be the completion of the stroke. Once you've mastered it, do it also on your weak side.

6. In your streamline position, push off and begin kicking. Starting with your strong arm, slide the arm out to the side, shoulder-width, and take your first stroke. As it begins its recovery, begin your stroke with your weak arm. Repeat that pattern, and when you're done, smile. You're swimming freestyle!

Now that you have a grasp on swimming in its simplest form, we'll break it down into selective pieces that allow you to fine-tune your techniques.

THE PROS KNOW

There are a variety of ways you can swim freestyle to enhance your fitness as well as your speed, but be sure to get a solid grasp on the hip-driven stroke before branching into the shoulder- or body-driven strokes. The hip-driven method is the basis for efficient swimming, so become comfortable with it first.

The Traditional Freestyle

The traditional, hip-driven stroke works because it is simply the most efficient. It allows a swimmer to move through the water effectively and with the least amount of energy possible, which prevents the early onset of fatigue. As you may have guessed, the hip-driven stroke finds its power in the movement of the hips. Like dancers, good swimmers are very adept at controlling their hips as well as realizing the necessity of the hips in performing well.

Hip-driven freestyle starts with one hand extended outward, palm facing down, and the body on its side. The hand slides slightly outward as the hip skates on its side. At the point where the arm pull—the propulsive force of the stroke—is beginning to be initiated, the fingertips point toward the bottom of the pool, the elbow comes upward, and the shoulder rolls upward. With the leg on the same side of the body, a strong kick will move the hips around and cause them to face toward the bottom of the pool, allowing the body to rotate into the next stroke, repeating the process on the other side of the body.

With each pull, the body is moved past the hand until it reaches the hip, where there is a release of the water and an exit of the hand, following the elbow out—which is your *recovery*.

The power part of the stroke has nothing to do with the recovery or style of arm recovery used in swimming. The recovery used is highly dependent on the swimmer in the water, and there are two main types of recoveries.

FUN FACTS

Johnny Weissmuller was best known for his on-screen role as Tarzan in the movies, but he was also a sports legend—having won five Olympic swimming gold medals in the 1920s!

Lift and Shift Recovery

This is a high-elbow recovery led by the elbow exiting the water first at the end of the stroke and staying upward as the shoulder rotates forward to begin the next stroke. This is the most common recovery seen among all kinds of swimmers and is essentially your standard recovery.

The lift recovery is a comfortable, basic recovery that uses natural body mechanics to return your arm to the entry position.

To properly execute this after you complete your stroke, you bend at the elbow to break the surface of the water and continue bringing it upward until your arm is entirely out of the water. Once clear of the water, you roll the shoulder forward as the body rotates into position to begin your other arm's pull, then place the hand back in front of you where it started the initial pull.

Straight-Arm Recovery

Straight arm recovery is exactly as it sounds. From the exit point to the entry point, the arm stays straight. Once one side of your body finishes a stroke, your pinky finger is the first thing that leaves the water, and you bring your arm around—like a windmill—and place the hand back in its starting position.

Recovering with a straight arm position is a more advanced, power-oriented recovery style.

Shoulder-Driven Freestyle

Swimming with a shoulder-driven stroke offers the chance to most use the power that comes from the rotation in the shoulders as well as the pull of the arms. You do this by moving your shoulder blades together while keeping your hips stabilized.

To get a more general picture of this freestyle style, imagine a group of football players being thrown into a pool. Most of them, traditionally being non-swimmers, would try to reach the other end of the pool with their heads up, arms wide, elbows high, and bouncing left to right as they pulled with their arms. The obvious technical missteps throughout the rest of the stroke aside, that is about as strong of an example of shoulder-driven swimming as possible.

Note two things with this style of freestyle: it isn't the most visually appealing way to swim, and it takes a lot of extra muscle. But it's an extremely fast way to swim when you want to get somewhere quickly. In fact, every swimmer in the finals of the 50-meter freestyle at the 2008 Beijing Olympics raced with a shoulder-driven stroke.

Instead of focusing on the rotation, this style of stroke requires a strong connection in the upper body. You want to focus on feeling the connection of the fingertips through to the middle of the shoulder and continuing on to the middle of the back.

Throughout the entire stroke, the hips stay solid and in one position while the kick is strong and fast to maintain balance and height in the water. A lot of sprinters have high kicks, where you see their feet kicking out of the water, but this doesn't mean it's propelling them forward. It keeps the hips secure so the shoulders can express power off the steadiness of the hips. Think of it as climbing up a step-ladder: if the ladder is creaking and wobbling, you won't be able to carry anything down that has any significant weight. But if that ladder is solid and stationary, you have a much greater ability to use your strength to do what you want.

A drill that was used at The Race Club, an elite training group of swimmers in Florida, was swimming shoulder-driven freestyle while wearing weights on the wrists to emphasize the rotation in the upper body. The extra weight created increased gravitational pull on the body, which made it easier for swimmers to follow the path of force and really feel the rotation.

FUN FACTS

The first ever crossing of the English Channel was by Captain Matthew Webb in 1875 in 21 hours, 45 minutes. The record today is held by Petar Stoychev, who crossed in 6 hours, 57 minutes in 2007.

Body-Driven Freestyle

The body-driven stroke is what you would consider the racing stroke. It's the tool you turn to when finishing a race, using up all the energy you have left to pull out the last bit of speed you can muster.

In general, this style of freestyle is very inefficient, but when used properly it allows you to finish strongly as opposed to tying up your stroke and losing power because of your muscles tiring out. This stroke, at its most basic element, allows you to attach additional muscle fibers to your swimming that haven't been previously fatigued during the race.

Like with the football team in the shoulder-driven example, we'll give you a simple picture of what body-driven swimming looks like. It may look strikingly similar to a stroke that a little kid starting to swim would use. You'll see that child go from side to side with his or her arms pretty much attached to his body and rotating right and left, right and left, with his or her head down and hips going up high. The child just goes back and forth, paddling through the water. That's body-driven swimming: tying the arms to the rotation of the body.

Instead of holding the hips tight and moving through the water with the power of your shoulders, you're using the full rotation of your body, recruiting the core muscles as you go back and forth to attach to the core motion of your arms. Clearly, this stroke uses a lot more muscle, which you couldn't maintain for long on its own— but it is the perfect adjustment within the last 5 to 10 meters of your race.

FUN FACTS

Grammy-nominated musician Yanni was a member of the Greek national swimming team!

Common Mistakes in Freestyle Swimming

Learning to swim any stroke always seems to involve an "ah ha!" moment. While it might seem difficult at first, once you get your body into a rhythm and practice for a bit, it all seems to click and come together. As with anything, though, what you practice becomes habit, so you'll want to ensure you are learning to swim as efficiently as possible using correct form.

With any new skill you will find some kinks that need to be worked out, so we've covered a few of the most common problems new swimmers have, as well as how to fix them:

- **Sinking hips:** Anytime your body leaves a flat and level position, you'll experience drag. This drag is often caused by your hips sinking down toward the bottom of the pool and is usually brought on by an elevated chin position. Make sure your chin is down and you're looking toward the bottom of the pool when you swim. This will straighten your spine, keeping you flat in the water and ultimately much more efficient. Also, remember to kick, because this helps keep the hips up and steady.

- **Swimming sideways:** Many people find it difficult to swim in a straight line at first. This is not an uncommon problem, and there's nothing wrong with you. What happens is that many people enter their hands in line with different parts of their body, generally favoring the arm on the side to which they breathe. To remedy this situation, make sure you're entering your hand in line with your shoulders on both sides of the body and are pulling completely down the length of each arm.

- **Flat arms:** Always think about pulling with as much of your arm as possible. Imagine your arm as a boat oar. If you're pushing down on the water instead of back, you won't get much speed. Remember to keep your elbow high so you're pulling back with your entire arm.

FUN FACTS

Australian Dawn Fraser became the first swimmer, male or female, to win gold in the same event at three consecutive Olympics. She won the 100-meter freestyle in 1956, 1960, and 1964.

The Least You Need to Know

- A fundamental of freestyle is maintaining body balance, so never lift your head when swimming. Keep it in line with your body as you move through the water.
- Because breathing can take the body out of its natural alignment, only take a breath during the natural rotation of the body so you can minimize the movement of your head.
- Efficient freestyle is maintained when the body stays in as close to a streamline, flat position as possible. To keep the hips high in the water and the body well-balanced, focus on a strong, even-paced kick.
- Because you always want to swim as straight as possible, enter every stroke in line with your shoulder, and pull each arm down the complete length of your body to maximize each pull.

Backstroke

In This Chapter

- The benefits of the backstroke
- The backstroke pull
- The backstroke kick
- Learn the backstroke in six easy steps
- Avoiding common mistakes
- Tips for outdoor swimming

The backstroke is likely the most relaxing stroke of all to swim—and it's a wonderful workout, too. It especially works your back and shoulder muscles—two groups that, when strong and healthy, will certainly improve your life on land as much as in the water.

In general, the backstroke is an extremely simple stroke to swim. But to swim it properly, which is to say most efficiently and in a way that best works your muscles, quite a bit of technique is necessary. A great benefit to this stroke, of course, is its "easy access" to air, and when taking the need to turn your head for a breath out of the equation, you can get a great deal of training done in short order. Let's tackle the backstroke, and very soon you will be gliding through the pool with ease.

The Reverse of Freestyle

It's not really a stretch to say that the backstroke is very much the opposite of freestyle, or the "crawl" (see Chapter 4). But instead of your shoulders and arms rotating forward, they're rotating backward. Instead of lying on your stomach, you're lying on your back. Rather than looking down at the bottom of the pool, you're gazing straight up toward the ceiling. Your feet don't feel like they're kicking downward but instead upward. You get the idea.

An added benefit of swimming the backstroke over freestyle is that it gives your shoulders a nice reprieve from the repetitive motion of swimming freestyle all the time.

Because it's the standard way to swim, most swimmers conduct the vast majority of their yardage in various forms of freestyle swimming. Whether it's through medium-paced long-distance work, sprint swimming for enhanced cardiovascular work, or even from drilling, you can put a lot of time (and rotations) into your shoulders from doing that. It's a good idea, then, both to avoid injury and to increase your muscular balance, to work both sides of your body and your muscles.

You have muscles all throughout your body that you should train, and no single exercise—in or out of the water—hits them all. So if you only do one stroke all the time, you're missing out on a lot of potential strength and muscle gain. By swimming more of the backstroke, because it is the one stroke so similar to the freestyle you're likely swimming most often, you're doing yourself a great favor and balancing out your workload and your body.

Additionally, you'll certainly feel the benefits of the backstroke in short order. Specifically, if you're not stretching or just not stretching very often, after a lot of freestyle work you'll notice your triceps and chest may feel particularly tight. When you flip over and start swimming the backstroke, you'll feel a slight stretch on those muscles with every stroke—and it'll feel exceptionally good!

Like all strokes, the backstroke begins on your back in the streamline position. You want to keep your body as flat as possible on the surface of the water. If your hips drop at all, you're creating drag that you have to fight through to move across the water. At all times during the backstroke, ensure that your entire body is in one solid line.

During actual backstroke swimming, you're going to be kicking throughout the entire stroke cycle—but for the sake of simplicity when teaching it, we are going to break it down into two portions: the pull and the kick. Both are very simple, but focus on just one thing at a time.

Backstroke Terminology

Most terms you'll hear around the swimming pool are pretty universal amongst strokes, but a few are more adept at describing instances or techniques in backstroke. As such, we'll go over a couple that you'll find pertinent here.

Turnover

Turnover is a simple way to describe the speed at which you're completing stroke cycles. If we mention increasing your turnover, that means to more quickly take each stroke. A great example is if you were to watch the 1,500-meter freestyle in the Olympic Games. You'll notice that swimmers seem to be taking strokes at a relatively calm pace, that the water doesn't splash a great deal around them, and that they can maintain this rate for a rough 15 minutes. If you then watch the 50-meter freestyle, the athletes are taking frantic (but well-attuned!) strokes with lots of white water and using a huge amount of energy. The greatest difference in the two races is, of course, turnover.

SINK OR SWIM

Before any race or high-intensity set, do a number of easier, gentler swims first to prepare your body, warm up, and prevent injury.

Position in the Water

Position in the water is relatively self-explanatory. You're either sinking, too low, high, or too high in the water. As a well-trained swimmer, you should never have to worry about sinking, so we'll focus on the other terms:

- **Too low:** If you're too low in the water, it means you're causing a lot of drag— which is holding back your efficiency, speed, and training. Anytime we discuss an occasion where new swimmers might find themselves "too low" in the water, you'll know what to watch out for.

- **High:** It just wouldn't sound right if there were a position called "just right" in the water, but that's generally what remaining high in the water means: you're right where you should be. This is a position where your body is in alignment, thus creating the least amount of drag, and it also allows you to move to any position necessary to perform proper technique. In the pages of this book, you will hear us use the phrase, "Stay high in the water" pretty often.

- **Too high:** Like anything, there is the possibility of getting too much of a good thing. Usually, you just have to keep an eye out for having your head too high in the water, because this will, as a result, push the rest of your body downward.

FUN FACTS

Aileen Riggin is the only woman to have won Olympic medals in both diving competition and in swimming. In 1924, she won silver in 3-meter springboard diving and bronze in the 100-meter backstroke.

Flat

If you've spent any amount of time on a pool deck, you've likely heard coaches talk about the need for backs to be *flat* during the backstroke. This is true, of course—to an extent. For this particular method of swimming, we're going to introduce a slightly refined definition of "flat."

The shape of the back is extremely important in the backstroke. Certainly, you don't want to be so rounded in your back that your hips are pointed downward, causing a V shape with the body and thus incurring a lot of drag resistance. But you need to think of yourself in terms of a boat. If you think about the hull of a boat, it's obviously rounded where it goes from beneath the surface to above the surface. In the backstroke, you don't want to be perfectly flat in the absolute literal sense because you won't cut through the water as well. Round your back just a bit for comfort—but not so far as to feel your hips being forced down.

Backstroke Pulling

The easiest way to learn the backstroke pull is to use a pull buoy between your legs to keep your hips and lower back afloat without the need to kick. When using a pull buoy, many people try to place it just above the knees, only to find it difficult to hold on to. Place it higher (between the thighs), which will make it easier to use but equally as effective.

Once you have the pull buoy in place, lean back into the water and straighten out your body with your hands down at your sides. You will be staring at the ceiling or sky and floating relaxed. Take this quick opportunity to go through the motions and positions of the proper backstroke before doing so and remember the keys: a slightly rounded back, hips on the surface, and shoulders rotating on the surface of the water.

To begin your first stroke, keeping your right arm straight with hand flat and fingers pointed, raise that arm upward in a clockwise motion, allowing the shoulder to lift and rotate upward with it.

In backstroke, each arm stays straight as it recovers above you.

Your fingers will point to the ceiling at the halfway point, and then as you begin moving the hand behind you, rotate your hand 180 degrees so that when you enter the water above your head, your pinky finger is the first thing to break the surface. You will want your hand to enter just outside your shoulder width (true for every stroke you take).

At this point, you will have one arm above your head, fully extended, and the other still at your side. This is perfect. Now we are going to focus on the movement of just the right arm for the time being.

You're going to bend at the elbow, making your arm into a bit of an L shape, and bring that arm down the length of your body. As you do this, keep your elbow relatively high in the water—just slightly beneath the surface—and your hand will stay flat and your fingers pointed to the side of the pool. Think of it as literally pushing the water down your body so that it moves you forward.

While your right arm is pulling water, your left arm will be repeating the initial stages you had just done on the right side: keeping it straight, lift it skyward and rotate your hand before it enters the water.

Try to keep your hands at exact opposite positions. When one is straightened above your head, the other will be at its full extension at the side of your body. While one is straight overhead pointing toward the ceiling, the other will be at your side, halfway through its pull. Repeat these steps with the pull buoy between your legs until you are comfortable with the general motions.

After you get the hang of the timing, we are going to clean up the stroke a bit. To become efficient, you have to take advantage of your body's own movement. In the backstroke, this involves shoulder rotation.

Going back to your first stroke with your right arm, as that hand enters the water the right shoulder should dip slightly beneath the surface. This action puts the body in a great position to really pull a great deal of water. Consequently, while the right shoulder goes down, the left shoulder will come up, offering a much easier way to bring the left arm around. This repeats itself in reverse, of course, and you will find it allows you to pull much more efficiently.

Although your shoulders are rotating, your head stays in the same position at all times. Your chin stays high and your head remains back, and it does not move at all. Some backstrokers have trained with objects such as half-full cups of water on their foreheads to practice ensuring that their head doesn't rock back and forth. You may not want to train with that particular method, but it does demonstrate the need for a rock-solid position of your head. With the cup of water, for instance, it makes it very easy to pinpoint at what part of your stroke you are rocking too much, thus causing the cup to tip.

THE PROS KNOW

According to Olympian Adam Mania, when swimming the backstroke, the head should remain very still. Pretend that you are spinning on a rotisserie but the head stays still. This is called T-Spine rotation. The shoulders turn from side to side, but the spine and head remain in line. In order to keep this movement steady, a constant near-vertical kick is required. Many swimmers have a tendency to scissor kick, splitting their feet apart too much and then crossing over when they kick. This causes the commonly seen "hopping backstroke," which looks as if the swimmer is hopping from side to side instead of staying on the "rotisserie."

As we suggest with all strokes, feel free to grab a pull buoy and work on your pull without kicking. This is especially beneficial in the backstroke because the body naturally bends at the waist in a position that would cause you to sink relatively easily.

Using a pull buoy, you will be able to give full concentration to your head, shoulders, and arms and ensure they are entering in the proper position.

Backstroke pulling may feel a bit more awkward at first than a freestyle pull because you aren't able to apply as much force with your pull as you are in freestyle due to the necessary reach above your head. To combat that, we involve more body movement, such as the shoulder rotation we just talked about as well as the hips, which gives us the ability to use more force while still remaining on our backs.

Now that we've covered this stroke in detail and you have a pretty good idea of how backstroke pulling is done, here are a couple of simple tips that may come in handy:

- Relate hand entry of the pull to a clock: your hands should be at the 10 o'clock and 2 o'clock positions.

- Remember your arm position: straight arms above the water, bent arms below water.

Double-Arm Drill

A terrific way to train for proper arm placement is to do a drill that has you using both arms at the same time to pull. One of the biggest issues in the backstroke is reaching too far with your hand to begin your pull, and this drill helps solve that. At this point, it is best to use the pull buoy.

While on your back as if you were going to go ahead and pull normally, raise both hands simultaneously above—keeping your arms straight—and rotate both arms so that your pinky fingers will enter the water first, at the same time.

Because you aren't focusing on rotation, you will get into a habit of properly placing your hands in line with your shoulders. If you were to try and reach too far, you would find it uncomfortable and awkward. You'll know you have this right when you feel an even amount of pressure on either arm when pulling and you don't push off to one side of the lane or the other.

Additionally, once you get the hang of traversing the pool with this drill, add to your focus the goal of pushing as much water as possible. With each pull that you complete, feel the rush of water down your sides and try and make each pull more efficient and more powerful.

One Arm at a Time

As with the double-arm drill, you can get a lot of training value out of swimming backstroke with just one arm. Because it's important to make sure that each stroke is placed in the same position relative to the shoulder on either side, you can gauge if you're out of alignment on a particular side by training a full length with just one arm pulling.

There are two ways you can do this. First, you can try just leaving one arm down at your side while pulling with the other. Or you can place and leave one arm extended above the head—pointed toward the opposite end of the pool—while pulling with the other. When you're done, look and see if you're in the same portion of the lane as when you started. Repeat with the other arm.

Backstroke Kicking

It wouldn't be too much of a stretch to say that kicking for the backstroke is just freestyle kicking done on your back, but being as your body is face-up instead of face-down, there are some additional ways to look at it and a few minor changes you need to make.

The kick always starts from your hips. In the backstroke, the kick is a little more profound than it is on freestyle. Whereas your freestyle kick is very much a stabilizer for your hips in an up-and-down motion, the backstroke includes more rotation.

Your hips will rotate along with your shoulders. Some excellent backstroke swimmers have a rotation so profound it looks as if their hips almost reach an entirely vertical positioning on each side. You don't need to try to go that far, but do allow your hips—and subsequently your legs—to comfortably follow the lead of the shoulders in rotating left to right as you kick.

When it comes to the feet themselves, similar to freestyle, still think of your legs as being part of a whipping motion with a snap at the end. In the backstroke, you can very much liken this to flicking a shoe off your foot.

THE PROS KNOW

A great way to get your backstroke kick down is to simply kick on your back in a streamline position. Keep your arms extended above your head and just kick your way up and down the pool. This will allow you to gain a feel for the kick as well as practice keeping your hips up near the surface of the water.

Backstroke for Beginners in Six Easy Steps

As in the freestyle lesson in Chapter 4, we're going to add fins to this practical backstroke lesson. They help you float, will assist in ensuring that you point your toes properly and will put you at ease while we break down simple steps to backstroke swimming. Unlike the freestyle six-easy-step program, though, we won't need a snorkel:

1. Put on your fins and push off the wall on your back in a streamline position so that you're floating on top of the water and kicking with your legs. You will maintain this steady kick throughout the entire process.

2. Keeping your arms straight, slide your right arm to just outside your shoulder (as if you were making half of a narrow Y shape with your body) and turn your palm to face the wall (your pinky finger will be down).

3. Bend at the elbow now so that the tips of your fingers point toward the side of the pool.

4. Maintaining that same position with your hand, push it down the length of your body, down past the hips, until your arm is straight.

5. Repeat steps 1 through 4 with your left arm.

6. As your left arm is taking its stroke, bring your right arm back to its starting position by keeping it straight and lifting it toward the ceiling and turning it as it passes your head so that your pinky finger is the first part of your hand to re-enter the water.

Common Mistakes in Backstroke Swimming

Rome wasn't built in a day, and neither was the perfect backstroke. In fact, swimmers today are still getting faster and faster than their counterparts of even just a few years ago. So clearly, the "perfect" stroke has yet to be found. But what we have discovered over the last several decades are some basic mistakes that swimmers tend to make when traveling through the water on their backs. With these simple tips, you'll be able to avoid these problems—or if you're currently experiencing them, you can solve them with haste.

Over-Reaching

Over-reaching is the term used when a swimmer enters his or her arm too far out of proper alignment. By doing so, the swimmer causes himself or herself to not only swim at angles instead of straight but also causes the fluid motion of the entire stroke to be ruined.

If you feel your stroke is a bit awkward, try this for a quick fix. Think of yourself lying on the center of the black line on the bottom of the pool. When swimming a proper backstroke, your hands will be entering just outside of your shoulder width, which would be on either side of the black line. Now if you're over-reaching, your hand will likely be entering on the line, which is not correct technique. Focus on keeping your arms farther out to the sides.

Enter the arm in line with the shoulder, as shown, while the opposite arm begins the recovery phase of the stroke.

Getting Water Up Your Nose

If you're swimming the backstroke and notice water splashing onto your face or up your nose with each stroke, you're likely keeping your chin too far down toward your chest. Lift your chin as if you're pointing it toward the sky. You don't need to be looking down at your feet when you're swimming anyway, and this will allow you to move your arms more easily *and* keep water out of your nose.

 FUN FACTS

When Krisztina Egerszegi of Hungary won the 200-meter backstroke gold medal at the 1988 Olympics, she was the youngest Olympic swimming champion in history—just one month after her 14th birthday.

Letting the Hips Sink

If you find yourself sinking in the backstroke or if it just feels like you're swimming against something (as in you're feeling a lot of resistance), the most common possibility is that your hips are too low in the water. Remember, you want to keep your hips up near the surface of the water so that you're extremely flat and floating near the surface. Think of yourself as a boat skimming the surface.

You may be able to solve this problem with the same solution for getting water up your nose: lift your chin. The body is all connected, obviously. When you lift your chin, your chest will rise, followed by your hips, and your hips will allow your legs to float higher and thus kick more efficiently.

If you feel a bend in your lower back, lean back, get that chin up, and lift those hips. You'll find yourself swimming faster and easier than ever before!

Not Adjusting for Distance

Something that will become more familiar to you the more you swim is the need to adjust your stroke for the particular set you're doing. It can be quite the damper on your training or competition if you take your swim out too hard or too fast and find that you don't have anything left in the proverbial tank to finish strong. On the flip side, it's also disappointing to finish a training set you intended to be very challenging, or a race where you wanted to beat a best time, only to touch the wall at the end and discover you had plenty of energy left to utilize. When this problem is seen in the backstroke, it's often derived from overuse or under-utilization of the legs.

For the backstroke, look at proper body positioning varying slightly based on the length of your swim. If you're in a long swim, you're going to want to kick without quite as much force in order to prevent yourself from tiring too quickly. For swims of a greater volume—those that are longer in yards/meters—lean yourself back a bit farther into the water to provide additional assistance to your legs, and focus on kicking more efficiently rather than more forcefully.

In a shorter race, make sure you give it a strong effort from the start. Your body positioning will be sitting up a slight bit more, and you'll want to focus on kicking hard and fast and increasing your turnover rate in the arms.

FUN FACTS

In 1922, American Sybil Bauer, who would later win an Olympic gold medal, broke the world record in the women's 440-yard backstroke. It was also faster than the men's world record in the same event by four seconds!

Tips for Swimming the Backstroke Outdoors

Not all of us have the luxury of swimming outdoors most of the year (or at all in some areas), but a large number of people are blessed with the opportunity of getting outdoors and exercising in a pool under the warmth of the sun. If you are one of the latter, believe us when we say that millions of swimmers around the world are jealous!

Now with that said, a lot of people avoid swimming the backstroke outside for one of two reasons (and sometimes both).

First, and probably the biggest complaint, is that the sun is too bright. Unless the clouds happen to be passing overhead or you're in a rare outdoor pool with a canopy spanning overhead, the sun can definitely be a problem. The best way to combat this is to get mirrored or reflective goggles. Several manufacturers make these, and they're the closest thing you can get to sunglasses in the pool. They're extremely effective, very sleek, and generally made in the same styles with which you're already comfortable. If you swim outdoors, we highly recommend these both for your comfort and eye safety.

Second, and this is especially pertinent for people swimming in crowded outdoor pools, is that it can be difficult to keep track of where you are within the lane when swimming outdoors because you have no ceiling in which to follow a marker of any sort. And when you aren't sure you're swimming straight, it's very possible (and quite likely) you'll end up in the wrong spot and collide with a fellow swimmer. That can be both embarrassing at the least and painful at its worst.

The best solution for ensuring you swim straight is simply to practice proper technique. The main reason people end up moving left or right in the lane in the first place is improperly placing the hand on the entry—either overreaching beyond the shoulder or not far enough. Once you are able to consistently place your hand correctly, you'll find you can literally swim straight in a calm pool with your eyes closed. But until then, keep practicing and make sure you also take advantage of your peripheral vision.

Without dropping your head to do so, casually glance to your left every few strokes as your left arm is entering the water. This is a very easy time to check your placement in your lane because your body is already rotating to that direction. By doing this, you'll easily be able to make any corrections that you find necessary with your stroke to keep you safe and out of "oncoming traffic."

The Least You Need to Know

- The backstroke is a perfect complement to freestyle swimming by strengthening and balancing the upper body muscles.
- Balance is important to a smooth backstroke, so always enter your arms in the same place each stroke; never over-reach.
- The kick should be fluid and rhythmic and not forced, which can be assisted by keeping the chin high for proper body position.
- Take advantage of training tools such as fins and pull buoys to improve your backstroke technique.
- Never allow your head to rotate; it should remain stationary while the shoulder and hips take care of the rotation.

Breaststroke

In This Chapter

- The breaststroke: your "ultimate gym"
- Proper pull-out technique
- Learn the breaststroke in six easy steps
- How to fix common problems before they happen

The breaststroke is likely the most storied stroke of all, and it has changed significantly over the years in the competitive aspect. Rule changes have continually brought changes in the technique of the stroke, which has made it both faster as well as a better workout. To properly swim the breaststroke, it's really quite valuable to understand its past and what makes it such a great swimming stroke.

Although the "easiest" stroke at the outset may be perceived as freestyle, or the "crawl" stroke, the breaststroke is actually the most popular and common way to swim overall. Because the body leans forward in the water with the legs parted and hands gliding in and out, it makes it exceptionally easy to float. For new swimmers, this provides a huge sense of comfort. For people in the water with no swim training of any kind, this is a very natural feeling—and many people move through the water with a very basic version of the breaststroke and don't even know it. Further still, because there is no part of the stroke that requires both hands to extend over the water, it can be much easier on the joints of the shoulders for people trying to rehabilitate an upper-body injury. All in all it's a fantastic stroke that can fit anyone of any age from new swimmers to those recovering from injury.

What Is Breaststroke?

In the fitness sense, when it comes to using swimming for muscular strength and conditioning, think of the breaststroke as the "ultimate gym," or whatever late-night infomercial you currently see on television promising an everything-in-one machine. The difference is, the breaststroke delivers—and you don't need to make three easy payments or pay shipping and handling! No stroke uses more muscles than the breaststroke, and no other stroke is so complete—ensuring an absolutely full body workout when you swim it. Just like the countless millions who currently take advantage of this stroke, we're sure you'll find it quite enjoyable and rewarding as soon as you give it a try.

In the competitive sense, the breaststroke is the "slowest" stroke, with the current men's 100-meter world record being roughly 10 seconds faster in freestyle than it stands in breaststroke. But speed isn't everything, and the breaststroke has a huge "fan base" (so to speak). It's swum by millions and millions of people around the world for its physical benefits, competitiveness, and sheer technical beauty.

The breaststroke kick, which is most commonly referred to as a "frog kick," is the most natural to new trainers and is also the easiest way to stay afloat or move forward in the water. Whereas the flutter kick requires more ankle flexibility and technique, even the most rudimentary of breaststroke kicks can greatly assist a swimmer in remaining high in the water. Because of this, by learning the breaststroke kick, new swimmers develop a comfort level in the water that carries over to everything else they will learn and do in a swimming pool.

Quite simply, the body has a natural affinity for the breaststroke. The body position makes it easy to float, the arm and leg motions are gentle, and the kick is easily learned. As such, the breaststroke in some form or another has been around for hundreds or perhaps even thousands of years. In the days before the modern Olympic Games, swimming competitions were held around the world, and the breaststroke was the name of the game. It was considered graceful and "proper."

 FUN FACTS

Even after athletes began using a stroke that was much like the freestyle we know today, many stuck with the breaststroke because the new stroke was considered "barbaric" due to the way the arms thrashed into the water. It would take decades before the world as a whole would catch up to faster methods of swimming—and in time differentiate each stroke into the separate arts that they are. Today, of course, we have four separate competitive strokes, but in the beginning, it was only breaststroke! The earliest drawings of swimmers show a breaststroke-like swimming technique and books written as far back as the 1500s and 1600s describe the breaststroke!

Terminology Explained

Because of its unique structure and patterns of pulling and kicking, a couple things used to describe the breaststroke are necessary to get the hang of first. Additionally, whereas in freestyle (Chapter 4), backstroke (Chapter 5), and butterfly (Chapter 7) you use a "kick-out" off the start and turn, in the breaststroke you use something quite different: a *pull-out*. The variety from other strokes is just one more reason why people love the breaststroke.

Pull-Out

A pull-out is the series of motions that a swimmer conducts after each turn or push-off before starting to swim the breaststroke. It's how a swimmer goes from being in a streamline position to the position needed to take a first stroke. The pull-out involves breaking from streamline by moving the arms outside shoulder width and pulling down the length of the body while keeping the elbows high near the surface.

Body position after the initial phase of the pull-out, with the arms straight at the swimmer's sides.

After the arms have pulled down the length of the body and are straight against the sides, the swimmer slides the hands (palms up) underneath the stomach while keeping the elbows close to his or her side and pushes the arms forward while thrusting forward with a kick. Doing this lifts the swimmer's body close enough to the surface that he or she may easily take that first breaststroke pull.

"Snapping" Your Kick

We've already talked about whipping the leg all the way through to the toes in freestyle and backstroke. Clearly, the same technique couldn't apply to the breaststroke, but the term still does. "Snapping" in the breaststroke sense is still used when discussing the kick, but it's more inclusive of the ankles than in a flutter-kicking stroke.

We'll get into more specifics about the breaststroke kick shortly, but when we do, remember that each kick needs to be completed all the way through so that the bottoms of the feet touch or nearly touch each other.

The breaststroke kick starts with the heels coming up to your rear, rotating the feet so the toes point to each side of the pool, then kicking the legs back behind you. As your legs are just about straight again, "snap" the kick together by releasing the water as you point your toes behind you and bring your feet close together in a fluid motion.

"Rounding the Corners"

This term simply refers to how your arms move through the water on the front part of your pull. As your arms bend at the elbow to start your insweep, you want to make sure that you are not dropping any of the water you just sculled out. By keeping the constant water pressure on the palm of your hand, you are doing a good job of "rounding the corners."

The Breaststroke Kick

The breaststroke is the one stroke where it is significantly easier to learn the kick than it is the pull. And in effect, the pull becomes easier to learn once the legs know what they're supposed to do—because they help keep the body lifted in the water and floating. And when we aren't sinking, swimming is easy!

The first step toward learning the breaststroke kick is to grab a kickboard. Hold the sides of the board near the top, and lean forward in the water. With only slight kicking movements of the leg, you'll find yourself staying quite comfortably on the surface of the water. This is an ideal learning position for this kick. With your legs extended straight out behind you, you're in the position where each breaststroke kick begins.

SINK OR SWIM

Always warm up your legs well with some sort of dry land or pool exercise before doing any powerful breaststroke kicking. Kicking the breaststroke too hard without warming up can cause injury to the groin and/or knees.

To start, place your legs about shoulder width apart and bring your heels up to your rear. You will want to ensure your feet stay below the surface of the water—meaning you don't want your heels touching the air while they move—so bend at the knee while you slightly tilt your hips up to facilitate the range of motion you'll need.

Next, without moving the knees outward, turn both feet so that your toes point to the sides of the pool. This will take some ankle flexibility and is developed over time, so don't worry if you can't quite do it yet (but remember to practice stretching after your workout). Just turn your feet as far as you can comfortably go. At this point, you're prepared for your kick and are ready to propel yourself forward. To do so, kick back behind you, focusing on pushing water *back* and not *down*. Think of yourself as pushing off something while jumping on land. You square up your legs and push off evenly, driving with the bottoms of your feet. That's exactly what you want to do here: kick with the bottoms of your feet, driving water behind you, your toes pointed still to the sides of the pool to provide maximum surface area—and then as you near the end of your kick, snap your feet together.

Think of the kick as involving different steps:

1. Your feet come up toward your rear with your knees close together.

2. You turn your feet out as far as you can toward the sides of the pool. The farther you can turn your feet out, the more water you will "catch" and the faster you will go.

3. Snap your kick and finish with your legs together.

The Breaststroke Pull

Even novice swimmers can tell that the vast majority of propulsive force in the breaststroke comes from the kick. It's just that obvious. The legs are bigger and stronger, and the body position of the stroke simply bodes well for the lower half when it comes to creating power in the stroke. Whereas freestyle is an upper body–dominated stroke and the legs provide more balance and stability than anything else, the breaststroke is quite the opposite. The legs are the driving force while the arms and the rest of the upper body are used to put oneself into position for an efficient kick. Because most of the power in the breaststroke comes from your legs, your arm pull only plays a small part in the actual speed and power of the stroke. Although it only accounts for a small amount of the power if you make your arm pull too big or too wide, you can actually slow yourself down because a big arm pull can get in the way of an efficient breaststroke kick.

Before each pull, a swimmer will be in a broken streamline. The body will be flat and near the surface of the water (arms and legs both extended), but instead of being in a normal streamline position where the biceps are pressed against the head and the hands overlap one another, the arms are in more of a "Superman" pose, extended out straight from the shoulders.

When broken down, the breaststroke pull really has three separate parts:

- The scull outward
- The insweep
- The underwater recovery

These work in unison with no pause between any step.

For the scull outward, you'll have your palms facing downward while your body is flat. From here, you move your hands out toward the sides of the pool so that they ultimately put your body in a Y shape.

For the insweep, you will bend at the elbows—while keeping the elbows themselves up near the surface—so that your fingers start pointing toward the bottom. You will then pull your arms back, your head breaking the surface of the water for a breath as you do, ensuring that you keep everything from beneath your elbow (forearms, wrists, and hands) all the way to the tips of your fingers straight and in line. As your hands begin to pass by the sides of your head, you will stop pulling backward. This is the part of the stroke where it is very important not to make your pull too wide. Many swimmers make their pull very big and actually pull way down by their stomachs because they feel more powerful this way (and rightfully so). You are actually pulling a lot more water this way. But you are also taking your body so far out of alignment that this type of breaststroke pull is very counterproductive. And for the competitive swimmer, it's also illegal, as it is not allowed to pull back that far.

The recovery phase is where you complete the stroke and ultimately return your hands to the starting position. After you have discontinued pulling back, bring the hands underneath your head. To do so, you will bend at the elbow while turning the hands up so that your palms are facing you. The fingers from one hand will overlap on top of the fingers of the other, and once you're there, push your arms back out ahead of you and return to the position where you started.

As the hands move forward on the breaststroke recovery, the elbows stay high near the surface of the water.

The Glide

Because of the amount of technique involved in swimming the breaststroke properly, many swimmers get too caught up in going through the motions. One largely overlooked aspect of the breaststroke is the glide phase. As soon as they complete one stroke, many swimmers immediately begin the next and completely skip the gliding phase. This is the time in which your body is back in the nearly streamlined position and you are being propelled forward by the force of your most recent kick. It's an efficient body position that is valuable to your swimming because it reduces the drag your body creates, allows you a bit of a resting period between strokes, and sets your body up for launching efficiently into the next stroke. It is also, in fact, a phase that should be appreciated even when breaking the stroke down into parts, such as a pull set or a breaststroke kicking set. By skipping or shortchanging yourself on the glide, you're ultimately expending more energy in exchange for less speed.

To swim the breaststroke properly and efficiently, make sure that after each kick you extend your body out to your streamline starting position and allow yourself to glide through the water. Only when you start feeling yourself slow down should you begin your next stroke. This is something you will have to play with, because it won't be obvious the first time you swim the breaststroke when you start to lose speed—but in time it will be very natural, and you'll be able to time the transition between strokes perfectly.

THE PROS KNOW

In the glide phase, it's important to keep your body as straight as possible. Many swimmers have a tendency to lunge down at the end of each stroke instead of forward, causing the stroke to be much more wavy than it needs to be. By lunging straight forward on the glide, you will propel forward more with each stroke—and in turn, take fewer strokes per length.

Pull and Kick Timing

The breaststroke is a very technical stroke with many important facets. Whereas some strokes may allow slight flaws in stroke technique to be hidden, the breaststroke is one that needs a great deal of fluidity to be done properly. Flaws at any juncture can throw off the rhythm of the stroke and not just slow you down but also make it feel awkward to swim. On the flip side, though, when the breaststroke is swum with correct technique and proper timing, it is a fun and fluid way to exercise and move through the water.

The timing between the pull and the kick is critical. If timed incorrectly, your kick will face a lot more opposition in the form of drag. When the kick is timed properly, your body is in a very hydrodynamic position that will allow you to move forward quickly and freely.

When you begin your pull, your body stays flat as your arms spread apart. As you begin to pull back, at that point it's okay to tilt your hips and begin setting your feet up for your kick. It's very important to play around with this and ensure you don't drop your knees straight down in the water, because it will create a huge amount of drag as well as make kicking very awkward. Tilt your hips just enough so that you can bring your heels back over your hamstrings, and turn your feet out.

As you are putting your hands back out in front of you, begin your kick. Be sure that you do not begin your kick as you are still pulling back. Wait until your hands start their forward momentum before driving with your legs.

An easy way to remember when to kick is to think, "Kick your arms forward"—meaning the powerful part of your kick should come when your hands are reaching forward into the glide phase.

Breaststroke for Beginners in Six Easy Steps

The breaststroke is a very rewarding stroke physically and mentally. Once you're gliding along swimming in this way, you'll feel accomplished and your muscles will quickly become bigger and stronger. At first, we're going to begin without incorporating a pull-out. To get you going right away, follow these easy steps:

1. Push off the wall, starting in your streamline position.

2. Keeping your arms straight, move them apart so that they create a Y shape with your body.

3. Bend at the elbows and point your fingers downward, starting your pull backward.

4. Start drawing your heels up behind you to set up your kick, ensuring that you are not bending so much at the hips that your quadriceps become a wall against the water to create drag.

5. Scoop your hands up underneath your body and push them out forward in front of you to complete your recovery.

6. Kick your legs, focusing on a strong driving kick that will push water behind you and propel you forward.

Body Alignment in the Breaststroke

An often-overlooked aspect of the breaststroke is the alignment of the body. In the backstroke and freestyle, the concept of how the body should be positioned is much easier to grasp because it generally lies on a single, flat plane that is set high in the water. The breaststroke is different due to the undulation, albeit slight, that the body naturally goes through when swimming the stroke. Even with these intricacies, though, the proper position for various parts of your body is easy to understand when put into practice.

As we've already discussed, it's critical to not drop the knees. Remember that the heels get drawn up to the rear; they don't get put into position by dropping the knees down toward the bottom of the pool. The knees do have to move to clear the way for the heels, but the motion should be derived from tilting the hips slightly, opening a path for the feet. You shouldn't need to actually think at all about moving your thighs or knees, as the simple motion of the hips will take care of the necessary movement. Your heels will then slide up to you just beneath the water's surface.

Now as for the upper body, the easiest way to grasp proper body position is to think about a splint being placed from your lower back, straight up your spine, and past the back of your head. Your head, neck, and spine shouldn't move independently at all in the breaststroke and should instead maintain one cohesive bond that's held throughout the entire stroke.

Common Mistakes in Breaststroke Swimming

Because of the level of detail involved in swimming the breaststroke properly, it is possible to overlook an aspect or two as you're picking up the stroke. It's completely normal, and we're going to cover a few of the common problems to help you either avoid them completely, notice them if you have them, and fix whatever you may need to.

The breaststroke is a very simple stroke that can be extremely technical. It takes time to develop a great stroke, but because each one is so independent (by starting back out in a streamline), every pull and kick is a new opportunity to improve. With a little practice and patience, you'll have a beautiful, graceful stroke to not just get fit with but to show off, too!

FUN FACTS

The first crossing of the English Channel was done by Matthew Webb, and he did so swimming the breaststroke.

The Kick

Because the kick is so integral to the breaststroke, there are a few problems that can result from the same technique issue, including:

- **Scissor kick:** If you find yourself using a scissoring motion, where the legs kick inward and together, this is a scissor kick.

- **Flutter kick:** Another issue that can come up is that your feet end up doing a motion that's very much like the flutter kick in freestyle, where they seemingly kick straight down instead of back.

- **Directional kicking:** Directional kicking is a kick that sends you off to your right or left instead of straight ahead. If you find that even though you start in the middle of the pool lane, but after a couple strokes you're getting closer and closer to a lane rope, this is likely an issue for you, caused by one leg kicking more forcefully than the other.

To fix any of these issues, simply focus on pushing *back* when you press your kick. You can get a good sense of this by practicing your kick while holding on to the wall of the pool, extending yourself out, and working on your kick. With each attempt, think about turning your feet so the bottoms are pressing directly toward the other end of the pool. It does take coordination, so go through the motions slowly until it becomes second nature. If you try to do it too quickly, your legs will naturally want to simply extend at the knee, which will cause you to kick downward.

Incorrect Timing

Many beginning breaststroke swimmers have issues with getting any force from their kick because they are too low in the water. This happens when you are attempting to kick before your upper body is pressing forward and your arms are going out. You can fix this by ensuring you're not kicking too early. Some of the best breaststroke swimmers in the world look as if their upper bodies are almost fully extended before they begin their kick. To get a sense of proper timing, try overexaggerating the delay between pulling and kicking. Once you get a better feel for the speed of your arms, you can better time the pressing of your kick.

Lifting the Head

By far the most common problem even advanced breaststroke swimmers run into is that they lead their stroke with their head. That is, after they scull outward to begin their pull, rather than allowing their arms to pull back and lift their upper body and head out of the water, they lift their chin and draw their head back first. This throws off the entire rhythm of the stroke and can make the pull and kick less powerful by taking them out of their areas of strength.

Remember that your head should be kept in a solid line from the top of your head through to your hips. Think of yourself as standing on land, walking, and looking straight ahead of you. Your chin is level, your eyes are forward, and the back of your neck is smooth. This is how you want to remain during the breaststroke.

The back of the head should remain in line with the back during the breaststroke.

A main component that causes people to lift their head is that they focus on wanting to look at the other end of the pool. It's quite natural; if that's where you're going, that's where your eyes want to stray. But despite whatever the natural occurrence may be, avoid it. Your eyes during the breaststroke will go from looking at the bottom of the pool at the onset of the stroke to looking at the water at an angle when you pull. Other than during your turn, your face should never be vertical to the wall.

Pulling Back Too Far

The arms in breaststroke have a lot to do with the alignment of the rest of your body. If you pull your arms back too far, it's just natural body mechanics that your shoulders will drop, followed by your elbows, and your spine will curve. In time, the hips will sink, which—as we've covered over and over again—will cause problems with your kick, either delaying it, causing your knees to drop and create drag, or prevent you from kicking backward.

Play around a bit with your arm placement; you may need to make it feel like you're leaving them too far out in front to get the proper position, but you'll feel when you're doing it correctly as your shoulders won't slope downward.

The Least You Need to Know

- Never allow the knees to flare out of the body line when kicking.
- The elbows should always stay high throughout the pull.
- Keep the head in line with the back, and never lean too far forward or behind.
- Always think "back" when kicking, never down.

Butterfly

In This Chapter

- The latest stroke in swimming: butterfly
- How to learn a difficult stroke
- Proper timing to ensure a flowing butterfly
- Learn the butterfly in six easy steps
- Preventing common, drag-causing mistakes

The butterfly is the most recent innovation in swimming. By that, we mean to say that of all the strokes, it's the newest as far as competitive terms go. While the other strokes have been around in some form or another for hundreds of years, the butterfly (or "Fly," as it is often affectionately referred to) got its start in the 1930s.

The interesting story behind the butterfly stroke is that it didn't actually come together on its own. It was really a two-part creation process by swimmers looking for a faster way to swim the breaststroke, and what resulted was a beautifully crafted and fantastic fitness stroke.

What Is Butterfly?

The butterfly is really very much a hybrid stroke. Like all strokes, there are two parts to the butterfly: the pull and the kick. The difference compared to other ways of swimming is that unlike freestyle and backstroke, the pull is done with both arms simultaneously while entering from above water (in contrast to the breaststroke, where the hands are generally underneath the water for the duration of the stroke). The kick, too, is different because it is actually made up of two kicks instead of one.

There is a small dolphin kick upon entry, when the body is elongated with arms out in front and legs lengthened, and another as the hands are passing the torso during the pulling phase.

Now, as mentioned, this stroke was developed in two parts. The dolphin kick (which we will cover much more in depth later) was, by letter, against the rules of competitive swimming. The arm movement of taking the hands simultaneously above and over the water for the recovery phase, though, was not. So starting in the 1930s, some very intelligent breaststroke swimmers found it would greatly increase their speed to use what we now know as the upper-body motions of the butterfly but apply it to the breaststroke. If we saw this today, we would think it looked incredibly awkward: a butterfly recovery with a breaststroke-like frog kick. But what's out of fashion today was all the rage decades ago. It would take upward of 20 years before this all changed by the allowance of the dolphin kick, and shortly thereafter, the creation of the stroke as we know it today.

THE PROS KNOW

Today, there are four strokes in the Olympic Games: freestyle, backstroke, breaststroke, and butterfly. The latter is the newest entry into the games, having only first been swum on its own in 1956 at the Melbourne Summer Olympics.

Two Ways to Swim Fly

The way that the butterfly was developed is also a great outline for how it should be taught. Anyone who watches someone such as Olympics gold medalist Michael Phelps swim the butterfly stroke will say, "Wow, that looks beautiful!" And the butterfly is an extremely graceful-looking stroke. But the same people who are commenting on how great it looks will tell you that it also looks extremely daunting. It takes a great deal of coordination and rhythmic sequence to swim this stroke properly. Because of that, mastering the technique of each piece of the stroke *before* trying to combine them is extremely beneficial.

While it doesn't take as many muscles to swim the butterfly as it does the breaststroke, that doesn't mean it's necessarily easier to do. In fact, most swimmers would say that the breaststroke is much easier to swim than the butterfly. The reason is because there are really two ways to swim the butterfly—gracefully (properly), or what coaches would say, "muscling through it"—and many swimmers try the latter.

If you try to just use your strength to get through the stroke, you'll find yourself tiring out very quickly and having a lot of difficulty being able to swim this stroke for any decent length of time. On the other hand, if you try to elongate your strokes, stay relaxed and flexible, and focus on proper technique, this becomes a fun stroke you can keep your form with for quite a while.

As you learn to swim the butterfly, a small trick to remember is ensuring you don't remain tight throughout the chest muscles. If you feel your chest flexing throughout your swimming, you're probably thrashing your arms down on top of the water and trying to just use brute force to propel yourself forward. Remember, you can't bench press water, and if you're constantly feeling your upper body tighten, you're just pushing down instead of pulling water behind you (which is the goal).

While true for every stroke in different ways, it is especially important to stay relaxed during the butterfly. It takes a lot of flexibility, especially throughout the torso and down through the legs, to be done properly. Take your time and learn it the right way, and you'll be on your way in no time.

Terminology Explained

Despite looking significantly different from the other strokes from above water, the body position of the butterfly shares a lot of similar characteristics with the other strokes. Here are some quick term explanations to help you understand what we're talking about as we go through the motions.

Getting "Up" on Your Elbows

During the pull of the butterfly stroke, the elbows should stay high in the water. They shouldn't be so high that they are breaking the surface as you pull back, but once they enter in front of you to begin the pull, they should remain near the water level with your fingertips pointed down toward the bottom of the pool—almost creating a 90-degree angle in your arm. This is called being "up" on your elbows.

Staying "Low" on the Surface

Sometimes it can be a bit confusing with terms such as "low" right next to the definition of "up" when discussing the same stroke. But fortunately, they are easily differentiated.

There was a time when a big wave motion of the body was considered ideal. Swimmers would enter the water and dive down a bit so they could rocket themselves back up and take another stroke. In time, we've discovered that swimming with a big undulating motion is neither the most energy efficient nor the fastest way to swim.

Take, for instance, the contrasting styles of the world's two greatest butterfly swimmers of the past and present: Mark Spitz (winner of seven gold medals at the 1972 Olympics) and Michael Phelps (winner of eight golds at the 2008 Olympics). If you watch the two swim, you'll notice a striking contrast (other than Spitz having an awesome mustache and great '70s hair, as compared to Phelps's hydrodynamic cap and clean shave): height in the water. With each stroke Spitz took, his head rose relatively high out of the water—and you can see a wave of water against his chest. If you watch Phelps swim, his chin barely lifts out of the water when he breathes. The reason is that we've discovered it's better to stay flatter in the water. As a result, our body isn't rising high above the surface and instead is staying "low."

The Butterfly Pull

It's a little simplistic, but a very general way to think of the butterfly pull is to think of just doing two freestyle pulls at the same time. Both hands enter extended in front of you, just outside shoulder width; you bend at the elbow and keep the elbow high in the water and pull back the length of the body. We'll break that down to specifics, but if you keep that general picture in mind, you'll have no problem grasping the concepts.

First, we highly encourage you to put on a pair of swimming fins before trying the butterfly pull. While it seems kind of contradictory because you won't be kicking, fins do a great job of keeping your body on the surface. If you're sinking, this becomes much harder to learn because you can't get your body in the proper position. So throw on a pair of fins and make your life a lot easier. As another option, you can also use a pull buoy if you prefer—but because they help elongate the body, we recommend fins.

FUN FACTS

Benjamin Franklin invented hundreds of useful things during his lifetime, many of which we still use today. One of his many inventions includes swimming fins.

Once you're in the pool, extend your body out on the surface of the water facing the bottom of the pool. Make sure your legs are straight behind you and your arms are extended out front. Your hand placement should be just as we discussed; slightly outside the shoulders is great. Your palms will be facing downward, and your eyes will be looking toward the bottom of the pool (not the opposite wall).

When you're ready to take a pull, you will bend at the elbow so that your fingertips now point down. Your elbows shouldn't move much and should remain at the same height in the water. Now is the time to propel yourself forward, which you will do by pushing water behind you, down the length of your body, and past the hips. The key is to ensure you stay up on the elbows in order to use maximum surface area.

Think of it this way: you'll push a lot more water using your entire arm than you will with just the back of the triceps. Yet the latter is a common problem many beginning butterfly swimmers have because they allow their elbows to drop. And once that happens, the entire stroke tends to break down because you need a strong pull to maintain the rhythm of the stroke. If you can't set up your body position for a proper kick because you weren't able to maintain height in the water (due to the arms dropping), it becomes extremely hard to fight that resistance. Remember: swim smarter, not harder!

From the elbow down to the fingertips, the arm will stay straight all the way through the pull until the hands begin to pass the hips. As you're pulling, make sure your arms aren't wide and away from the body. The pull is relatively compact, and the hands glide just outside the body throughout the duration of the pull.

Pulling Pattern

Butterfly and freestyle (see Chapter 4) have, over the last decade or so, undergone a bit of an ideology change when it comes to the pattern of the pull. It used to be common for swimmers to pull with an S-type pattern with the hands. The theories for this were varied, but this technique had garnered a lot of followers. More recently, many coaches are teaching swimmers to take a straighter path from hand entry point to hand exit point. This can allow for greater use of the muscles involved in the pulling.

When your hands enter in front of you, you bend at the elbow while leaving your hands in the same plane along the sides of the body. Draw an imaginary line in your head as to where those hands started, and as you pull back, make sure they exit the water on that same line behind you.

The Recovery

In Chapter 4, we discussed the straight-arm recovery. In the butterfly, you're doing something very similar but with both arms simultaneously.

As you finish your pull, your arms will be at full extension and your hands will be past your hips. At this point, your palms will be facing up, so we have to rotate the arms as we exit the water.

When your hands break the surface, rotate the arms so that the thumbs are facing down. Keeping your arms straight, make half moon–like shapes with both and recover them both back to the same position in which you started. Keep the arms low, and avoid the temptation to just throw them forward. If you raise your arms up too high, the first thing that happens is your shoulder blades come together—and it acts almost as a weight on your back. Your chest will get pushed down and your body position will suffer, causing a lot of drag and preventing you from staying relaxed and fluid with your stroke.

The arms stay extended during the recovery phase; bending them can result in pushing the chest down.

 SINK OR SWIM

Be sure not to raise the arms higher than needed out of the water on the butterfly recovery. Doing so can put unnecessary stress on the smaller muscles of the shoulder.

Timing Your Breathing

Breathing during the butterfly is done on an as-needed basis. Some swimmers like to breathe every stroke, others like to go one-up, one-down (one stroke with a breath, one without, then repeating that pattern), others go one-up, two-down, while others maybe two-up, two-down, or any combination thereof. It comes down to your own comfort and conditioning as to what works best for you.

What doesn't change, though, is the portion of the stroke where it is done. Whereas in freestyle, for instance, you can choose to breathe on either side of the body, in the butterfly it is simply done by lifting the chin up and clearing the mouth above the water's surface and breathing in.

As you're beginning your pull backward, surging your body toward the other end of the pool, tilt your head back just enough that you are able to open your mouth without taking in water. This will certainly take some practice, but with each breath, do so with the intent on staying as low as possible. As we've mentioned, the more out of alignment you make yourself, the more liable you are to cause a drop in your torso and your hips. This is one reason why many coaches teach their swimmers to take as few breaths as possible, because it causes the least disruption in the body line. Swimmers who have a high level of skill in keeping that line while taking a breath, though, are certainly less affected by this.

The chin should only break the surface of the water as much as is necessary to take in a breath.

Play around with different patterns and find what works best for you when it comes to how often you need to breathe. When you're learning, it may be more beneficial to try to breathe the least amount possible so that you can focus on getting the pull itself down. Don't hold your breath so long that you're gasping for air when you do finally lift your head, but if you're in the initial stages of swimming and don't need to breathe every stroke, give that a shot. It's much easier to learn the proper pulling technique without breathing.

The Butterfly Kick

The kick used in the butterfly stroke is called the "dolphin kick." This is somewhat misleading, though, because hearing the word "kick" naturally makes people think of using just their legs. The dolphin kick is really derived from the core and is a motion that works itself through the entire body. We'll get into the finite details of the dolphin kick in Chapter 9, where we discuss kickouts, because the dolphin kick is easier to grasp when in the streamline position coming off a wall. For now, we will cover the basics of the motion and how you can put it together quickly and easily to get you swimming "Fly" right now. And to make it as simplistic as possible, we still suggest wearing fins until you get the hang of things.

The dolphin kick is done with the legs together, moving as one. Think of a dolphin, mermaid, or even a shark: their propulsion is from one motion in the lower extremity that gently and easily pushes water behind them and moves them forward. If you can picture doing that yourself with your legs, you're already on the right track.

Properly conducting a dolphin kick starts in the upper body, pressing the chest down and then having the rest of the body follow suit with a whipping-like motion that extends through the toes. When doing this kick, you'll maintain a slight bend in the knees—and make sure you point your toes to the end of the pool behind you.

The dolphin kick used when swimming the butterfly is not a standard kick because there are actually two kicks done per cycle. There is a kick done when the hands first enter the water and another as the hands are passing the midsection. The two kicks that make up one normal butterfly dolphin kick are not of equal stature. The first kick can almost be looked at as a "setup" kick for the bigger second kick.

As the hands enter the water for your pull (where your arms are extended), press the chest down into the water and allow that motion to continue down the body and kick downward with your feet. As you go through your pull, the legs will rise back up toward the surface a bit—and as the hands are pulling past your midsection, do a second, more powerful kick. This second kick (when done properly) will make it easy for you to stay high in the water and get your arms back around to the initial starting point.

> **THE PROS KNOW**
>
> The dolphin kick is the only kick used in every stroke. Aside from being used in the butterfly, it is also often used off turns in freestyle and backstroke—and one dolphin kick is allowed during a breaststroke pull-out.

Butterfly for Beginners in Six Easy Steps

Although it may appear daunting, swimming the butterfly is really no more difficult than any other stroke. Like the other strokes, it simply needs to be broken down into easy-to-understand steps:

1. With fins on, push off the wall in the streamline position.

2. Slide your hands just outside shoulder width and bend at the elbows, keeping the elbows high while the lower half of the arms starts to point downward.

3. Pull the arms back, focusing on keeping the elbows up, and ensure that your head stays in line with the rest of your body.

4. Exit the water with both hands simultaneously to begin your recovery, ensuring you keep your arms straight. As your hands move back ahead of you, your thumbs should be just above the water's surface.

5. Enter the water with the hands, making sure that you don't slap the water on entry. Entry should be gentle and smooth.

6. As the hands move back to the position to start the next pull, press the chest downward and do your first dolphin kick to set up your next stroke cycle.

Common Mistakes in Butterfly Swimming

Almost all problems with butterfly swimming come as a result of body position, which is a bit unique. In the backstroke, there's the tendency to place the hands improperly or allow the waist to bend; in freestyle, head position can be an issue; and in the breaststroke, there's a lot of learning to go through with the pull pattern.

That isn't to say these types of things don't affect the butterfly, but because the motions are rather standard, the most common problems tend to come as a result of where the body is in the water and not from a lack of knowledge.

THE PROS KNOW

Here's some advice from Olympic gold medalist Tommy Hannan: to make your butterfly stroke smoother and longer, when performing the recovery, focus on relaxing the arms and hands and work on pressing the upper chest down. Try to make the hands the last thing to enter the water. Also, during the butterfly, your hands and hips are high when your chest and feet are low. Think of your body as a wave that moves through the water at a constant height. You do not want to have any part too high out of the water, and you don't want any portion too deep in the water. By decreasing your wave height, you can increase your wave length.

Pushing Down on the Water Instead of Back

If any number of coaches were asked about the biggest problem they run into with teaching the butterfly, the majority will tell you that their swimmers have a tendency to push down on the water with the pull rather than back behind them. This presents the obvious problem of bringing the chest too high out of the water, along with dropping the elbows—but an issue new swimmers may not grasp right away is that it also places the hands significantly farther below the water's surface at the end of the pull. Rather than the hands being easily lifted into the air, the hands must push through several inches of water (drag).

The body should never feel like it's being significantly lifted upward while swimming the butterfly. You should always be thinking *forward*. Even when you take a breath, it may be lifting the body upward slightly, but it should still feel *forward*. If you have a tendency to feel as if you're pushing yourself toward the ceiling instead of the other end of the pool, make sure you are keeping your elbows high and pulling behind you, not downward.

This common problem is often linked to the initial entry of the stroke. If a swimmer is slapping downward on the water to enter instead of gently setting the hands into the water, the natural momentum of the arms can cause a downward motion to begin—rather than allowing the athlete to get up on the elbows.

THE PROS KNOW

According to Olympic gold medalist Mel Stewart, many swimmers have a habit of slowing down during their stroke because they don't place enough emphasis on the first kick in the butterfly. Focus on giving power to that kick so that you keep your stroke momentum, and balance yourself out for a faster, more efficient butterfly.

Incorrect Timing on Breathing

Because butterfly breathing is really rather unique compared to the other strokes, getting the proper rhythm down is often a little tricky. And because it isn't something practiced every stroke (usually), it can take a bit of time. Fortunately, practice with this skill makes perfect—and with a little work, you'll have it down in no time.

The most common issue with breathing is that swimmers have a tendency to lift their head far too early in the pull phase. Beginning swimmers tend to like to lift their heads as soon as the arms begin to move backward, which can rob them of a lot of strength. If the head gets lifted too soon, the body can't recruit the larger muscles in the back to give strength to the pull.

Wait until the hands are passing by the head on the pull before lifting it to breathe. Play around with this, and you'll notice how much easier it is to take a breath at this time than upon entry or near the exit of the hands.

Lifting the Head Too High

Some cities at altitude may have mottos that liken to, "The air is better up here," encouraging you to go take in the fresh air on mountaintops. And maybe that's true (particularly if you live in a smog-filled metropolis), but the few inches of lift you can give yourself in a swimming pool while swimming the butterfly make no difference. So stay low! Focus on lifting your head only high enough to take in air and not water, then get your head back down.

The Least You Need to Know

- Keep the arms straight above water during the recovery.
- Lift the head only enough to breathe, and return it to the water as quickly as possible.

- The first kick during each stroke cycle is a smaller kick, with the second being the source of the most power.
- Always pull straight back with the arms underwater; avoid the temptation to make your pull curve.

Starts and Turns

As with any sport or activity, there are elements that make everything flow together; consider the details in this part those elements. In a way, what this part covers is the "glue" of the sport. In swimming, those techniques are the starts that get you into the water smoothly, turns that keep you moving without interruption, and also a neat little technique called the "butterfly kick" that's so versatile and effective it's the one thing you can do in *every* stroke. It's so valuable in fact that it's often called "the fifth stroke," and you will surely learn to love it and utilize it as you train. After this part, you'll know the proper and quickest way to enter the water and the best way to move from one stroke to another, no matter which stroke you're swimming or which stroke you want to do next.

On Your Mark, Get Set, Start!

In This Chapter

- The different types of starts
- Proper entry into the water
- Backstroke starts made simple
- Avoiding common start mistakes
- Relay starts
- Exercises to improve your starts

There are many ways to get into the pool and start your training. You can slide in at the end, use the ladder, or climb down the stairs that some pools have built into them—or if you're looking for something new, dive in off the blocks. Your pool may have rules against using the blocks during a regular open swim, but if you're on a club team, odds are you will have the opportunity to use them if you would like. There is a little more to it than just diving forward and hoping you don't belly flop, so we'll cover the differences and intricacies of the various kinds of starts you can use when swimming. They're relatively easy with some practice, fun, and definitely boost your confidence when it comes to your in-water abilities. So let's dive in!

Block Starts: Not Just for Competitors

The vast majority of swimmers around the world don't enter organized races, but that doesn't mean there's no value in block starts. The same way the avid weight trainer might try an Olympic lift although he isn't a power lifter or a non-boxer may occasionally give the speed bag a go, it's simply another way to vary your training and a tool you can use to enhance your enjoyment of the activity as well as your overall fitness level.

One of the main benefits of using a block start is additional speed when doing sprint work. It puts your body in an extremely efficient position, which allows you to get your arms and legs moving quickly at the beginning of your swim, rather than waiting to surface from a slower push start off the wall. For fitness purposes, this can be a wonderful beginning for a more challenging swimming set.

Push Start from the Water

A push start—pushing off the wall from the water—is the most common way swimmers begin their sets during training or when going for a leisurely swim. The key component to remember each time you push start is to get into a tight streamline position before leaving the wall. If you push off before extending your arms or locking in your streamline, you will create a huge amount of drag that will hinder your motions in the water and make it a lot more difficult to take your first few strokes. As you progress in your swimming abilities, you will find that each length begins to feel "shorter" and that it does not take as much effort to reach the opposite end of the pool. Swimming becomes easier when you don't cause yourself to exert extra effort due to inefficiency at the beginning of each length.

When you're ready to go, drop beneath the surface of the water with your feet on the wall and knees bent, extend your arms past your head, point your fingers to lock in a nice and tight streamline, and give yourself a strong push off the wall.

When you're ready to break the surface of the water off each turn, you will begin your first stroke. In freestyle swimming, it's best and most efficient to get into the habit of not breathing during your first stroke cycle off the turn. Advanced swimmers also ensure they do not breathe on the last stroke going into the turn, which ensures they're not creating additional drag and are able to get into and out of the wall as quickly as possible. For the fitness swimmer, this is also a great way to help build lung strength and aerobic capacity.

When it comes to backstroke and breaststroke, you can breathe right away just by virtue of the mechanics of the stroke because your face will be out of the water. As for the butterfly, try to take at least one stroke off the turn before taking your first breath.

SINK OR SWIM

Always check the depth of the pool water before using the starting blocks. Rules and regulations have changed over the years for required safe starting depths and can vary depending on your area. Older pools in particular may have very shallow starting ends and may not be suitable for use by newer swimmers due to the risk of diving too deep and hitting the bottom of the pool. For your safety, never conduct starts if you are alone.

Starting from the Deck

Despite the starting blocks available, no one says you have to actually use them. Even in U.S. Masters Swimming competition for example, it's entirely acceptable to start from the deck if it's more comfortable for you. And just for general practice, it's a lot less daunting to learn how to start from the deck rather than from the blocks. Here's a step-by-step breakdown of how to do just that:

1. From the deck, place your toes over the edge of the wall and bend at your knees slightly. You can start from this position by either bending at the waist and touching the wall between your feet and waiting there for the starting sound or by extending your arms in front of you and waiting there. Whichever you choose, if you are in a race, you will need to stay still once you hear "Take your mark."

2. Once the signal has been given and/or you're ready to start, send your body weight forward by driving with your legs and push yourself out over the surface of the water.

3. While you're in the air, straighten your legs and place your arms into the streamline position so you can enter the water smoothly. Think about causing the least amount of disruption as possible to the water.

Entering the Water

Proper entry into the water is critical for a variety of reasons—the first of which is efficiency. Think of any diving competition you've ever seen, especially at upper levels such as the Olympics. The athletes aim to enter the water as smoothly as possible, and the underwater footage you see on television is really profound when you consider how deep into the diving well they go. Now imagine if these athletes belly-flopped instead. They would lose just about all their momentum as they slapped the surface of the water. Not only would that slow them down, but it would hurt, too!

The best way to think of correct entry is to picture a small circle in front of you in the water, and your goal is to pass your entire body through that one target.

To enter properly, focus on getting your body to follow a straight, arrowlike line. From your fingers down to your toes, everything needs to go past the same position. When you start entering the water, your fingertips will be the first part of your body to go in, and your arms, head, chest, midsection, legs, and toes all need to go through that exact same spot.

Entering the water in a straight line with as little splash as possible is the key to smooth, efficient starts.

Once your entire body has entered the water, you need to level your body out so that you don't continue on down to touch the bottom of the pool. As your toes breach the surface of the water, adjust your body position by pulling back slightly toward the surface with your arms. This will flatten you out, and the momentum you have from the start will be sending you forward now instead of down, which is exactly what you want.

To bring yourself to the surface, begin your kick once you've lost the extra speed given by the start—and depending on the stroke you will be swimming, continue with the appropriate *breakout*.

 DEFINITION

Breakout refers to the portion of a swim where a swimmer's body breaks the surface of the water and he or she begins a stroke; it occurs after starts as well as turns.

Flat Start from the Blocks

Once you decide to give starts from the blocks a chance, there are two ways to do so. Flat starts are the easiest way to get going from the blocks. (They're generally also the best method of getting acquainted with starts from above the deck.) With the flat start, you are on the block with your toes curling just over the front edge and your feet just about shoulder-width apart. And as you may have guessed, your feet and heels will be flat against the blocks.

Here are the steps involved in the flat-start technique:

1. While keeping a slight bend in your knees, lean forward and grip the space of the platform between your feet.

2. To put yourself in the best position to create momentum once you start, ensure that your chin and eyes are aimed down and back, not forward out to the pool. Only bring your head forward once you begin your start. When it's time to blast off the blocks, always think *forward*. Never think *up*.

Especially important on the flat start is keeping your hips lined up over your feet to create stability and power.

3. The first thing you will do when beginning the start is push your body toward the pool while throwing both hands forward and preparing them for a streamline position.

4. Push hard off the block with both legs and dive out as far as you can, getting your body into a straight streamline position before your fingertips break the surface of the water.

Track Start from the Blocks

If you want to try something a little snappier and more advanced, there is another option: track starts. Track starts are called such because they are the swimming variation of the track-and-field race start. In this position, you have one leg—generally your weaker leg—back rather than lined up with the other that's at the front of the block. Where your weak foot will be precisely depends on your build and size and the length of the block itself, but between 1 foot and 18 inches is common.

Track starts rely on a transition of power from one foot to the other, so it's important to have good footing.

The process for starting properly with a track start is similar to that of a flat start, but relies a bit more on fluid body motion when pushing with the legs:

1. Place your stronger leg forward and wrap your toes over the edge of the block. Place your opposite leg back between 1 foot and 18 inches, then lean forward. Your strong leg will be slightly bent, and your weak leg will be balanced on the ball of the foot. As for your upper body, unlike the flat start, during the track start your hands will grip near the ends of the block, just outside the feet.

2. Keep your chin and eyes down, ensuring you are not looking forward and out to the water (which would alter the positioning of your spine).

3. Push off to create your initial force with your back leg, and project yourself forward.

4. As your hips pass over your forward leg, push with that leg as well while launching your hands forward—and, as with the flat start—preparing yourself for entering the water in a streamline position.

Which Start Is Right for You?

The question of whether you're best attuned to be a flat- or track-type starter is largely a matter of personal preference. The flat start is easier to begin with and more comfortable for people who don't get to practice starts often. Many would argue that you are able to generate more power, and thus more propulsion upon entry into the water, by using a flat start. Others are advocates of the track start because it is generally a faster way to get off the blocks, which could make up for the slight difference in initial momentum.

If you've ever run track in your life, whether on a club team or in high school, you may just naturally be more comfortable with the track start. If you've never done any type of start before, get comfortable with the flat start first and feel free to play around with track starts later.

THE PROS KNOW

The most important piece of the start is not which style you use but clean entry into the water. You can always change how you decide to start later on, but a constant should be perfecting your entry regardless of foot positioning on the platform.

Backstroke Starts Broken Down

One more type of start that's available to you is the backstroke start. This type of start finds swimmers starting in the water instead of above it and launches them into the swim with a perfect body position for a great dolphin kickout and backstroke swim. The backstroke start takes a little more getting used to than other starts, but it's a lot of fun once you get it down!

The backstroke start is a little more complicated than a track or flat start simply because it's fully done by feel. You start in the water, facing the block, and grip the handles that are beneath the platform. The height of these will vary from pool to pool, and their structure is also likely to change (some are handles; others are bars).

With your hands on the grips, place your feet on the wall about shoulder-width apart and your toes just beneath the water's surface. From here, tuck your chin down toward your chest and lift yourself so that your hips are near the surface of the water. It does take a lot of upper-body strength to pull yourself up, so this is a pretty good exercise itself. You can also help yourself get this technique down when not in the pool by working out your back muscles, specifically focusing on exercises such as pull-ups.

Stay close to the wall when doing a backstroke start to ensure you are able to push off with power. Keeping yourself distant from the wall will prevent an adequate push.

When you want to start, push hard with your legs, arch your back, and throw your head back. The best backstroke swimmers in the world have a beautiful arch on their entry, and you should practice doing the same. As you're pushing off the wall, quickly bring your arms behind you and put them into a streamline position to prepare for your entry into the water.

Common Start Mistakes

As with each individual stroke, many intricacies must be ironed out before you become really comfortable with starts. It isn't uncommon to end up with a red belly a few times before learning to enter the water smoothly, but we'll give you some tips to avoid unnecessary discomfort.

THE PROS KNOW

Unlike in track and field, where a false start is allowed, in Olympic swimming competitions if a swimmer false starts—by flinching or by starting early—he or she is disqualified from the race.

Belly Flops

Starts that are felt by your stomach first instead of your fingertips are relatively normal among beginning swimmers. The main cause is that swimmers too often think about getting distance with their starts instead of proper technique. Remember that how far you go isn't nearly as important as *how* you enter the water.

The main goal of a start is to give you a powerful and efficient beginning to your race or set. Entering the water from a start is far quicker than just pushing off the wall, and the momentum you create will also last longer. But if you end up creating a big splash more akin to a cannonball than to a start, you won't be carrying any speed at all with you. Focus on entering in a straight line a comfortable distance from the wall, and don't worry if you think it's not far enough. Wherever you can enter smoothly is a perfect start.

Starting Too Deeply

Some swimmers discover that after learning to enter the water smoothly and with little splash, they're a bit like a rock that is thrown into the pool: they head straight for the bottom. This happens when swimmers don't adjust quickly enough underwater to level out. As we mentioned, you'll want to pull your arms back a bit once your body is fully into the water. If you feel as though you're doing this but it isn't soon enough, try starting a bit sooner. You're moving fast when you enter the water, so you might be waiting too long (much after your body has all broken the surface). By thinking about it slightly sooner, you may end up doing it at just the right time.

Rules About Relay Starts

For people who want to swim competitively, one of the most enjoyable times at swim meets are *relays*. You get to race with and against friends and teammates, and you have a variety of options when it comes to distances. The one thing you will need to know to take advantage of these opportunities is how to do a proper relay start.

DEFINITION

A **relay** is a team of four athletes swimming together as part of a single race. The term can refer to freestyle relays, where all athletes swim freestyle over an equal distance; or a medley relay, where each athlete swims a different stroke in the order of backstroke, breaststroke, butterfly, and freestyle.

Relay starts are generally a lot faster than standard flat or track starts because you don't have to stand still. You can be in motion to build momentum and already begin your start progress while your teammate is still swimming into the wall.

For a relay start, it's essential to gauge where your teammate will need to be for you to start your body motion. For example, if you know based on how fast you react that you can make a legal relay exchange by starting your movement when your teammate is five strokes from the wall, you can save quite a bit of time for your relay.

For a relay start, stand with your toes over the edge of the platform the same way you would for a standard start, keeping your knees bent a little more than you would regularly. And now, instead of gripping onto the block with your hands as well, keep them down but slightly forward. When your teammate is getting close to his or her finish, swing your arms up around in a clockwise motion to build momentum. As your arms swing around and pass your hips, push yourself forward and dive into the water, getting yourself into a solid streamline position before breaking the surface. This takes practice to time properly, because your feet can't leave the block until your teammate has touched the wall.

Dry-Land Exercises for Explosive Starts

Great starts are all about explosive power off the blocks. Whether you're using the flat start or track start, you'll need to have some strength in your legs to ensure you get a great leap into the water. From there, it's all about technique—but before you can slice perfectly through the surface of the water, you have to make sure you get yourself well into the air and have enough of a boost to allow your body to get into the appropriate position!

There are several things you can do, without a pool and even without weights, which will help give you additional leg power. As with all exercises on dry land, make sure you are warmed up before beginning—and if you feel any kind of pain, discontinue immediately.

Squat-Jump

Stand up straight with your feet apart and lined up a couple inches outside your shoulders. Your toes should be pointed forward, and it's a good idea to wear comfortable athletic shoes when doing this exercise.

Bend at the waist and slowly squat down until your hips are below your knees. As you're coming down, you can either let your arms hang in front of you or extend them out in front of you.

Pause briefly when you reach the bottom of your squat, then powerfully drive from the legs upward and jump into the air, bringing your legs together and your arms to your sides.

As you are about to land back on the ground, make sure you have a slight bend in your legs and land on the balls of your feet first (to protect your knees). Then move your feet back to their starting positions and repeat. Start with a couple sets of 10 jumps with a minute break in between, and increase your sets and jumps slightly as you become more comfortable and stronger. See how high you can jump!

SINK OR SWIM

When doing any kind of jumping exercise, always ensure that you are on level and clear ground. Jumping above obstacles or on rocky, uneven, or otherwise rough flooring/ground can lead to serious injuries.

Broad Jump

Broad jumps are actually quite similar to relay starts and are great for improving your jumping abilities. It's a simple movement: a standing long jump. In track–and-field events, you see the running long jump, and this simply removes the running portion.

Stand with your feet apart and hands at your sides. Bend at the knees now and pull your arms back as far as you can, then swing them in front of you as you jump forward for distance. You can return to your starting position and repeat this process if you're low on space, or you can pause briefly and do several jumps in near-consecutive motion if you have room to do so.

One-Leg Squats

This movement is more advanced and takes some getting used to but can do some great things for your leg development, your starts, and your swimming as a whole.

Stand up straight and put both arms straight out in front of you. Now also put one leg straight out in front of you. With the leg you're balancing on, squat down as far as possible, pause at the bottom, and push hard to stand yourself back up. Balance will come into play, but do your best to keep your arms and legs straight. It's perfectly okay to not reach parallel at first; just do what you can. You can also practice by holding on to something lightly for balance if it allows you to get deeper into the movement. Be sure you're working toward a goal of being able to do it unassisted. There's no specific number that's necessary to reach for this to be a benefit to you. Work up to being able to do several sets with each leg using only a minimal amount of rest in between sets.

The Least You Need to Know

- There's no consensus on one start being better than another; choose what's right for you after practicing both and finding which is most comfortable.
- Balance is very important on starts. To best maintain poise when preparing to start from a flat or track position, keep your hips over your feet, and don't lean back.
- Enter the water in a solid line with your body and create as little splash as possible.
- Strengthening the lower body and increasing flexibility in the lower back and legs can significantly increase the comfort of doing starts from the blocks.

One Good Turn (Deserves a Few More)

In This Chapter

- The details of dolphin kicking
- The different types of turns
- Open turns and flip turns
- Turns used in the individual medley
- Exercises to improve your turns

Over the course of your swimming career, you will perform tens of thousands of turns, so it's quite a good idea to get comfortable with them. Fortunately, you'll have a lot of practice and ample opportunity to perfect your craft. Consider this: Olympians can swim upward of 20,000 yards a day. That's *800* turns a day. Over the course of their average six-day training week, that's *4,800* turns each week, 19,200 per month, roughly 230,000 per year ... you get the picture. And while the majority of us aren't Olympians, if you figure the average Master's workout is still around 3,000 yards a day for five days each week, you're still doing 120 turns a day, 600 a week, 2,400 a month, and almost 29,000 a year. It's a good thing turns are fun!

Swim Like a Fish; Kick Like a Dolphin

The *dolphin kick* is also sometimes referred to as "the fifth stroke" because of how integral it has become to efficient swimming. The dolphin kick is a beautiful motion because of its fluidity, and to achieve that, a good amount of coordination is required. You will use dolphin kicks in conjunction with every turn you do, with the exception of the breaststroke open turn. On top of that, just kicking with this method is a great core workout.

> **DEFINITION**
>
> The **dolphin kick** is the swimming kick where the legs remain together and move in a whiplike manner, maintaining only a slight bend at the knees.

Why Dolphin Kicking Is So Important

There are two ways to look at the dolphin kick and its importance. First, for everyday swimming, it sets you up off each turn to break the surface of the water smoothly while building your speed before getting into your actual swimming stroke. If you don't kick (or don't kick properly) when coming up from under the surface, you'll be at a standstill and practically have to start from scratch. You want to build into each length, and a great kickout is the best way to accomplish that.

Second, if you ever choose to compete, the dolphin kick is the fastest way to come off each wall (with the exception of the breaststroke, where it isn't allowed). Further, it takes less energy to kick underwater in a streamline position than it does to take an equal number of stroke cycles.

For the fitness swimmer, knowing how to properly dolphin kick underwater is great because it affirms your talents in the pool. You're doing something you love, you're doing it well, and it's impressive in the minds of others. Clearly, you're not exercising for their sake—but it never hurts to inspire others. And most importantly, dolphin kicking is a great workout! You involve muscles throughout the length of your body, and in no time flat you'll develop an impressive set of abs and a stronger lower back and pair of legs.

Dolphin Kicking Broken Down

With the exception of when you're swimming the butterfly stroke, anytime you dolphin kick you will be doing so from the streamline position (see Chapter 4). Kicking from this position requires coordination that runs the length of your body. To do this properly, think of yourself as a long, continuous instrument that flows together rather than works in individualized parts.

Start from Your Core

Because you're in the streamline position, your body is as long as it can possibly be and is in a tight and powerful kicking position. Although it sounds very much like a leg-only motion, dolphin kicking actually begins much farther up the body in your midsection. This is where you want to start creating your power. If you think of yourself as a whip, you can see why this is necessary. If you have a long whip but only move the tip, you won't create any power. But if you start back at the handle of the whip, you'll have a profound and powerful snap at the tip. In the case of swimming, that snap you're creating will equal a terrific amount of propulsion in the water. To begin the dolphin kick, start "whipping" your body at the core by pressing your midsection slightly downward.

Hip Motion

As you continue that whipping action in the core, the motion is going to start moving through your hips. Think of your hips as a station that transfers the power you've started to generate in your core through to the legs, and allow the hips to rotate forward and put the legs in position to "snap" like the tip of a whip. Another great way to think about this is to picture yourself kicking a soccer ball or football. If you stand still with your hips immobile, you won't be able to send the ball very far compared to when you rotate your hips into the kick. When you do that, you can launch the ball a great distance. The same applies to swimming. When you allow your hips to generate power for your kick, you will then create tremendous propulsion.

Knee Action

Just as a whip is never completely rigid at any point during its throw, neither are any points in your legs. The knees maintain a slight bend throughout the kicking motion so that you can create more power in the end. Never lock your knees during the buildup in the kick, because this will prevent your body from flowing properly. As your body motion comes through to the knees, you bend them just slightly more so that you can send your feet up for the big snap that finishes the kick.

Whipping Through to the Toes

The snap of the toes at the end of the dolphin kick is just like the final snap of a whip. Point the toes and finish your flowing body motion all the way through to their tips.

SINK OR SWIM

It's important to keep the whole body loose in order to perform a proper dolphin kick. If the body is too rigid and stiff, it won't be possible to use proper technique and the body will sink, making kicking—and swimming—much more difficult.

Types of Turns

Now that you have the dolphin kick down, we'll move into the actual turns you'll be conducting with each particular stroke.

Even people who have no swimming background can tell the difference between swimmers who are comfortable and smooth in the water and those who are timid and inexperienced just by watching them turn around. Whether you're in a yards or meters pool, eventually you'll have to head back the other direction—and there are several ways to do it (and do it properly).

When you're training, the last thing you want to do is practically stop every lap and start all over. You wouldn't go out for a run and stop to a standstill at every corner before starting again, and there's no reason to do so in the pool, either. Swimming is such a smooth and graceful activity that any break in that pattern is purely annoying. And fortunately, it is also unnecessary. Depending on what stroke you're swimming, there are generally three ways to keep you moving efficiently.

Open Turn

The open turn is the most basic and easiest-to-grasp turn that you can do in the pool. In simple steps, you glide into the wall with both hands, bring your knees up toward your chest and place your feet on the wall, and push back toward the other end. When doing this, try to stay in a tight ball when rotating to reduce your drag. It is called an "open" turn because your head comes up out of the water.

The open turn is used for both breaststroke and butterfly swimming, although you also see some novice swimmers do it during freestyle, although that isn't recommended (freestyle has its own faster turn, called the flip turn, which we'll cover next).

Flip Turn

When you see a swimmer approach the wall, tuck their chin, somersault and push off the wall without a second thought, that's a flip turn. The flip turn is the most common turn in the pool because it's used for freestyle (and, let's be honest, it's pretty fun). You also see a variation of this turn used when you're swimming the backstroke.

Backstroke Turn

The most common turn for the backstroke is a hybrid flip turn of sorts. As you swim in toward the wall from the backstroke, you turn onto your stomach and in one continuous motion take a final stroke and then flip. The main difference between this and a regular flip turn is that once you push off the wall underwater, you remain on your back instead of turning back over to your stomach.

Open Turns Broken Down by Stroke

Now that you have a general understanding of what these turns are and how they're done, we'll go into more detail. Keep in mind that these aren't things only "racers" should know, but they are also valuable tools that will increase your comfort in the water as well as your level of fitness.

An *open turn* is used when swimming the breaststroke or butterfly. This is an efficient turn because it becomes a natural extension of either stroke. With the breaststroke, each stroke finishes and begins again in an outstretched position with both hands forward. For the butterfly, the hands are outstretched during the onset of each new stroke. You will use these same positions for your turn.

DEFINITION

An **open turn** is a method of turning done predominantly when swimming the butterfly and the breaststroke. It involves both hands touching the wall simultaneously, and the swimmer bringing the knees up toward the chest, placing the feet on the wall, and pushing off in a streamline position to return to swimming.

The best way to practice any turn is to start a few yards away from the wall and swim into it, do your turn, and stop in about the area where you started. From here, you can relax, think about how your attempt felt, and adjust. Setting aside specific practice for turns allows you to grasp the concept better than doing long swims and only practicing when you reach the wall. This also keeps you from getting tired and not being able to maintain good form. On turns, especially open turns, there is a period of time you will be holding your breath, so it will serve you well to practice these fresh.

To begin mastering breaststroke turns, start about three strokes worth of distance away from the wall. Swim these just as if you had a full length of open water in front of you. Work on making yourself long with each stroke, and on the last stroke, finish your pull and kick without starting another pull. You want to glide for a short distance into the wall.

Now for the actual turn: first, with your arms extended in front of you, glide into the wall and touch it with both of your hands.

On each open turn, your body should be flat when touching the wall to allow smooth transitions.

Second, as your momentum continues to move the rest of your body toward the wall, pull your knees up under the body toward the wall—and as you're turning your body onto its left side to face the side of the pool, place your feet on the wall just a few inches below the surface of the water.

Next, allow your body to fall back into the water on its left side as you place your arms out into the streamline position before pushing off the wall with your legs.

The body should stay compact as you go through the turn to allow easy motion and quick rotation.

With every breaststroke turn, always practice your pullout as well. They go hand in hand, and not practicing one when practicing the other takes away from your development. You're already in a tight streamline positioning coming off the wall, so put into practice the pullout you learned in Chapter 6.

Move your arms out slightly toward the sides of the pool, dolphin kick, then bend your arms and pull down the length of your body. Get a feel for the momentum you have at this point, and only start your recovery when you feel yourself slowing down.

Once it's time to move into your recovery, bring your hands up from underneath your body—keeping your head in line and looking down—and kick as your hands get placed out in front of you. Once your body is extended, take a couple strokes and stop so that you can turn around when ready and try practicing another turn.

Butterfly Turn

The butterfly turn is similar to the initial portions of the breaststroke turn, but there are a few slight differences you should know.

In the breaststroke, there is more of a natural glide at the end of each stroke, which allows for a very slight pause between the end of your stroke and when you will want to touch the wall. In the butterfly, try to end your final stroke before turning as close to the wall as possible. This will take a little practice, but in time you will be able to take a full stroke that ends perfectly with your fingers just slightly off the end of the pool.

The next piece of the puzzle is the same as the breaststroke: bring your knees up, place your feet on the wall, lean back into the streamline position, and push off. As we just talked about, get a feel for when you slow down. Once this occurs, start dolphin kicking.

Kick in a streamline position until you feel your body reaching the surface of the water, and once you're just about to the top, start by taking a stroke. Take a couple, rest, and practice another turn by focusing on ending your final stroke as close to the turn as possible.

THE PROS KNOW

A key to quick turns is the ability to know when it's the right time to move into your next phase. This varies from person to person and is based on power, technique, and body composition. Feel it out and find what works best for you.

Flip Turns in Four Easy Steps

As you're nearing the wall for a flip turn, take a final stroke that leaves you within a distance that after you flip, your feet will be touching the wall in a position that allows you to push off with bent legs. This will vary depending on your height, so play around with it a bit before trying it with swimming. Once you have that sorted out, the rest is simple.

After your final freestyle stroke leading into the wall, both of your hands will be down by your sides, your head will be in line with the rest of your body, and you will be flat in the water. Follow these steps:

1. Tuck your chin to your chest.

2. Bend at the waist and roll your body forward just as if you were doing a somersault on land.

3. Once you have turned over in the water and are on your back, put your arms into the streamline position with your fingers pointing to the other end of the pool.

4. Push off the wall with your feet, then rotate over onto your stomach.

Turning Over in the Backstroke

A backstroke turn is largely similar to the flip turn. The actual turn itself is the same; the difference is in getting your body into the position needed to somersault over.

Backstroke turns are done in a continuous motion that take you from your stroke, onto your stomach, into the flip, and right back into position to start swimming again.

When swimming the backstroke into the wall, you will gauge your distance from the flags that hang over the pool on either end. First, you determine how many strokes you need to take after passing the flags so that when you turn over onto your stomach, you will be in the right spot to flip. For a lot of swimmers, it is three strokes; for others, it is four; and for some really efficient and powerful swimmers, it can be two. For the sake of this lesson, we will say yours is three.

As you come underneath the flags, take three more strokes—for example, right arm stroke, left arm stroke, then one last right arm stroke—and as you're finishing that stroke and pulling the arm down the length of the body, start turning over onto your stomach, rolling to the side of the arm you are using.

As you're on your stomach and still moving in toward the wall, using your opposite arm—in our scenario, it would be your left arm—you then take one freestyle stroke that finishes as you're tucking your chin and flipping over.

Once you flip and get back into your streamline position, push off the wall and kick out with a flutter or dolphin kick until you begin swimming again.

IM Transitions

IM *transitions* is a simple way of saying individual medley turns. These are the turns that swimmers use when changing strokes.

In swimming, the individual medley racing events are done in the order of butterfly, backstroke, breaststroke, and freestyle. Because you're switching strokes as you go, the turns have to be adjusted. You can't do a flip turn efficiently into the breaststroke, for example. And if you ever enter a swimming race, it isn't even legal to turn that way. And on top of being necessary for sport, it also just makes swimming in general much easier and fluid.

DEFINITION

In swimming, a **transition** is the process of switching from one stroke or technique to another. The individual medley involves three transitions: butterfly to backstroke, backstroke to breaststroke, and breaststroke to freestyle.

Butterfly to Backstroke

This turn is fairly straightforward and very simple to execute. As you're swimming in toward the wall in butterfly, time your stroke so that you touch in the same manner you would when doing a butterfly open turn. But instead of turning onto your side once you are ready to leave the wall, you're going to lean backward. As you touch the wall, allow the momentum of the stroke to continue through and bring your legs up toward your chest, just like an open turn. Place your feet solidly on the wall, lean back into your streamline position, and push off firmly and as straight as possible.

Backstroke to Breaststroke

There are two ways you can do this turn with preference given to whichever you find most comfortable after a bit of practice.

The first method revolves around the concept of just bringing your legs down underneath you and onto the wall. After determining how many strokes you are from the wall once you see the flags, reach back on the last stroke and touch the wall, turning over just slightly onto your side. For our example, we'll say you're touching with your right hand. As your right hand is on the wall, your left should be down toward your hips in the position of a finished stroke. Bend at your knees as you turn your body to face the side of the pool entirely, and bring your feet to the wall by passing them beneath you. Once your feet are on the wall, fall to your left and into the streamline position before pushing away from the wall.

The second method is a little more difficult but fun to try. As your hand touches the wall, instead of turning and bringing your feet under your body, you instead do a 180-degree turn on top of the water by twisting your body around. In order to do this without any of your body sinking and causing resistance, you'll need to twist as soon as your hand reaches the wall. Once you have turned, you will place your feet on the wall as you turn your body and push off into a streamline.

Dry-Land Exercises for Better Turns

Despite how much we may want to do so, we can't spend all of our day in the pool, and sometimes it's just hard to actually find a pool in which to train. If you're traveling or for one reason or another are away from the water, there's no reason to prevent your training from moving forward.

There are a variety of things you can do even when you're not in the pool that will help you be more efficient, faster, and simply train better when you return to the water. As you probably have discovered by now, turns are very reliant on the core muscles of the body. Even the dolphin kick on its own is a phenomenal workout for your abdominal and lumbar muscles. So of course, you can aid your water workouts by working your core in your spare time with some extremely simple weight- and machine-free exercises.

Leg Raises

Lie on the floor on your back, in the streamline position. Keep a slight bend in your knees and point your toes, just as if you were about to do a dolphin kick in the water. Lift your heels off the ground; you will feel your abdominal muscles tightening right away. Now while keeping your legs straight, lift them until they point straight up. Pause there for a brief second, then return to your starting position with your heels slightly off the ground. After pausing there for a second, repeat the exercise.

If you haven't done any abdominal training in the past, this can make you quite sore, so start slowly. Try to do 3 sets of 10 lifts the first day and see how it goes. You can build up from there if that was too easy and eventually work up to doing multiple sets of 20 to 25 raises each set.

Crunches

Most people are familiar with the standard abdominal crunch, but we will add a few tips to make it a little more effective and safer.

Start by sitting on the floor with your toes underneath a heavy chair or couch and knees bent. Lie back on the ground and prepare for your crunches. The only real difference we suggest from the standard crunch is placing your arms crossing over your chest and not behind your head. If you're pulling on your neck once the exercise gets tough, you can injure your neck muscles. From here, begin your crunch with a focus on bringing your chest upward, rather than focusing on reaching your knees. This will ensure you activate your entire abdominal region and place less strain on the lower lumbar muscles.

Another variation we suggest is not crunching up so far that your elbows touch your knees or so your back ends up vertical. For one, this takes the tension off your abs, and it can also hurt your lower back. Test it out over a few repetitions, but you will probably want to stop at about three quarters of a full crunch and return to your starting position.

SINK OR SWIM

When doing any kind of abdominal exercise from the floor, be sure that you don't "bounce" between repetitions. If you use momentum to fulfill your next rep, you'll be cheating yourself and not getting the full benefit of the exercise.

When doing these abdominal exercises, do several sets of a comfortable number to start. Be sure you aren't doing so many that your abs begin to cramp up, but do challenge yourself. If 15 repetitions would be the most you could do, for example, start by doing a few sets of 8 to 10.

Elbow Push-Ups

A great abdominal exercise for building muscular endurance in your core—a huge key in swimming—is quite similar to a push-up.

Start on the floor flat on your stomach and on your toes, just like you were going to start a push-up. But instead of pushing up with your hands, bring your elbows in about shoulder width and push yourself up on your elbows. Your forearms should remain flat on the ground, and you can keep your hands rolled into fists.

With this exercise, keep your head, back, and legs as flat as possible. In short order, you will really feel the tension on your abdominals. Hold it for 30 seconds or so to start and then rest before repeating, doing three or four sets to start with. Add time as it becomes more feasible.

Exercise Ball

If you've flipped through television channels, you've probably seen a workout "guru" on what looks like a big, round bouncing ball. He or she may have arms on it, feet, or the back, or he or she might just be rolling around like a child having a grand time. Well, what they're doing is actually quite good for you. The ball you see is called an "exercise ball," and it comes in a variety of sizes. The advantage of these tools is that you can train on them, specifically your abs, with no real pressure on your lower back. It makes for a great variation on the standard crunch!

To give this exercise a try, sit on an exercise ball and place your feet flat on the floor with your knees evenly spaced apart (the farther apart, the easier it is to balance, but don't go any wider than you need to because it can lessen the effectiveness of the exercise). Slowly lean back until your abs flatten, cross your arms over your chest, and do a crunch—focusing on "up" motion, not "forward" motion—the same as you would as if you were doing the crunch on the floor. Most people find this not only more challenging to do on the exercise ball, but a lot more comfortable because the foundation below them forms to the body rather than remaining solid.

Another added benefit of exercise balls is that because they move very freely, you have to use stabilizer muscles that you may not otherwise be exercising. This is akin to swimming, where you start using every muscle in your body to move through the water. That's what makes swimming just about the best exercise you can do: it targets your entire body.

The exercise ball, just like advanced swimming sets, is simply another tool you can use when time permits or your situation requires it to keep your fitness routine on track. No matter where you are—whether near or far from a pool—don't neglect your abs!

The Least You Need to Know

- If you want to practice your flip turn technique when you're not in the pool, practicing somersaults like a kid is a great way of training on land!
- When still getting comfortable with swimming and turning, feel free to use open turns even on freestyle and backstroke, but begin practicing flip turns as soon as possible.
- Individual medley practice is a great way of getting used to all of the types of transitions and turns in swimming.
- Turning technique is directly related to beginning each lap efficiently, so it's important to be in a great streamline position when pushing off of the wall, no matter what stroke you're swimming.

Train Smart

Legendary football coach Tom Landry is widely credited with saying, "If you are prepared, you will be confident and will do the job." There are a lot of ways you can interpret that statement, but however you do, it's a very applicable quote when you're training to improve yourself and your health. Whether you want to be a great swimmer or just be in great shape, you have to be prepared to do the proper work required to achieve the results you want. In this part, we'll cover a variety of additional training techniques you can use to ensure you're not just prepared but are also confident to do the job. We'll cover everything from stretching to strength training and a variety of drills and tools that will put you on the road toward results … fast! Many types of exercise leave you feeling like it's another job, but with swimming and its associated training tools, you will enjoy training every step of the way.

Stretching for Swimmers

In This Chapter

- Seven types of stretching
- The basics of safe stretching
- Stretches for your upper body, core, and lower body
- Staying strong and flexible as you age

Stretching is as important as training when it comes to swimming. Tight muscles don't react the way you need them to, and they also can create quick discomfort once you begin to exercise. In the water, when your entire body is working in unison to propel you forward, you need to be comfortable and relaxed. In order to achieve that, you have to maintain a physical structure that is capable of moving you the way you want. And the benefits of stretching go far, far beyond helping you in the pool. Being flexible and actively including a stretching program in your daily life provides many benefits.

Regular stretching improves your muscle flexibility as well as your joint range of motion. This can make just about everything in your life more comfortable, from leaning over to pick something up off the ground to reaching up to grab something on a high shelf. Flexibility improves your balance, too, which is of even greater benefit to the elderly.

Additionally, consistent stretching can relieve muscle tension brought on by anxiety and stress and can improve your body's natural blood flow to surrounding tissue. The benefits are so great there is just no reason to not stretch!

Seven Ways to Stretch

When most people think of stretching, they can name a few movements that involve some basic stretches—but that's about the extent of their flexibility knowledge. By now, you already know what good increased range of motion can do for you, but we want you to also know the process behind it. All stretching is definitely not equal: in fact, there is quite a variety of movements that will help loosen up your body.

There are actually seven "types" of stretching, but not all are useful or even healthy. Unfortunately, that doesn't mean you won't see them in action—because a lot of people are unaware of putting themselves at risk by performing these unhealthy stretches. The explanations that follow will help ensure that not only are you conducting the stretches most beneficial for your body, your sport, and your overall health and fitness, but it will also ensure that you avoid the most common mistakes when undertaking this effort.

SINK OR SWIM

Because every body is different and each individual's health history unique, always consult with your physician before beginning an exercise program.

Active, Isolated Stretching

"AI" stretching, as it is also called, works on the ideology that when an isolated muscle contracts, its opposite relaxes. A lot of positions in yoga, for instance, are examples of this type of stretch. These are usually done in short duration as they aren't always easy. Ultimately, these types of stretches don't often have a home in the swimmer's repertoire. That said, knowledge is power—so it's good to have a grasp of what's available to you.

Ballistic Stretching

You may have heard the phrase, "We're going ballistic, Mav!" a time or two if you have watched the movie *Top Gun*. While it sounds like a great idea for a pilot on the silver screen, it's not a great idea for your body. In fact, ballistic stretching is one of the most often-noted types of stretching in gyms around the country—but it's generally the most dangerous.

Ballistic stretching involves the over-lengthening of a muscle caused by force or momentum. Swinging your arms behind you to stretch your chest or bouncing down to touch the ground with your hands are just two types of ballistic stretching.

Remember that stretching should be done slowly, and you should always be in control of every inch your body moves. Bouncing or forcing muscles beyond their comfort zone is a surefire path toward injury, which won't just keep you out of the pool but will also most definitely derail your overall fitness lifestyle.

Dynamic Stretching

Dynamic stretching can be considered the well-behaved child of the stretching family. While ballistic stretching uses force to stretch a muscle past its abilities, dynamic stretching uses a controlled swinging motion that you allow to take you to the limit of your flexibility and gently away.

A dynamic stretch that swimmers often use is a leg swing in which they allow the leg to act almost like a pendulum, swinging easily forward to its comfort limit and doing the same behind them—repeating the process until reaching desired levels of warm-up or stretch.

Isometric Stretching

If you have ever used force against a solid object to stretch, you've likely done isometric stretching without knowing it. This type of stretch involves muscle tension and resistance to develop flexibility.

An example for stretching the chest is placing your arm lengthwise against a wall and turning away to the point of stretch. By trying to "push" the wall away from you, you are increasing your stretch in the targeted muscle group.

Passive Stretching

Passive stretching is sometimes called "relaxed stretching." It includes the involvement of another part of your body, another person, or even a solid object in the stretch that holds your stretched position for you.

PNF Stretching

Proprioceptive Neuromuscular Facilitation (PNF) stretching is a combination of techniques originally developed for rehabilitation needs. This type of stretching generally requires someone to help you because it involves stretching a muscle with passive movements, then remaining in that position and stretching with an isometric moving, before returning to a deeper, passive stretch (which is now available due to the isometric movement).

Static Stretching

This is the most common and basic type of stretching. Along with passive stretching, it's also the most beneficial. With static stretching, you slowly get set into your stretch and hold it. You should feel your muscle stretching over its length but not any pain or pulling on the joints.

THE PROS KNOW

Quite often, people confuse passive and static stretching or use the terms interchangeably, which is a mistake. Static stretching holds a singular position at the limit of the muscle's flexibility, whereas passive stretching involves an additional element that creates or contributes to the stretch.

Essential Stretching Rules

Before getting into some of the stretches that will benefit you, keep in mind some simple rules:

- **Go slowly.** You can imagine that jumping into the splits would not be a comfortable thing to do. Use that same caution with any stretch to avoid injury.

- **Never bounce.** Once you get into your stretch and feel the tension on a muscle, hold it there. Never force a muscle to stretch farther than is relatively comfortable, and never ease off so that you can then force it farther with momentum.

- **Hold your stretch.** A common mistake made with stretching is that people hold a stretch for just a couple seconds before moving on. Stretching isn't a race, so hold each position for at least 15 to 20 seconds.

- **Be consistent.** Your muscles are tight now because they haven't been taught to elongate and relax. If you aren't stretching on a regular basis, even after doing these stretches for a good amount of time, you can end up right back where you started. Make stretching a priority.

SINK OR SWIM

Exercise caution when stretching. Stretching too far—to where you feel painful discomfort—can lead to injury. Not everyone can do every stretch, so listen to your body and back off when it says to stop.

Upper-Body Stretches

The upper body has many muscles that need to work in unison to keep a smooth stroke going during your time in the pool. The following sections detail a number of stretches that will help you stay loose and feel fluid in the water stroke after stroke.

Streamline

Just as if you were in the water, place yourself in the streamline position. Stretch and make yourself as tall as possible, slowly leaning to one side and holding that position as you stretch your back. Return to your starting position, then slowly lean to the opposite side.

Streamline stretch.

You can also do the streamline stretch on the ground or floor and simply make yourself as long as possible. When doing it this way, you are also able to point your toes and stretch your ankles as well.

Triceps

Raise one arm straight into the air above you, and bend at the elbow as if you were going to pat yourself on the back. Using your opposite arm, reach over and gently pull on the outside of your elbow.

Triceps stretch.

Back

Face a wall and place your palms flat on the wall, shoulder-width apart, two feet or so above your head. Slowly move back so that your arms are almost straight, and lean your head and chest forward between your arms.

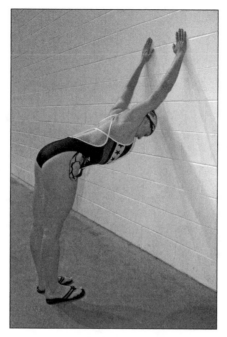

Back stretch.

Chest

For the first chest stretch, start by facing a wall or other solid object and extending your arm against it with your palm open and flat on it. Keeping your arm in this position, slowly turn your body away and feel the stretch throughout your chest. Repeat this stretch with your other arm.

For the second chest stretch, go to a corner of a room with two flat walls. Position yourself so that you are looking directly into the corner where the walls connect. Place one hand on each wall, slightly about the level of your head, with your palms flat. Gently lean forward into the corner until you feel your chest begin to stretch, and hold that position.

Chest stretch.

Forearms

For the first forearms stretch, with one arm horizontal in front of you from the elbow down, point your fingers toward the ceiling. Using your other hand, gently press back on your fingers. Repeat this stretch for both arms.

For the second forearms stretch, sit on the floor with your legs out straight in front of you and your back straight. Extend your arms down your sides, and place your open hands on the ground so that your fingers are pointing forward and your palms are completely connected with the floor. From here, slowly pull your hands behind you, keeping your hands on the ground. You should quickly reach a point where you feel your forearms begin to stretch.

From the initial sitting position, you can also turn your hands around so that your fingers point behind you (with your hands still completely flat on the floor) and lean back gently to stretch.

Neck

Stand up straight and use your left hand to grasp your right wrist behind your back. While keeping yourself facing forward, lean your head to the left as if you were try- ing to touch your ear to your shoulder. Use your left hand to steady your right arm so it can't rise up, thus allowing you to stretch. Repeat with the positions reversed to stretch the other side of your neck as well.

Core Stretches

Most people consider stretching to be of vital importance for the major muscle groups, but they tend to forget that the muscles around the midsection are just as important. Especially in swimming, when everything is essentially connected, it's necessary to be flexible throughout the entire body. In the following sections we share some basic but beneficial stretches to ensure your core is just as prepared as the rest of your body.

Lower Back

Sit in a chair (with or without arms), and place your feet so that they are flat on the floor in front of you about shoulder-width apart. Ensure you are sitting up with proper posture and that your head is in line with your body. Slowly turn your upper body to one direction while preventing your hips and legs from moving. Use either the arm on the chair or press against the outside of your leg to increase and hold the stretch. Repeat this stretch for your opposite side as well.

Abdominals

Lie face down with your stomach on the floor. Without moving any muscles in your lower body, push yourself up with your arms and hold once you feel a stretch in your abdominals.

Abdominal stretch.

Obliques

Stand up straight with your feet about shoulder-width apart. Lean slowly to one side until you feel a stretch in your side. To increase the stretch, you can also raise the arm on the side of the body you are stretching and reach as you lean.

Lower-Body Stretches

Much of the discomfort some people experience during their day, particularly if they have a job that causes them to sit for a long period of time, can be credited to the legs. Whereas most people assume lower-back discomfort comes from the lumbar region itself, often it has to do with leg muscles—particularly the hamstrings—being too tight. If sitting becomes uncomfortable, you can only imagine how much inflexible leg muscles may be holding back your swimming. Try the following stretches and see how much better you feel not just in the water, but throughout your day.

Quadriceps

This stretch will have you standing on one foot, so you may want to stand near a wall or other object that you may hold for balance.

Quadriceps stretch.

Moving only the lower half of your leg, bend at the knee, bringing your heel toward your backside. Use the hand on the same side of your body and gently pull back on your toes. Repeat this stretch with your other leg.

Hamstrings

This is quite possibly the simplest stretch of all: with a slight bend in your knees, slowly lean forward and reach your fingertips to the ground. When you reach the point you can go no farther, don't bounce forward to try and reach deeper. Just hold a steady stretch.

Another variation you can use to stretch your hamstrings without having to bend as far forward is to place your leg straight out on something that is a comfortable height, then lean into the stretch. You can use a chair, the arm of a couch, or—if you're at the pool—the starting blocks. During this stretch, keep a very slight bend in the leg that is still on the ground.

Hamstring stretch.

Lower Back

This stretch also takes place from a flat chair. With your feet flat in front of you and in a position so that you are resting near the end of the seat, place your feet shoulder-width apart and lean forward, placing your hands on your calves or on the backs of your ankles. Lean forward slowly, keeping your chin down and allowing your back to stretch.

FUN FACTS

Your heart is a muscle—easily the hardest-working muscle you have. The heart pumps more than 2,500 gallons of blood each day and can beat more than three billion times in your life. Maintaining strong and flexible muscles allows blood to flow more freely throughout your entire body.

Calves

Facing a wall, stand about a foot away and place your hands on the wall with your palms open. Start by slowly moving your right leg back while keeping your foot flat on the ground, toes facing forward. As you're doing this, you will bend slightly with your left knee. Stretch until you feel a stretch in your right calf muscles. Repeat with reversing the roles of each leg.

Calf stretch.

Hips

Lie flat on your back and choose a leg to start with. Bend at the knee and bring it toward your chest. From here, cross it over your body and set it on the ground while keeping your back flat on the floor.

Hip stretch.

Groin

Sit on the floor with your legs in front of you, pull your heels in toward your center, and press the bottoms of your feet together. In this position, your knees will be facing out to the sides. Place your hands around your ankles and use your elbows to very gently press down against the inside of your knees.

Ankles

This is an extremely simple stretch. While standing with your feet even and shoulder-width apart—feel free to hold on to a chair or wall for support, if you'd like—place one foot on its toes about a foot behind where you started. Then slowly move the heel forward while leaving the toes in place until you feel the top of your foot stretching.

The second ankle stretch requires a partner. Sit on the floor with your legs extended flat in front of you. Lean forward slightly and point your toes forward as far as you can. When you reach your limit, have a partner gently push down on the foot near the toes until you feel a deeper stretch in the upper part of your foot.

More Stretching Tips

We've covered a lot of ground about stretching already, but there are a few things that are worth reiterating and some common things that are often overlooked. Once we cover these last couple tips, you'll have all the knowledge you need to be more flexible and more comfortable than you have ever been!

Warm Up Before Stretching

Stretching cold muscles can be uncomfortable and also put you at risk for injury. If you're going to stretch at the gym or even at home, it's always a good idea to warm up your muscles first.

If you're at the gym or have the equipment or weather available to do so, go for a brisk walk or a light jog for even a few minutes. Don't be afraid to do a few push-ups, sit-ups, body-weight squats, and other light body movements. Just get your blood flowing and get your body warmed up a bit, then get into stretching.

Breathe

Being reminded to breathe during a stretch might almost seem somewhat laughable, but before you do that, you may want to go back and check out your own habits. Most people don't even realize when they've been holding their breath during a stretch until their heart rate increases when they release the muscle.

Stretching requires relaxation, so ensure that you inhale fully and exhale deeply. Get into your stretch, breathe in slowly through your nose, and exhale completely and gently with your mouth.

Dress Appropriately

Often overlooked is the effect that your clothing has on your stretching. To get the most from your efforts, dress accordingly. Don't wear clothes that are too tight or too baggy (which could obstruct your movement). Jeans, for example, are a bad choice because of the limits they place on your legs. Loose-fitting clothing such as T-shirts and sweats are great, as are tennis shoes or going barefoot (which is preferable when the option is available to you).

Don't Overstretch

There is a possibility of stretching too much, so make sure that in your eagerness to increase your flexibility you don't do too much too quickly.

If you think of your muscles like taffy candy, then you can understand the analogy that they can be damaged if applied with too much pressure when cold. But when warm, they can stretch quite a bit. But like anything, there is a limit. If you feel you have to go into some awkward angles or start feeling pain sensations in your joints because of how you need to move to feel a stretch, you're going too far.

Don't stretch too long or too often. If you're stretching your entire body at once, you should be able to complete your program in 15 to 20 minutes. If you're stretching much longer than that or if you're stretching for that kind of time period several times a day, you may want to scale it back a bit for your own safety.

Age and Fitness

A lot of people worry that as they get older their quality of life will decrease due to physical factors that they feel are out of their control. Fortunately, this just isn't the case. You may be getting older as the days go by, but you are in control of your fitness and activity levels—and thus your quality of life for as long as you live. As the old saying goes, if you don't use it, you lose it. So … use it!

FUN FACTS

In 1900, Americans had an average life expectancy of 47 years. Today, it is more than 75. Along with advances in health care, proper understanding of nutrition and exercise has allowed people to thrive for decades longer than was common just a century ago.

By learning to swim—or, if you were already a comfortable swimmer, by getting involved with a regular swimming routine—you're doing immeasurable good for your body. When you add extra physical activity such as regular stretching, you're building upon that great foundation of fitness you have already created—and it will last with you as long as you continue to use it.

Take a look around. Everyone knows a number of people to whom they could say, "There's no way he or she can really be that age!" This happens when people remain vibrant and active long past what our society's conventional wisdom says is normal.

Age isn't necessarily what prevents people from doing the activities they loved doing for years. It is, instead, simply the slow reduction in use. As we get older, it becomes increasingly important to make sure we stay active. Strong and flexible muscles are vital to quality of life. Think of this: by age 80, sedentary people will have lost about half of their body's muscle mass. So be sure you aren't sitting still when there is plenty of water in which to swim!

For people of all ages, but especially those getting older, stretching should be an integral part of life. As we age, bones in the body become weaker and more susceptible to fracture should we slip and fall. Muscles that are flexible and well-trained, though, are resilient and often able to stabilize the body from such an event, which can prevent serious injury. And of course, when we're healthy, we have more time to swim!

The Least You Need to Know

- Being flexible will benefit you in all aspects of your life, not just when you're in the pool or exercising, so be sure to stretch all of your major muscle groups daily.
- Proper form is just as important when stretching as it is when swimming or weight training. Never bounce when stretching, overstretch, or stretch beyond your comfort level.
- For overall and general muscle health, make sure you train regularly as well as stretch and stay hydrated.
- Many stretches can be enhanced by partnering with someone who can help add tension to your muscles. Just be sure your partner moves your body positioning slowly.

Basic Principles of Conditioning

In This Chapter

- Determining your heart rate
- Different types of exercise
- How to define your training intensity
- Signs of overtraining

Your level of physical conditioning is what determines how much stress your body can handle. This stress can come in various forms, including heavy lifting, running for sprints, and of course long-distance swimming.

We all have had occasions where we have found ourselves doing some new sort of labor, either on a job or in the gym or pool, where we've become quickly fatigued. The next day, we also find ourselves extremely sore, even out of the range of our ordinary amount of soreness after a tough workout. This is because the body hasn't been conditioned to handle that particular task or level of effort. The more you work out properly and train your body to handle a variety of tasks, the more viable you will be at new types and volumes of training. In turn, this will allow you to reach new peaks of fitness and accomplish all the goals you have set.

Now before we begin, it is important to note that more does not necessarily mean better. Pushing yourself for the sake of pushing yourself is not wise; overtraining can put the brakes on your progress in a hurry. We're going to teach you how to challenge yourself without draining yourself too far mentally or physically—and how to come back to your training each day better than the day before.

Heart Rate

Before we can effectively describe various types of exercises, you will need to know how to measure your heart rate. Aerobic and anaerobic exercises, which we'll discuss later in the chapter, are linked to your heart rate—and it's a number you will occasionally want to know to ensure you're in the proper zone for the conditioning you're after.

The easiest way to keep track of your heart rate is to use a heart rate monitor. Most health stores and sporting goods outlets offer a variety of these, ranging from smaller units that attach to your wrist to others that strap around your chest. Both are effective, but both options are relatively expensive, with models ranging from around $20 up to more than $100. Some are even waterproof, which you can—and are encouraged to—wear while swimming.

Taking Your Heart Rate

Fortunately, you don't actually need to buy anything at all to get a general idea of your heart rate. While taking your heart rate manually is not as exact as using a heart rate monitor, it is plenty accurate enough for your needs. To find your heart rate, simply take your pulse at your wrist or your neck and count. Count for 6 seconds and multiply that number by 10, or for a slightly more accurate count, take your pulse for 10 seconds and then multiply by 6. Further, you could simply count out your heartbeats for a full minute and get a relatively precise count.

You can use this technique while you're sitting at home, at work, or anywhere you go. When doing it while not under any kind of exercise-related duress, this is your resting heart rate. While you're exercising you can take your heart rate, such as after a set, and gauge the intensity you put in.

Before doing so while working out, practice by taking your heart rate while sitting around at home. It's a good idea to gauge your resting heart rate anyway, as you will discover after you start exercising often that this number will decrease. This is a sign your heart is pumping blood throughout your body more efficiently due to the improved cardiovascular health you've created for yourself. So for example, if you count 11 heartbeats in 10 seconds, multiply by 6 and you have a rate of about 66. The average for a healthy person at rest is about 60 to 80, although this, too, varies greatly. In general, though, resting rates lower than 50 are relatively rare.

FUN FACTS

Athletes in general have much lower resting heart rates than sedentary people, with ultra-endurance competitors having some of the lowest ever recorded. But one of the most impressive belongs to cycling champion Lance Armstrong, who has recorded a resting heart rate as low as 32. And if you think that's impressive, it has been reported that a couple of his cycling counterparts have been reported in the high 20s!

Maximum Heart Rate

Another number you need to know is what is considered your maximum heart rate. This is important because much of your conditioning exercise sets, in and out of the pool, are based around an effort level that is defined by a given heart rate. While it's an inexact science because the true answer varies widely from person to person, the generally accepted formula to discover your maximum heart rate is to take the number 220 and subtract your age. So if you are 30 years old, your maximum heart rate would be roughly 190. You will want to remember that number as we go forward.

Once you determine your maximum heart rate, you'll have an idea of how close you are to hitting "full throttle"—for example, when doing a set that requires an all-out effort.

Not All Exercise Is Created Equal

You know that not all exercise is the same. Going for a walk is easy, and if you walk with a friend and chat the entire time, it may not even feel like exercise. But that little walk is heart-healthy, burns calories (and thus, burns body fat!), works your leg muscles, and benefits your cardiovascular system.

Now, in contrast, think of the last time you went for a run. You probably couldn't imagine doing it for the same length of time as walking, and it would be pretty difficult if you tried to carry on a conversation while doing it. It's certainly exercise, but the factors behind running are different than walking. Due to the increased effort and number of strides you take, running burns more calories and gets your heart pumping at a much different rate. The same can be said for lifting weights or doing jumping jacks, alternating from push-ups to sit-ups, or jogging up the stairs—the options are nearly limitless when it comes to exercise, each causing a different reaction from your body.

SINK OR SWIM

According to the Centers for Disease Control and Prevention (CDC), more than a quarter of the population in America performs no leisure-time physical activity. These people are at a significantly higher risk of premature death by factors such as cardiovascular disease. Regular exercise is critical for good health!

Aerobic Fitness

Aerobic exercise is broadly defined as any type of exercise that utilizes oxygen in the body. Aerobic exercises are those performed at moderate intensities that increase your heart rate and last a relatively extended period of time. Think of this as your "endurance" training zone. Swimming is the ideal aerobic exercise because it not only works your cardiovascular system but is easy on the joints and bones while also providing the opportunity to build muscular strength and endurance (which we will cover later in the chapter). Other types of aerobic exercise include cycling, walking, jogging, playing soccer, and even skiing if the intensity is done at the appropriate level.

DEFINITION

Aerobic literally means "with oxygen" and is the term for actions that require oxygen to be present. In exercise terms, it's a type of exercise that can be continually supported by the body's respiration and use of oxygen.

A good target for your aerobic training zone is about 65 to 70 percent of your maximum heart rate. So for example, if you're 30 years old with a maximum heart rate of 190, maintaining a pace of exercise that keeps your heart pumping between 124 and 133 would be just about right (65–70 percent of 190 = 123.5, 70 percent of 190 = 133).

Basic health guidelines encourage every adult to get at least 30 minutes of this type of aerobic exercise every day. If for some reason you can't make it to the pool one day, go for a walk or a jog, take the dog out for a run, or hop on a bike. Just get your blood flowing … your heart will thank you!

Anaerobic Fitness

Anaerobic exercise is a result of exercise involving an intensity level that surpasses aerobic efforts and generally causes the heart to pump at 85 percent of maximum or higher for its duration. This type of exercise lasts for only a brief period due to the fuel requirements and limitations of the body. Anaerobic bursts of exercise primarily bypass oxygen as a fuel source and instead use the glucose stored in the body to function. When you are doing sets that require an all-out effort, and you start gauging your efforts based on the maximum heart rate number we found previously, this is the perfect example of anaerobic exercise.

DEFINITION

Anaerobic means "without oxygen" and in fitness is the term for actions and efforts that take place without the presence of oxygen. This type of exercise requires a fuel other than oxygen.

When you watch the 50-meter freestyle during the Olympic Games, for instance, you will notice most of the swimmers don't take a breath for the entire span of the race. This is because they are well conditioned and because their bodies aren't really using oxygen as a fuel source for their race anyway. In contrast, the energy requirements of a 200 freestyle causes swimmers to swim at a less-intense pace, so they can maintain a better overall speed for a longer period. They start their breathing patterns a couple strokes into the race to keep their bodies fueled with fresh oxygen. This latter example is a combination of both aerobic and anaerobic exercise. Efficient middle-distance and distance swimmers take their races out in an effort they can maintain before pushing themselves to the limits of their abilities for the last portion of the race.

As an athlete with a goal of general health and fitness, you will find yourself doing far less anaerobic training than aerobic—but both have their place in a well-rounded program. Sprint swimming and running as well as heavy weight training are a couple of examples of anaerobic conditioning exercises.

Lactate Threshold Training

Lactate threshold training occurs when the intensity of the undertaken exercise causes the body to build up lactic acid, also known as lactate, which is a substance that is produced by the body as a result of anaerobic glucose metabolism, faster than it can be processed. This training method is particularly important to athletes who are looking to push themselves at maximal effort for long periods of time.

As we have discussed, anaerobic efforts are relegated to brief occurrences because the body is limited to how long it can support it. Aerobic exercise is also technically limited—but on a much, much larger basis. How much lactic acid the body can process is yet another limitation of exercise. All these things can be improved with practice.

Athletes who train in a short-duration sprinting fashion but for repeated bursts on brief rest intervals are conditioning their bodies to respond to a buildup of lactic acid. Because the body is being called upon to support another maximal effort before it has recovered from the prior one, it becomes more efficient at this task over time.

Strength Training

An important facet of your exercise program should be about getting stronger, which helps not only in your athletic endeavors but also in your everyday life. It makes life easier in all that you do, from walking around to carrying your groceries into the house. But strength shouldn't be confused with muscular size.

A common myth exists among women that lifting weights or doing strength-oriented exercises will cause them to become "bulky." It just doesn't work that way. It takes a lot of effort, nutrition, and time to build muscular size, and you can ask anyone who has tried: it's not a terribly fast endeavor. But strength is something that you can develop in short order and something you shouldn't overlook. You want to challenge yourself and cause your muscles to adapt to additional weight resistance. You can probably squat dozens and dozens of times if you're only using the resistance of your natural body weight, but if you put a bar with some weights on your back, you're going to be creating real strength. This is very valuable, because the strength you create can be used in everything else that you do, making moving around in life easier and more comfortable.

This, of course, is all in addition to helping you handle pushing water in greater volume and with greater efficiency when you're in the pool. A well-developed cardio-vascular system is a wonderful thing, but it isn't the only important piece of the physical puzzle. Don't overlook strength training. The benefits are vast, including helping protect bone density (particularly in women).

THE PROS KNOW

Most people reach their peak bone mass—the point where the body stops building bone tissue—at age 30. Regular, moderate exercise helps slow the decline.

Muscular Endurance and Conditioning

Walk into any gym and you're likely to see a few men and women who stand out from the crowd with their sheer size and strength. Professional body builders and Strongman athletes have taken their muscle proportions to limits that are hardly believable by the average person. They are impressive sights to see, and the total poundage of weights they can move from point A to point B is truly amazing. Clearly, they have taken their anaerobic conditioning to a very high level—but what about their aerobic abilities?

Although a professional body builder's physique is more developed than the average amateur swimmer, if you're placing them head to head in an endurance competition, you may just want to put your money on the smaller person. For all their size, the endurance capacities of professional physique athletes are, on average, relatively low. In fact, some admit to getting winded just by walking up several flights of stairs. That's not to say they aren't well-trained athletes; it's instead an example of how the body adapts to a stimulus. Their goal is very specific: to get bigger. This takes a great deal of anaerobic training followed by copious amounts of food and rest. A swimmer, on the other hand, won't be comparable on a body-building stage but could literally swim circles around most heavily muscled counterparts. This is the same type of example we used earlier, when we mentioned football players generally aren't very good swimmers if they haven't been training in the pool.

When it comes to strength athletes, some people can bench hundreds and hundreds of pounds more than the average person. It is just incredible how strong these types of athletes are. They train to see how much weight they can lift just one time or for a very low number of repetitions; that is their solitary goal. And while they can do that extremely well, they may not be able to lift a significantly lower amount of weight for an impressively high number of repetitions. They haven't trained that way.

Now we have detailed three extremes: well-trained strength athletes, well-trained physique athletes, and well-trained endurance athletes. Your goal, to maximize your health and wellness, should be a healthy mix of all three. You don't want to just be able to swim forever, just look great, or just be strong. Unless you're entering a sport with grand aspirations of turning professional in a league that focuses on those attributes, you should ensure you have a well-rounded program that improves your cardiovascular function while building strength, burning body fat, and adding lean muscle. One of the ways to do this is improving your muscular conditioning, which in turn provides endurance capabilities that allow you to train and better yourself.

Muscular conditioning comes from the repeated use of a muscle or muscle group against tension. This is developed through volume that occurs during singular workouts as well as over time. The easiest example is to think about the first time you went swimming. You were probably sore after your first time in the pool, with your back and triceps muscles particularly fatigued. But the next time you got in the water, it wasn't quite as difficult—and you didn't feel quite as sore afterward. And over time, it became easier and easier. Your body adapted, made itself stronger, and conditioned your muscles to handle training volume. This is something that happens with all kinds of activities in life and sport, and the underlying message is to train and push yourself in the manner in which you want to improve. Believe us: your muscles will respond!

THE PROS KNOW

Stretching is indeed considered exercise. It's an important one, too, because it trains your muscles. Make stretching part of your regular routine before you get into the pool. (See Chapter 10 for more on stretching.)

Establishing Your Training Intensity

Deciding how hard you should train for optimal results has long been a point of debate in the fitness industry. Train too hard and your body and mind break down to the point you just don't want to train anymore. But if you don't train hard enough, you're spending a lot of time doing something that could be done in far more brief periods. Unfortunately, the answer can't be mathematically decided. There's no formula based on your height, age, or weight that tells you how much you should exercise and how often and how hard. The factors are based on a variety of things that you have to consider for yourself.

Deciding when enough training is enough has to do with everything else you do during your day. In the next sections, we look at common factors for the average trainer. Depending on your schedule and what goes on during your daily life, the list of considerations you personally need to take into account might be twice as long.

Sleep

Your training program is only as valuable as the recovery you give to your body. You can have a great workout where you swim longer than ever and lift weights that are heavier than you ever have before—and for more reps than you dreamed possible—but if you don't allow your body to recover to nurture those new milestones, you're liable to lose them.

Your muscles don't grow bigger or stronger while you're in the pool. They do it outside the pool while you're asleep. What you do in the water is the catalyst for positive change, but it's only one part. You absolutely must ensure you are getting enough sleep to recover from your given workload. (And by workload, we don't just mean physical training. If you have a stressful job, that can tax your mind too and thus require you to get more sleep.)

"Eight hours" has been preached for ages as the magical number you need to sleep. For you, it just may be the ticket, but it also may not be enough. Listen to your body. If you're tired, you likely need more sleep, so find a way to give your body what it needs or cut back on your training.

Nutrition

Coming in near the top of the factors critical to positive body change is nutrition. This rivals sleep because both are mandatory; you need good fuel for the body just as much as you need good sleep.

If you work out hard and for extended durations, you need quality carbohydrates, fats, and proteins to fuel your efforts as well as to recover from them. We will talk extensively about nutrition in Chapter 17, but for now, just remember that if you put low-quality fuel into your body, you'll get low-quality performance. Similarly, if you don't have time to eat the proper meals in the proper amounts, scale back on training until you can work it out. You shouldn't train while starving, and you shouldn't have to wait too long after your workout to eat a good meal. You wouldn't try to drive a car longer than the fuel in its tank will last, so don't do it to your body, either.

Work

Work comes into play in a couple ways when considering how much training you should do. First, lots of people give up their lunch breaks to hit the gym. It's admirable, and the thought process is somewhat sound, but the body needs fuel just like it needs stimulus on its muscles. If you can't eat properly *and* work out, you really shouldn't be working out. We will cover a process called "catabolism" in Chapter 17 when we discuss nutrition, but it's the byproduct of not eating properly in combination with training. It's not a good thing and should be entirely avoided.

Second, consider the type of work you do. If you sit in an office all day, you can likely handle more training than someone who pours concrete or lifts trash and recycling bins all day. If you find yourself exhausted at the end of the workday, or if certain muscle groups are sore from a hard week at work, you should create a schedule and program that works *with* your job. Just because you're sore from something you're doing at work doesn't mean it's any different than the type of resistance you get in the gym. Heavy is heavy!

Family Obligations

If your family enjoys biking together, hiking, or getting together for any other type of physical activity, make sure you take that into account. If you go on a long walk or ride with your spouse or kids, you're likely getting plenty of cardiovascular exercise. There's no need to head to the gym afterward and walk on a treadmill.

Experience Level

With everything you do, consider your experience level. If you're a brand-new swimmer, don't try to swim five miles on your first day. Start with a few hundred yards; we'll give you some specific beginner's workouts in Chapter 12 that will be perfect for that. Just because you're excited doesn't mean you should overdo it; bottle up that excitement and hold on to it. Fitness is meant to be a lifetime of fun.

Finding the Right Intensity for You

"Trial and error" isn't exactly the best way to look at the equation that makes up how much training you're supposed to be doing, but sometimes it works out that way. And if it does, that's entirely acceptable—and it's actually a good indicator of where you are.

Almost everyone starts a new exercise program a little overzealous. It's even kind of a good thing. It means you're excited about the positive changes you're bringing into your life. But be aware—it's going to make you a little sorer than you may have expected. When you start, just train until you're fatigued—then rest. Don't keep pushing because you think it's what you're supposed to do. Everyone has limits, and for new trainers, it's extremely easy to reach yours. Volume is a great thing, but it will come in time—so don't rush it.

When it comes to speed in the water, don't try to race from the start. Take it easy and slowly. You're not competing against anyone: this is all about you. Trying to swim too fast too soon will actually hinder your progress, so keep that in mind if you ever feel you should be going faster than you are. The reality is that no, you shouldn't! You should swim at a comfortable pace.

FUN FACTS

Some people have the ability to nearly redefine the word "intensity." Englishman Lewis Gordon Pugh is one of them. In 2006, Pugh became the first person in the world to have completed a long-distance swim in each of the world's five oceans!

Don't Overdo It!

"Overtraining" is a term used in the fitness world to essentially describe the point of diminishing returns. Like watering your lawn past its limits, at some point you start making things worse rather than better. There are no specific signs that scream, "Stop! You're overtraining!", but there are some warning signs.

Sure, we all love a warm bed and soft pillow with comfortable sheets, but not wanting to leave them and feeling immense discomfort doing so are entirely different things. If you wake up in the morning with your heartbeat racing and you feel horrible all over, you are likely trying to do too much. Take a day off. It's okay to do that if you've overtaxed yourself.

If you're suddenly feeling weaker in the water or find that your endurance is lacking, it's possible you've been training too much. Your performance is a relatively stable indicator of improvement, so if suddenly you have a reduction in abilities, you should consider your training immediately.

Other mental factors include your mood and even depression. If you're noticing that you're just not quite yourself and if you lack energy and enthusiasm, you're likely in need of some rest. Lacking a desire to eat, not being able to sleep as usual, and pain ranging from muscle aches to headaches are all also potential signs of overtraining. Don't think you need to be a hero and push through when these symptoms occur. Do yourself a favor and back off until you're back to your old self.

Overtraining can significantly suppress your immune system, so it isn't something to take lightly. Be cautious and aware of the things your body is telling you. If you listen to your body, you'll find yourself having a lot more fun in the pool than if you ignore it.

The Least You Need to Know

- Do the majority of your training at a pace that increases your heart rate but that is also sustainable.
- Exercise comes in many different forms, from swimming to stretching to walking and more. Do what fits your schedule on a given day; the important part is to just keep moving for part of every day.
- Consider everyday factors such as sleep, nutrition, and work before jumping into a hard workout in the pool.
- Don't continue training if you have symptoms of overtraining; allow your body to rest.

Beginning Your Training Program

In This Chapter

- Creating your own training schedule
- Fourteen days of workouts for beginners
- Intermediate- and advanced-level sets
- Tips to keep your training on track

Now that you have your skills down, it's time to put them to use! This will not only allow you to develop your abilities further but will also help get you in great shape at the same time. Whatever your goals— fat loss, cardiovascular conditioning, or muscle building—you will achieve them through well-constructed workouts.

Workouts in the pool are constructed of "sets," or portions of your daily workout that are similar in nature, have a particular theme, or are looking to accomplish a specific goal. A set can technically be compromised of any duration and length of swim and stroke combinations, but to get the most from your time in the water, you will want them to be designed with certain targets in mind. It isn't wrong or even uncommon to have a set with all four strokes, plus some drills and/or kicking mixed in, but the end result you're after should be the same. Further, you don't necessarily have to make an entire workout follow the same goal. Depending on how long you have to swim, you may have lactate threshold sets, endurance sets, and technique sets all in the same workout.

Most swim teams have enough time allotted in the pool each day that they are able to mix their workouts with significant variety and sets that serve many purposes. But if you don't have the time to devote a couple hours to your workout each time you swim, don't despair. A good method for you would be to pick a specific goal for the day and take sets from that topic to use. We'll provide plenty in the pages that follow, but the idea is that after reading this chapter and using some of our workouts, you will be able to design your own in the future. Everyone has a different level of ability for certain skills, and each person has his or her own goals. Therefore, the best way to reach them is to find what works best for *you*. Let's get to it!

Training on Your Own

You don't need a swim team or club to keep you motivated to swim every day. You just need a plan. Some people can get themselves to the pool and come up with their workout on a whim, but the majority of people need more structure so they don't arrive, jump in, and get bored.

The main advantage of swimming on your own is that you can do it on your own time and work it around other priorities in your life. But you do need to make sure you give it focus. If you treat it like a secondary endeavor, it becomes far too easy to overlook the importance of your exercise plan.

When training on your own, not only can you get to the pool when you want, but the workouts can also be more specifically tailored to yourself—meaning yardage and even *intervals* are all up to you.

 DEFINITION

An **interval** is a specified amount of time to complete a swim, finish it, allow yourself a bit of a break—which could be as little as a couple of seconds—and begin the next swim.

To be prepared for your next workout, have your swim bag ready (suit, goggles, sandals, towel, and water bottle) and your accessory bag with it (pull buoy, kickboard, and hand paddles). Take them to the pool each time you want to swim so you're always prepared. Have a prepared workout either written down or well thought out in your head. Lots of people write their workout on a piece of paper, place it into a zip plastic bag to keep it dry, and stick it to their kickboard. Do whatever works for you!

Create Your Own Program

The first step in creating your program is to determine how much time you can dedicate to swimming. You may be able to go five days a week, or maybe you can only go three. Whatever you can work in, get it on your calendar and don't let yourself get in the habit of putting it off. Then consider how much time you have to exercise on days you can't get to the pool. Remember that you should shoot for at least a half hour each day of physical activity at a minimum.

Start slowly when you start exercising. Even if you have time to devote to a more rigorous program, save that until you're ready. To start, go with three or four days a week. Get your body used to the idea that it's going to shed fat and build muscle, and after a couple weeks you can consider whether your recovery and other factors allow you to add more.

After a month or two of regular workouts, you will want to round out your training to a full week (but with some days more strenuous than others). Here is an example:

> Monday: swimming workout
>
> Tuesday: walking—30 minutes
>
> Wednesday: swimming workout
>
> Thursday: walking—30 minutes
>
> Friday: swimming workout
>
> Saturday: swimming workout
>
> Sunday: walking—30 minutes

The days when you're just out for a walk can be as simple as taking the family pet out or going for a stroll with your family. Just adjust this for what works for you. If you can make it to a pool every day and your body is ready for it, by all means go for it if that's what makes you happy (and really, how can swimming not make you smile?). Just be sure you aren't pushing yourself to the max seven days a week; as we talked about in Chapter 11, overtraining is a very real possibility you want to avoid. The key is simply to stay active and get your blood flowing every single day.

Your First Two Weeks

You have to crawl before you can walk, as the old saying goes. And once you can walk, you're ready to run—and once you're off and running, only you can stop yourself. The biggest obstacle most people have with getting on board with a new, healthy swimming program is getting started. It's that first step—that very first dive into the water—that can sometimes make people nervous. But rest assured that's completely normal. Everyone gets a little bit anxious when starting anything new, whether it's swimming, a new job, or even driving off the dealership lot in a new car. New things just take some getting used to. Once you're experienced and comfortable, though, there's no telling how far you can take something—especially a new skill such as swimming that opens so many doors for you.

The following is a step-by-step, set-by-set breakdown for any new swimmer to follow for the first 14 days of a new program. They are numbered in sequential order to keep workouts in order; they certainly don't imply you must go train 14 days straight. While we don't suggest taking too long of breaks between each workout—and once you see how great you feel after you start, we don't think you will want to anyway—just do them as you can, on your own time. After getting comfortable by using these sets, you will be able to use the materials that follow to put together your own personalized workout for each day going forward.

Day 1

Warm up with: 6 × 50 freestyle on the first length, backstroke on the second length

(This means you do six separate 50-yard swims, swimming freestyle as you first head down the pool, and after you turn, swim backstroke until your return to your starting position.)

Main workout: 1 × 100 kicking with a kickboard, or kicking on your back

Finish with: 2 × 50 pulling with a pull buoy (your choice of stroke). When doing this workout, really focus on perfecting your stroke technique on the first six 50s. Then loosen up your legs on the 100 kick and your arms on the 50s pull.

Day 2

Warm up with: 8 × 25 (your choice of stroke). Mix things up a little and try one of the drills you will read about in Chapter 13.

Main workout: 4 × 50 (your choice of stroke); kick with a kickboard. During this workout, feel things out and see what you are comfortable with. You may find you like one stroke better than another!

Finish with: 1 × 100 alternate freestyle and backstroke by length

Day 3

Warm up with: 6 × 25 freestyle, working on your breathing pattern and technique

Main workout: 3 × 50; kick with a kickboard. Continue working on getting comfortable in the water. Start thinking about the way your body moves and how your body position in the water affects how fast you go.

Finish with: 4 × 50 (your choice of stroke); pull with a pull buoy

THE PROS KNOW

According to Megan Jendrick, two-time United States Olympian in 2000 and 2008, there is no time limit on how quickly you have to progress. Use the workouts that are comfortable for you as long as you need them. Megan started swimming when she was 9 and was so bad she was put in a group with 4- and 5-year-olds; everyone improves at a different rate. Trying to get too advanced too quickly will only hold you back, so focus on the basics before taking the next step.

Day 4

Warm up with: 4 × 25 freestyle swimming on any amount of rest you need before starting again; 4 × 25 flutter kicks, pushing off on your back in a streamline position on any amount of rest

Main workout: 6 × 25 swim—alternating pattern starting with freestyle, then backstroke, then breaststroke; repeat that twice; 4 × 50 kick—use a kickboard and kick using either a flutter kick or breaststroke kick

Finish with: 2 × 25 easy freestyle swimming on any rest interval

Day 5

Warm up with: 4 × 25 freestyle swimming on any amount of rest you need before starting again; 4 × 25 flutter kicks, pushing off on your back in a streamline position on any amount of rest

Main workout: 6 × 25 freestyle one-arm drills—push off the wall and use only your right arm to swim one length while leaving your left arm straight out ahead of you, then alternate arms for the next length (focusing on a strong kick); any amount of rest; 6 × 25 kick—using a kickboard, alternate each length by going one where you kick easily, the next kicking as fast as possible; any amount of rest

Finish with: 4 × 25 alternate easy freestyle swimming and easy breaststroke kick without a kickboard; any amount of rest

Day 6

Starting with this workout you'll notice we are moving into some specific rest periods, rather than having you choose your own. You'll see in the main set there is a "2 × 25 at 1:00 rest" set "as fast as you can go." This means we want you to race a length of the pool, freestyle, as fast as you can. One minute later, we want you to race freestyle back down the pool.

To make it simple, if you're watching a pace clock, wait until the hand reaches the very top of the clock (which will be the number 60). As soon as it touches 60, race away! Once you finish and as you catch your breath, keep an eye on the clock. When the hand touches 60 again, start racing. The amount of rest you have will be determined by how quickly you finish the interim swim. If your first swim takes you 30 seconds—meaning you touch the wall when the pace clock is on the 30—you will have 30 more seconds to rest before starting again.

Warm up with: 4 × 25 freestyle swimming on any amount of rest you need before starting again; 4 × 25 flutter kicks, pushing off on your back in a streamline position on any amount of rest

Main workout: 2 × 25 your choice of stroke, kick going as fast as you can; 2 × 25 at 1:00 rest, freestyle, as fast as you can go; when swimming the 25s fast, try to have just as good of technique as when you are swimming slowly; repeat twice

Finish with: 6 × 50 alternating freestyle and backstroke by length

Day 7

Warm up with: 2 × 100 your choice of stroke; nice, easy swimming

Main workout: 6 × 25 alternate freestyle and backstroke as fast as you can go; 3 × 50 easy swimming or kicking with a kickboard; now that you are a little more comfortable in the water, start being aware of the way you push off each wall; work on your streamline and the transition between your kickout and your first few strokes

Finish with: 2 × 100 backstroke

Day 8

Warm up with: 6 × 50 at .30 seconds rest; freestyle

Main workout: 2 × 50 at .30 seconds rest, easy kicking with a kickboard; 8 × 25 at .30 seconds rest, kicking as fast as you can; see whether you can make each of the 25s a little better than the last, either by going faster or improving your technique on each one

Finish with: 1 × 200 easy swimming, your choice of stroke

FUN FACTS

South African swimmer Natalie du Toit became the first amputee to compete in the Olympic Games when she swam in the inaugural 10K Open Water event at the Beijing Olympics in 2008.

Day 9

Warm up with: 1 × 100 at .20 seconds rest; long and easy freestyle

Main workout: 1 × 100 at .20 seconds rest, your choice of stroke, kicking only; 12 × 50 at .20 seconds rest, long and easy swimming; the goal with building your endurance is swimming with good technique, keeping your heart rate fairly low, and taking minimum rest

Finish with: 1 × 100 (your choice of stroke), long and easy swimming

Day 10

Warm up with: 4 × 100 at .30 seconds rest, working on breath control; try breathing every 2, 3, 4, and 5 strokes by length

Main workout: 4 × 100 at .20 seconds rest, kicking on your back or with a kickboard; 2 × 100 at .20 seconds rest, your choice of stroke, pulling with a pull buoy

Finish with: 1 × 100 easy backstroke swimming

THE PROS KNOW

When you are working on building your endurance, remember to keep track of your heart rate (see Chapter 11). The suggested amount of rest we give is an average, but if you feel your heart rate is a little too high, take a bit more rest between swims.

Day 11

Warm up with: 4 × 100 IM order (butterfly, backstroke, breaststroke, and freestyle) by length

Main workout: 8 × 25 at .30 seconds rest (your choice of stroke), swimming half the length fast and half the length easy; 4 × 50 at .30 seconds rest, kicking with the first 25 fast and the second 25 easily; make sure you are working on a good streamline and perfect technique, even when you are sprinting on this set; remember, it is better to swim correctly even if that means you will go a little slower

Finish with: 1 × 200 alternating freestyle and backstroke by length

Day 12

Warm up with: 6 × 50 (your choice of stroke); 2 × 50 kicking with a kickboard (your choice of stroke)

Main workout: 5 × 100 at .20 seconds rest freestyle with a nice, long stroke; when you are doing this set, you can try a pair of paddles and see how you like them; remember, when you swim with paddles, you really want to focus on the technique of the stroke and pulling as much water as you can with each pull

Finish with: 1 × 100 backstroke, easy swimming

Day 13

Warm up with: 1 × 200 alternating freestyle and backstroke by length

Main workout: 4 × 75 at .20 seconds rest, alternating swim, kick, and swim by length; 3 × 50 at .20 seconds rest freestyle, working on a breathing pattern; for example, breathe every third stroke and stick with that for all 3 × 50s; 2 × 25 at .40 seconds rest, your choice of stroke, as fast as you can go

Finish with: 6 × 50 kick on the first length; swim on the second length

Day 14

Warm up with: 1 × 300 alternating freestyle and backstroke by length

Main workout: 5 × 100 at .30 seconds rest, pulling with a pull buoy and paddles; when pulling on this set, really focus on where your arms are entering the water and how you can pull the most water with each stroke

Finish with: 1 × 200 alternating freestyle and backstroke by length

Intermediate Sets

A common characteristic of swimmers all around the world, from the beginning level to the Olympic level, is that they all tend to want to challenge themselves. They find themselves improving rapidly and because it feels so good to move fast through the water, they really want to test how fast they can go. Proper technique is the key to speed, so as long as the focus is on gaining speed through efficiency and not just brute power, development tends to occur at an incredibly fast pace. Once you feel comfortable understanding sets and are enjoying your time in the pool, give these more in-depth, intermediate sets a try.

The focus on the following set is to build your endurance while maintaining your technique. So you want to keep your heart rate around 70 percent of maximum and work on your best technique for each length:

> 1 × 200 at 3.10 alternating free and backstroke by 50
>
> 1 × 100 at 1.40 your choice of stroke, pulling with a pull buoy
>
> 1 × 100 at 2.00 your choice of stroke, kicking with a kickboard
>
> 4 × 25 at .45 half the length fast, half the length easy
>
> 3 rounds through this set

When you're doing the following set, make sure you do the same stroke on each round; that way, you can compare your times and will know whether you are maintaining the same speed for each 50:

> 20 × 50 at .50; 4 50s fast, 1 easy, 4 rounds through for a total of 20 50s

This next set is designed to work your legs through quite a bit of kicking. When doing the fast 50's kick, try and maintain the same times on each of the 50s, even when the sendoffs start to get faster:

> 1 × 150 at 2.30; easy kicking
>
> 4 × 50 at .55; kick as fast as you can
>
> 1 × 150 at 3.00; easy kicking
>
> 4 × 50 at .50; kick as fast as you can
>
> 1 × 150 at 3.30; easy kicking
>
> 4 × 50 at .45; kick as fast as you can

Advanced Sets

The following set works on both building your endurance and working on your sprinting ability. It is referred to as a "threshold" set because your heart rate is held near its peak for a relatively long period of time. The word *descend* refers to the interval on which a swim is performed; to increase speed/effort as a set goes on to reduce the amount of time each swim takes to complete.

3 × 200 at 2.50; descend 1–3

1 × 100 easy

6 × 100 at 1.30; descend 1–3, 4–6

1 × 100 easy

3 × 200 at 2.50; descend 1–3, trying to go faster than your first set of 200s

1 × 100 easy

12 × 50 at .45; descend 1–3, 4–6, 7–9, 10–12

1 × 100 easy

This next set works on your sprinting abilities but limits you to doing the same number of strokes for each length of the pool, making it harder each length as your body starts to wear down. Pick a realistic stroke count at the start of this set and see whether you can hold it for the entire time:

4 × 75 at 1.20; stroke count fast

6 × 50 at 1.00; stroke count fast

1 × 100 easy swimming

Repeat 3 times through this set

On the next set, you want to hold your "fastest average," so you want to assume a pace that is hard—but you will be able to hold even when you start getting less rest:

4 × 100 at 1.40 kick

4 × 100 at 1.35 kick

4 × 100 at 1.30 kick

4 × 100 at 1.35 kick

How to Avoid Training Burnout

It's possible to get too much of a good thing, even in swimming, if you don't occasionally mix in workouts that are easier than your normal routine. As we've said, your muscles grow and improve at rest, not while you're working out—so you need to make sure you aren't taxing yourself to the limits every time you train. There are a couple of methods you can use to make sure all your time spent working out is quality time, and this will not only be appreciated by your body but also by your mind.

Taper Your Training

Each season, competitive swimmers have a portion of their training called a *taper*. This is where their training gets reduced in volume, which allows their bodies to recover and primes them to swim fast at their championship meet. Most people don't have this big competition in their future, but that doesn't mean that the occasional taper isn't for you. In fact, it might be just right if you modify it.

DEFINITION

In swimming, to **taper** means to decrease training volume and total intensity over a period of time with the goal of peaking for a competition by being well rested and ready to swim fast.

After several months of intense and consistent training, your body will have become very well accustomed to what you're doing. To keep progress moving forward, it's a great idea to change things up for a brief period. Think of it like a job: even if you have one you really enjoy, a vacation every once in a while will do your body and mind a lot of good.

If you have been hammering out workouts of several thousand yards for an extended period of time, scale it back a few hundred yards a day until you have a few workouts of around 2,000 instead. Spend the extra time you have in the hot tub or sauna. After a short amount of time, you will notice your body feeling a lot more energetic than usual—and if you've had any aches or pains, they should subside. Once you feel reenergized, get back into your routine and push yourself to see what you can do!

Take Time Off

The combination of training, work, and other additional stress can create a point in time where you may just need to take a week off. Don't agonize over whether it's okay or whether it means you're really dedicated to your sport; that's nonsense. Even Olympic gold medalists take time off each season. It allows the body to recover and the mind to relax and allows you to keep a well-rounded life in all aspects. If you're finding yourself run-down, take some time off. Just don't overdo it, and you will be fine. In fact, when you come back, you'll likely be more focused and prepared to train than when you left.

Keep It Fun

Swimming is about having fun. Being fit is about enjoying life. If you aren't having a great time with your physical fitness program, in the long run it will fail. That's just the way it works. You have to be strict enough that you'll do the work necessary to achieve results, but you also have to have a good time so you'll maintain the routine. All our talk about setting things up and staying on track is fundamentally wonderful, but there may come a time when you're tired of doing it. If you hit that wall, then do something that's fun.

Maybe you're at the point where you love the water and don't want to take time off, but the idea of a workout is weighing you down. One suggestion is to find a local water polo group in your area and get involved. You'll still be in the water—the best place in the world to be—and you'll be learning another new skill. It's a great workout, and it's a change of pace that you may find you really enjoy. Plus, all your swimming talents will come in handy with this new sport.

 FUN FACTS

Water polo, an aquatic combination of rugby and swimming, is one of the oldest Olympic sports. It debuted in 1900 and has been in the Olympic Games ever since!

Last, don't think that just because you're at a pool you have to do a workout (or only do a workout). Splash around, hang out in the hot tub, blow bubble rings from the bottom of the pool, and just enjoy yourself however you want. Jump off the diving board and/or do some cannonballs in the deep end if you want to. Age isn't important; have fun and maintain that childlike excitement for splashing around. Ultimately, it will be what keeps you happy, healthy, and young.

The Least You Need to Know

- Always arrive at the pool with a plan of what you want to accomplish; set goals and define steps to reach them.
- It is important to be active seven days a week, even if you can't swim each day.
- Avoid burnout by ramping down your training every few months with reduced volume for a week.
- It's a good idea to take time off if you're feeling run-down physically or mentally.

Supplemental Drills

In This Chapter

- Why do drill sets?
- Drills for a more efficient freestyle
- Techniques for ensuring proper backstroke entry
- Recommended practice for rhythmic breaststroke
- Smoother, faster butterfly through drills
- Improving lung capacity from underwater work

Swimming no doubt provides a lifetime of fun. You have four strokes to choose from, and you can swim at a pace you choose—for as long or as little as you want. There's not much chance of getting bored with swimming, because with even the smallest amount of creativity, you can come up with something entirely unique. And on top of that, no one can argue with the results you'll feel each day because of your swimming routine: more energy, improved body composition, and stronger muscles. And to further the cause, you can always take it to the next step if you want and start practicing for competition. With that, you'll have an ever-increasing number of events to practice and race strategy to work on, and with every stroke you can be looking for ways to shave every possible second off your times. Maybe that's the drive that keeps you coming back to the pool every day, or maybe not.

But even with the infinite number of things you can already do in the pool, and whether you ever choose to compete or not, there's value in breaking things down and "drilling," which means taking time to work on just one or two facets of a particular stroke with some specialized swims. This chapter is all about those swims and will introduce to you a variety of techniques you can put to use and add some variety to your time in the water.

If you race, these drills can help you improve and perfect the technique that makes your stroke more efficient and faster than your fellow competitors. If you just enjoy swimming recreationally, don't flip the page too quickly: These drills are fun! And by improving your technique, you'll be able to swim more comfortably and more easily increase your yardage because of that. Let's dive in!

Drill Sets Explained

Drills in swimming aren't like you may think if you're experienced in other sports. Some people consider batting practice in baseball a type of drill, and others think of shooting lay-ups in basketball or a goal line defense practice in football. With swimming, we break them down by purpose, but we can also mix them up. Because what we do is dynamic—moving up and down the pool—we have the opportunity to continuously drill instead of having to reset to a specific line or stance. This opens a lot of doors for a variety of technique practices.

In the following sections, we've outlined a lot of our favorite, effective drills that will help you improve your technique, speed, and endurance. We've broken them down by stroke and purpose, so feel free to skip around and use what you think will help you most on your current goals.

FUN FACTS

The world-famous Wembley Arena in London, which has hosted concerts for the likes of The Rolling Stones, The Beatles, and Pink Floyd, originally housed a pool when it was built in 1934. The site, which was called the Empire Pool at that time, was also the venue for the 1948 Olympic swimming competition.

Freestyle Drills

Freestyle drills are fun and beneficial for many reasons, not the least of which is that they create a little variety in your everyday swimming. Because you swim freestyle more than any other stroke, it's worth ensuring the habits you're creating are correct, and drills break up the monotony of just taking stroke after stroke. The following drills will help you perfect your technique and improve your efficiency.

Drill Name: Catch-Up Drill for Freestyle

Drill Goal: To reduce overall stroke count

How to Do It: In this drill, focus on taking the least number of strokes possible per length as well as having a strong kick, especially between strokes, and having a good body rotation. To start, push off the wall in a streamline position. Start pulling with only one arm at a time while leaving your opposite arm out in front of your shoulder. Do not start pulling with your opposite arm until the arm you started with has returned out in the starting position in front of your shoulder.

Drill Name: Fist Drill

Drill Goal: Increasing surface area of your pull

How to Do It: If you've ever worn paddles in the pool when swimming freestyle, you know how much more power you can generate with each pull by using those paddles because of the large surface area they take up. Because so many swimmers only think of their hands as paddles in the water when swimming freestyle, the Fist Drill is important for reminding you that your forearm generates a lot of power as well. Swim freestyle just like you are used to, except close your fists tightly. This will greatly decrease the amount of surface area you are pulling with and force you to get up on your elbows in the water to pull more with your forearm. After doing a few lengths of the Fist Drill, swim regular freestyle and see whether you're able to pull more water with each stroke.

Drill Name: Stroke Count Drill

Drill Goal: To reduce overall stroke count

How to Do It: The goal of this drill is simply to take the fewest number of strokes per length. Make sure you're focusing on a strong flutter kick, trying to get full range of motion with your feet and ankles. Also, take long strokes, making sure you are reaching out as far as you can in front of you and pulling as much water as possible with each stroke. How few strokes can you take?

SINK OR SWIM

Drills are done with the strict intent of improving your technique and are very rarely done for speed. Because drills constitute a much smaller portion of your training time, they can be unusual for your body. Always conduct drills slowly to ensure proper body position and to protect against injury.

Drill Name: Quarter Drill

Drill Goal: Improve freestyle kick

How to Do It: This is a great drill for working on the strength and consistency of your freestyle kick. Push off the wall and go one quarter of the length solely kicking, followed by one quarter of the length doing the Catch-Up Drill, then return to just kicking for a quarter, and finally finish the final quarter of the length with a full swim. Because you are changing techniques every quarter of the pool, the goal is to keep a strong, consistent kick the entire length of the pool—making sure there is no lag in the kick when you switch between techniques.

Drill Name: Scull Drill for Freestyle

Drill Goal: Improve water feel and comfort

How to Do It: The Scull Drill can help beginner swimmers get a better feel for the water. Because your hands and arms never exit the water during sculling, this is an easy drill with great results! Push off the wall on your stomach, and start a small flutter kick. Sweep your arms through the water, leaving your elbows in one place and returning your arms to their starting position after each sweeping motion. Change the pitch of your hands in the water and see whether you're pulling more or less water with each sweeping motion.

THE PROS KNOW

Olympic gold medalist Scott Goldblatt offers this advice: Don't rush drills; they aren't races. Doing them slowly and correctly will allow you to improve your technique so you will be more efficient, and faster, in the water later on when you want to be.

Drill Name: Fingertip Drag Drill

Drill Goal: Improve freestyle recovery technique

How to Do It: For swimmers who recover in freestyle with a high elbow, the Fingertip Drag drill is great for working on that high elbow position. You are going to be swimming a regular freestyle, but instead of recovering with your fingers a few inches away from the surface of the water, drag your fingertips along the top of the water until they are fully extended in front of you. By dragging your fingertips over the surface of the water, you are overemphasizing the high elbow position in the freestyle recovery.

Just as the name implies, the fingers skim across the surface during the fingertip drag drill.

Backstroke Drills

By far the biggest problem most swimmers have with backstroke is initial hand entry. Placing the hand improperly into the water on the outset of the stroke can cause the entire stroke to be compromised as far as efficiency goes. The following drills will help ensure correct hand position so you can quickly begin doing it correctly without even thinking about it.

Drill Name: Double-Arm Backstroke Drill`

Drill Goal: To improve entry position for the backstroke

How to Do It: Because many swimmers over-reach in the backstroke and enter the water with their arms in line with their head instead of in line with their shoulders, the Double-Arm Backstroke is a great drill to work on entry position. Push off the wall on your back, and instead of swimming the backstroke with one arm at a time, pull with both arms at the same time—making sure that each arm is entering the water in line with your shoulders.

Entering with the arms simultaneously helps prevent overreaching.

Drill Name: Three Right, Three Left Drill for Backstroke

Drill Goal: Improve shoulder rotation

How to Do It: The focus for this drill is shoulder rotation. Because it is so important during the backstroke to have a good amount of rotation, while still keeping your head in line, this is a great drill where you can focus completely on the rotation of the shoulders. Push off the wall on your back, and take three strokes in a row with your right arm—leaving your left arm down at your side. Make sure you focus on leaving your head in good alignment while you rotate and get full range of motion from your shoulder on all three pulls. After you finish the third pull, leave your right arm down at your side and take three strokes with your left arm; repeat until you finish the length.

SINK OR SWIM

Drills are designed to improve your technique, but they can have the opposite effect if not done properly. Because drills can be challenging, it's easy to break proper form. But practice makes habit, so be sure to only drill when you're ready to do it right.

Drill Name: Spin Drill

Drill Goal: Increase turnover in backstroke

How to Do It: Only attempt this drill if your shoulders are very warmed up. It's not recommended if you've had any shoulder injuries in the past.

In sprint backstroke events, much focus is placed on the tempo of each stroke. The Spin Drill is a great way to work on increasing your tempo. Push off the wall on your back. When we talk about backstroke, before we talk about a good body line with your hips near the surface of the water and your head back, for this drill you want to let your hips sink a little bit and tuck your chin—almost like you're sitting in the water. Then start moving your arms, doing backstroke pulls as fast as you can—spinning all the way down the pool. As you near the wall, make sure you slow your tempo down to avoid hitting your hand.

Drill Name: Titanic Drill

Drill Goal: Improve leg strength

How to Do It: For this drill, focus on the legs. In the backstroke, you need to have strong legs to finish a race strong. Because the legs are so dominant in the backstroke, many swimmers tend to fade during the last part of a race because their legs are simply too tired to keep up a strong kick. Push off the wall on your back. Start kicking, and take your arms from the streamline position to perpendicular to your body, so your fingertips are pointed toward the ceiling or sky. Kick very hard, or you will begin to sink (hence the drill's name). For beginning swimmers, we recommend doing this drill with fins on.

Drill Name: Catch-Up Drill for Backstroke

Drill Goal: To reduce overall stroke count

How to Do It: Just like in freestyle, the focus is on distance per stroke, a strong kick, and shoulder rotation. After pushing off the wall on your back, start swimming slowly, making sure you don't start your next pull until your opposite arm is done pulling and touches the other arm in a perpendicular position above your head. In the Catch-Up Drill, you don't start the next pull until your right arm has "caught up" to your left arm.

Breaststroke Drills

Probably more than any of the other strokes, the breaststroke is a very rhythmic way to swim. To be smooth, it requires that all of the components are put together with the correct timing and technique. The following drills are excellent ways to ensure your breaststroke flows just right.

Drill Name: Flutter Kick Breaststroke Drill

Drill Goal: Improve breaststroke pull efficiency

How to Do It: This drill really puts the focus on the arms; specifically, the speed of the arms and pull. To stabilize your body in the water and make sure your legs stay near the surface, kick with a slight flutter kick. At the same time, pull as normal. The best way to do this drill once you are comfortable with the motions is to do your pulls as fast as you can in the water. This will really help with your stroke rate in breaststroke.

Drill Name: Pull Buoy Kick Drill

Drill Goal: To improve breaststroke kick position

How to Do It: One of the biggest mistakes people make in the breaststroke kick is bringing their feet up toward their bottom with their knees too wide. If you've had this problem, kicking breaststroke with a pull buoy between your legs is the perfect drill because it forces you to keep your knees closer together. If your knees separate too much as your feet come up, the pull buoy will pop out from between your knees. Find a kickboard and a pull buoy. Put the pull buoy between your legs, and push off the wall with your hands on the kickboard. Then slowly start kicking breaststroke down the pool, making sure to keep the pull buoy tightly between your legs.

Drill Name: Underwater Breaststroke Drill

Drill Goal: To encourage the catching of more water with each stroke

How to Do It: This is a great drill to help you get a feel for the stroke. It also helps you find spots in your pull or your kick where you may not be grabbing as much water as you could. Take a big breath and push off the wall about three feet underwater. Then swim breaststroke underwater without lifting your head for a breath after each stroke. If you are able to stay underwater for four to five strokes, you should be able to feel pretty easily if at any point beside the glide on breaststroke you are slowing down. Then when you go back to swimming the stroke, you can work on improving the weak part of your stroke.

Drill Name: One-Arm Breaststroke Drill

Drill Goal: To enhance body chemistry and synergy

How to Do It: In this drill, you will swim the breaststroke with only one arm at a time. Our body doesn't always move simultaneously at the exact same time, and with this drill, you can focus your attention on one arm at a time and make sure it's following the correct pull pattern. While you are pulling with one arm, keep the other arm extended out in front of you. Make sure you still do everything as if you were swimming the full stroke: focus on the legs coming up to the proper position, feet turning out, and kicking back. Also, make sure your head stays in alignment. This drill has the added benefit of encouraging proper head position, because you don't have both arms to steady you—meaning you will have to consciously ensure you aren't leaning your head back.

Drill Name: Opposites Drill

Drill Goal: Improve coordination

How to Do It: This drill will help you get a better feel for the water as well as help you build your coordination in the water. Push off the wall, and start your pull with your right arm only, leaving your left arm out front near the streamline position. Right after starting your pull with your right, start kicking with your left leg. Return to the starting position, and repeat the single arm and leg pull and kick with the opposite arm and leg.

Drill Name: Scull Drill for Breaststroke

Drill Goal: Improve water comfort and arm strength

How to Do It: There are two focus points when working on the breaststroke scull: getting a better feel for the water and working on your forearm strength. Push off the wall, and start a slight flutter kick. Position your arms with your elbows in line with your head and your fingertips pointed down toward the bottom of the pool, perpendicular to your body. Move your forearms and palms up toward your face and back down in the water toward the starting position. Your arms should not exit the water at any point during the scull. Continue moving your arms up toward your face and back to the starting position, making sure your elbows stay in one place. To make this a little more difficult, increase the speed of your arms.

Drill Name: Frog Kick on Back Drill

Drill Goal: Improve kicking position

The knees remain at the surface when kicking breaststroke on the back.

How to Do It: This is another option for the breaststroke kick if you would rather not use a kickboard. Sometimes it comes in handy if you have just finished a hard sprint set and go right into a kick set. Push off the wall on your back with your arms either streamline or down by your side. Do the breaststroke kick on your back, making sure you keep your knees just under the surface of the water.

Drill Name: Two Kicks, One Pull Drill

Drill Goal: Improve kick efficiency

How to Do It: This drill is done exactly the way it sounds. Take two kicks for every pull. The idea is to create much more power from taking two kicks instead of one. Because most of the power in the breaststroke comes from the legs, you can work a lot more on reaching and extending forward more with each stroke and have a little speed behind it. Kick while underwater in a streamline position, then break the surface for your pull before returning underwater to kick again.

The toes should point out to the sides of the pull during every breaststroke kick.

Butterfly Drills

Similarly to the breaststroke, the butterfly is best swum with a smooth cadence. Although butterfly can be done by simply muscling your way through the water, this is extremely inefficient and very tiring. Drilling with butterfly can prevent you from overexerting yourself and get you used to flowing into each phase of the stroke and, thus, moving smoothly through the water.

Drill Name: Three Right, Three Left for Butterfly Drill

Drill Goal: Allows for easier focus on stroke timing

How to Do It: As in breaststroke, it is sometimes difficult to perfect a technique while simultaneously moving both arms. For this drill, we will break the butterfly stroke down into swimming with one arm at a time so you can focus more on the technique of each arm. After pushing off the wall, take three strokes with your right arm, leaving your left arm out in front of your body. Then switch and take three strokes with your left arm. Continue this until you reach the other end.

All of the same technique rules apply in one-arm butterfly as the normal stroke, ensuring that the arms are straight and long above the water.

Drill Name: Angels in the Water Drill

Drill Goal: Improve body flexibility through relaxation

How to Do It: In butterfly, it is very important to swim with a relaxed body position. If you are tight and rigid, chances are your body won't flow through the water as easily as it could. If you feel like you could relax a little more in the water, Angels in the Water is the perfect drill for you! Push off the wall and start flutter kicking easily down the pool. With your arms, do a butterfly pull with no undulation in the water. As your arms recover, bring them just barely over the surface so you can stay nice and relaxed. The goal of this drill is to stay relaxed and go *very* slow.

Drill Name: Pull and Snap Drill

Drill Goal: Improved pull efficiency

How to Do It: The focus of this drill is on the underwater pulling motion of the butterfly as well as the timing of the breath. Get on your stomach in the water, doing a slight dolphin kick through the water. Put your arms out in front of your body in the same position as when you enter the water with a butterfly pull. As you start your underwater pull, slightly lift your head for a quick breath—and finish your pull all the way through so your hands finish down by your hips. Do an easy recovery under-water with your arms, and return back to your starting position to repeat the process.

Challenging Underwater Drills

Drilling is definitely a nice change of pace from your regular efforts in the pool, and they can help vastly improve the way you swim. That said, though, you might find some days you want to work on technique while challenging yourself in a new way. If that's what you're after, we have a few fun suggestions that can help. These are supplemental things you can do on their own or as part of your regular training as a full set.

Drill Name: Underwater Breaststroke Kick, No Breath Down, Two Kicks, One Pull Back Drill

Drill Goal: To improve lung capacity and exercise efficiency during training

How to Do It: This type of drill is done by 50s—down and back—so after two laps in a short-course pool, you can take a break. Do these on an increasingly challenging send-off, meaning take less rest in between each time you go through the drill.

Push off the wall and do a breaststroke pull-out—but instead of rising to the surface, remain lower in the water. Rather than coming up to swim breaststroke like you normally would after a pull-out, stay underwater and go into a streamline position and kick breaststroke repeatedly, without coming up for a breath if possible, until you reach the wall. Do a normal breaststroke turn, and on the second lap, do the Two Kicks, One Pull Breaststroke drill.

FUN FACTS

Underwater swimming was an actual Olympic event at the 1900 Paris Olympics. It was the only year the event was held due to a lack of interest by spectators, who couldn't see the athletes during competition!

Drill Name: Underwater Pull-Outs Drill

Drill Goal: Hypoxic training and pull-out efficiency

How to Do It: Like any other breaststroke set, push off the wall and do your normal pull-out. But again, instead of rising to the surface to swim, stay underwater and repeatedly do pull-outs. After your hands recover to their starting position in front of you, pull-out again. Try to make it to the other end of the pool without coming up for a breath.

Some people will only be able to do this drill for a couple pull-outs in a row to start before having to take a breath. That's okay; you'll get better in time. The main focus is that it takes energy—and thus, oxygen—to do each pull-out. The less energy you have to expend, the longer you can stay underwater. This means you will want to focus on making sure each pull-out is as absolutely efficient as possible so that you can take fewer of them. This will translate in time to your regular swimming (or competition, if you race) by allowing you to go farther on your pull-outs … and faster.

The Least You Need to Know

- Drills allow specific focus on individual technique issues and should be done regularly to ensure that each stroke is swum correctly and efficiently.
- Take drills seriously in order to garner the most benefits. Practice creates habit, so if drills aren't done properly, they can not only be a waste of time but create flaws in technique.
- Unless specifically drilling for intensity, drills should be done at a relaxed pace so the focus can remain on the drill rather than an increased heart rate.
- Use accessories such as pull buoys, fins, and paddles when necessary to focus on doing the drill properly as well as increasing the feel for certain drills.

Advanced Tools for Training

In This Chapter

- How to get more out of sets with fins
- Sets with paddles to build more upper-body strength
- Going high-tech to help your training
- Resistance training with chutes, cords, and tethers
- Have a ball!

In this chapter, we'll discuss how to get more out of some training tools you're already familiar with, such as fins and paddles, and we'll also introduce you to some other tech (and not so tech) gadgets you might find useful. Because swimming is a type of exercise that offers so much variety, you'll find there's really no limit to the things you can incorporate into your training to spice it up. Here, we'll cover some of our favorites.

Sets and Strength with Fins

Up to this point, we've mostly used fins for their buoyancy effects. Now that you are comfortable in the water and don't need them to help keep you afloat, we're going to give you some sets to try that will help increase your fitness level and challenge you.

Because fins and paddles offer larger surface areas to pull water, they increase the resistance you find on your body. It's as close to lifting weights as you'll find in the water, and your muscles will thank you later! As a final note before we get into the workouts, these intervals we give you are all subject to change. Don't think just because they're written specifically here you have to do them; adjust to your comfort level, but don't be afraid to challenge yourself.

SINK OR SWIM

Warming up is always essential, but especially so when using extra training tools because of the extra tension they apply to your body. Do a regular warmup without accessories, then before beginning your main set with them, do another short warmup using them in easier segments than your upcoming set.

Workout No. 1

Underwater kicking with no breath is excellent for building your lung capacity as well as strengthening your legs. Add fins to the picture, and you can probably make it all the way down the pool on a single breath of air. To start your strength-building sets with fins, make sure your legs are properly warmed up and ready for some breath control.

4 × 25 at .45 seconds rest; underwater kick, trying not to take a breath

(This means that you do four separate 25-yard underwater swims where you do your best to not take a breath, done with 45 seconds of rest after each one.)

If you are able to do this, move on to:

6 × 25 at .30 seconds rest; underwater kick, no breath, going as fast as you can on each 25

If you are able to do this, move on to:

4 × 50 at .45 seconds rest; underwater kick, no breath on the first 25, and swim as fast as you can on the second 25

Working on breath-control sets is effective toward improving your strength, lung capacity, and overall endurance in the pool.

Workout No. 2

Threshold sets help build your endurance at a fast pace, and wearing fins will not only help you go faster, but they will also help keep your overall heart rate down. Once you are warmed up, try the following set. This should be at about 90 percent effort, and you should take about 10 seconds rest between everything.

4 × 100; 90 percent effort

1 × 50 easy ("easy" is defined as swimming at comfortable pace)

3 × 100; 90 percent effort

1 × 50 easy

2 × 100; 90 percent effort

1 × 50 easy

1 × 100; 90 percent effort

1 × 50 easy

Varying your speed and tempo throughout a workout will help you burn more calories and increase your cardiovascular capacity.

FUN FACTS

At the 1976 Olympics, the U.S. men turned in the most dominating performance in history, winning 10 of 11 individual gold medals. The only one they didn't win was the 200-meter breaststroke, which David Wilkie of Great Britain won. Wilkie, though, trained at the University of Miami!

Workout No. 3

Adding fins to your workout builds strength in your legs, but did you also know it helps with your flexibility? With both flutter and dolphin kicks, you are pointing and flexing your ankles much more when wearing fins—and this point-and-flex motion increases the flexibility in your ankles. Try the following kick set with a pair of fins, and either flutter kick or dolphin kick.

1 × 300 at .30 seconds rest

4 × 25 at .10 seconds rest; fast

(The notation at the end for each 25 and 50 denotes if it should be swum fast or easy. On the previous swim, then, it is 4 separate 25-yard swims, done fast, with 10 seconds of rest after each.)

1 × 50 at .10 seconds rest; easy

1 × 200 at .30 seconds rest

6 × 25 at .10 seconds rest; fast

1 × 50 at .10 seconds rest; easy

1 × 100 at .30 seconds rest

8 × 25 at .10 seconds rest; fast

1 × 50 at .10 seconds rest; easy

After you've finished this set, make sure you do some ankle stretches so you're able to keep up with your flexibility (Chapter 10 notes a favorite of ours).

Those were just three basic workouts, but if you've tried them, you'll realize they are awesome for challenging yourself. These were just examples; feel free to mix and match and create fun and exciting sets of your own.

THE PROS KNOW

Only you know your body, so make sure you listen to it when you're training, especially when doing exceptionally difficult sets. You want to push yourself, but you don't want to push yourself too far. If you're feeling any kind of discomfort, despite what these workouts may notate, take extra rest before pushing off for your next swim.

Sets and Strength with Paddles

Paddles are great swimming tools for a few reasons. Because they help you pull more water with each stroke, they also help you feel where your strengths and weaknesses are in your pull. Additionally, because of the increased surface area, you can swim significantly faster—and fast is fun!

As with fins, paddles make pulling more difficult and thus activate greater muscle requirements. Don't be surprised if your triceps and back are more sore than usual after a good training session with paddles.

Again, the workouts that follow are just suggestions and are meant to be adjusted to your needs.

Workout No. 1

Although you're wearing paddles with this workout, pulling huge amounts of water shouldn't be the only goal; make sure your focus is still on your technique.

> 1 × 300 at .30 seconds rest; pull
>
> 1 × 150 at .20 seconds rest; swim
>
> 6 × 50 at .10 seconds rest
>
> 1st—focus on taking fewer strokes
>
> 2nd—focus on a stronger kick
>
> 3rd—focus on going faster
>
> Repeat for 6 × 50

You can go through this set multiple rounds, each time picking up a little speed. Find something specific to work on during each part of the set to make sure you are continuously improving, and note the changes you make each time your stroke feels more fluid and powerful.

Workout No. 2

For this set, we recommend doing either the freestyle or backstroke, as large hand paddles are usually not recommended in the breaststroke or butterfly.

For this set, you can do the entire thing either freestyle or backstroke or a combination of both. Make sure whenever swimming with paddles that the main focus is on technique and swimming properly. Any time a set says "fast," the action should be done as fast as you can—making sure that you are swimming correctly.

> 100 at .20 seconds rest; easy swimming
>
> 2 × 25 at .15 seconds rest; fast
>
> 100 at .20 seconds rest; easy swimming
>
> 4 × 25 at .15 seconds rest; fast
>
> 1 × 100 at .20 seconds rest; easy swimming
>
> 6 × 25 at .15 seconds rest; fast

Workout No. 3

The following set is hypoxic, meaning you want to swim at a pretty fast pace and take very little rest. This will bring your heart rate up and provide less oxygen to your muscles. If done correctly, you should feel like you have just completed a middle-distance race. This set can be swum either freestyle or backstroke.

>   3 × 100 at .5 seconds rest; 90 percent effort

>   1 × 50 at .20 seconds rest; easy swimming

>   2 × 100 at .5 seconds rest; 90 percent effort

>   1 × 50 at .20 seconds rest; easy swimming

>   1 × 100 at .5 seconds rest; 90 percent effort

>   1 × 50 at .20 seconds rest; easy swimming

THE PROS KNOW

Never sacrifice technique for speed. When a set calls for fast swimming, give it all you've got to the extent your technique will allow. Thrashing the arms and legs might feel more powerful, but that doesn't make it better for you, it certainly doesn't mean it's faster, and it could create bad habits.

Getting Technical

It's kind of funny to think about electronics and swimming—because we're pretty clearly taught all of our lives that the two don't mix. Fortunately, technology has caught up to the point where we can use some really fun things in the water to increase our enjoyment of training. We'll look at a few and see how they can help us become fitter and faster!

Waterproof MP3 Player

Perhaps the most surprising of tech pieces to find its way to the pool deck is a variety of MP3 music players. No one would ever dream of taking a Sansa or iPod into the pool, but if you have a specially designed, waterproof device such as those made by Finis (the SwiMp3; see Appendix B), you can swim for hours while listening to all your favorite songs. This device was so revolutionary when it came out that *Time* magazine actually recognized it as one of the top inventions of 2005.

The top waterproof MP3 players available today can store 2 gigabytes of music (several hundred songs). Some of these devices attach to your goggles while others can be slid in and stored under your cap. They range anywhere from about $75 to $200.

For people with the ever-increasingly popular iPod MP3 player, there are companies that make waterproof casings for this device. While you wouldn't need a new music player and wouldn't have to create new playlists to listen to your favorite songs, these cases tend to cost several times that of a device intended to go right into the water with no special protective casing.

All in all, an MP3 player can be a great companion if you're the type of person who gets motivated by listening to music. Whether there are lyrics that resonate with you and drive you to push harder or you just like the sound of a great beat while you're training, they might be just what you need to stay hyped up for your tougher sets.

Tempo Trainer

A Tempo Trainer can be a great training device when working on stroke rate in the water. This small pool accessory—about the size of a 50-cent piece—is typically used by more elite-level athletes and doesn't normally fall in the beginner category. A Tempo Trainer, made by Finis and available at swim shops and online retailers (see Appendix B), costs roughly $35, and the battery will last about two years.

The Tempo Trainer can be programmed to different time measurements down to one hundredth of a second. This device can be placed in your swim cap, and it will beep at the programmed interval to help you consistently swim at the same stroke rate. Stroke rate simply means the amount of time it takes you to complete one stroke cycle. Many times, to get faster, you will have to increase your stroke rate during your race. For example, Olympic-level female breaststroke swimmers have an average stroke rate of 1.1 seconds over the course of 100 meters. This means that they can complete a full stroke every 1.1 seconds. If you are just starting out using a Tempo Trainer and find your beginning stroke rate is 2.4 seconds, you can set your Tempo Trainer for a little faster interval to help you start to bring your stroke rate down.

Here is an example Tempo Trainer set for a well-trained athlete:

2 × 50 at .50 long stroke; focus on technique

4 × 25 at .40 at a 1.1 stroke rate (very fast; one stroke every 1.1 seconds)

1 × 100; easy

2 × 50 at .55 long stroke; pull with a pull buoy

4 × 25 at .35 at a 1.1 stroke rate; pull with a pull buoy

1 × 100; easy

2 × 50 at 1.00 long stroke; focus on technique

4 × 25 at .30 at a 1.1 stroke rate

THE PROS KNOW

Gadgets are fun and they can be phenomenal training tools. But if you're not comfortable enough to use them yet, save your money. Using tools that are more advanced than you're prepared for is only likely to frustrate you. They'll always be there, so just add things into your training incrementally, when you're ready.

Underwater Video

More and more coaches around the country are taking advantage of using underwater video equipment. Underwater cameras can be as small as a simple handheld waterproof camera all the way up to video recording devices set up at different intervals along the pool deck to record you at different places in the water, with TV monitors set up on the pool deck at a delay. This allows the opportunity for you to swim, get out of the pool, and immediately watch yourself on the monitor.

There are many advantages to using underwater video equipment, as it gives you a perspective that coaches cannot see from the side of the pool deck. Working with video equipment is also very beneficial because you can watch yourself swim in slow motion and pick up on minor flaws you may not have noticed before.

Even if you aren't interested in racing or if speed isn't your main focus, obtaining underwater video of yourself is a rather neat item to have due to how unique the perspective is. If you find yourself having any muscle or joint pain from repetitive motions in swimming, this also might be the angle needed to see what's going wrong and how to fix it to make the pain go away for good.

Hooking Up Using Chutes, Cords, and Tethers

All of these items provide an excellent opportunity to work on *resistance training*, which helps you burn more calories, work your cardiovascular system more, and get stronger and faster in the water. These devices all make it more difficult to swim through the water but provide valuable obstacles in improving your technique.

 DEFINITION

Resistance training refers to any type of training that causes a muscle to contract against a force or object with the goal of increasing muscular endurance, size, or strength.

Parachutes

Also simply referred to as "chutes," parachutes are used in resistance-training workouts or sets. Again, typically reserved for the more advanced swimmer, parachutes come in a variety of sizes depending on how much resistance you want. These devices have an adjustable strap that clips around your waist. Parachutes cost anywhere from $20 to $40 depending on the size.

Set No. 1

The focus on this set should be swimming long on the first set of 50s, making sure you're getting a good feel for the water. Next, you will move onto the 25s fast, doing the same stroke that you did on the 50s but without the parachute around your waist. You will feel much more powerful swimming fast without the chute because you've lost the resistance you had in the water.

> 4 × 50 at .20 seconds rest; swim with a long stroke with the chute
>
> 4 × 25 at .15 seconds rest; same stroke as above; fast without the chute

You can go through this set multiple times and change the stroke each time. You can also try a round of this set kicking with a kickboard to improve the strength of your legs.

Set No. 2

This set is more of an endurance set with the parachute. For most of this set, you will be kicking long and strong—so really focus on the technique of each kick, making sure you get a full range of motion each time. On every third length, *race!*

> 1 × 500 your choice of stroke kick with a kickboard and chute; every third length is as fast as you can go

After completing the 500, you may want to consider doing a few fast 25s without the chute. After building up your leg strength with the chute, you should feel very fast when you take it off.

Set No. 3

The following set can be done with your choice of stroke. If you do freestyle or the backstroke, you may want to consider also wearing paddles. Because this set is pull, the main focus should be on the speed of your arms and your head position when you breathe.

> 3 × 50 at .20 seconds rest, pulling with a pull buoy and chute; as fast as you can go swimming with great technique
>
> 4 × 25 at .15 seconds rest, same stroke as above; fast

You can go through this set multiple times, doing different strokes each time.

Stretch Cords

Stretch cords are used as another form of resistance training. They are usually attached to a hook on the wall or to lane lines with one end and attach to your waist with an adjustable clasp at the other end. Stretch cords are a great training tool that can be used for every stroke. They come in varying sizes depending on what kind of resistance you're looking for. This training device runs about $20 to $35.

Set No. 1

Because the cord is attached to the wall or lane rope at one end, you will really only be swimming against the cord for the first 25 of each 50. Once you reach the wall at the other end of the pool, lie on your back and allow the cord to pull you back to your starting end of the pool.

10 × 50 at .20 seconds rest, going as fast as you can and taking the fewest number of strokes per length

4 × 25 at .10 seconds rest without the cord; fast

Do the same stroke for the 4 × 25s that you did on the 10 × 50s. On the 4 × 25s, see if you can take fewer strokes than you normally do.

Set No. 2

For this set, you are going to push off the wall and kick as hard as you can for one minute straight. Try not to let your body inch its way back toward the wall as you start to get tired. Take .45 seconds rest after each 1-minute interval.

5 × 1-minute kick with a kickboard against the cord

You may choose to wear fins on this set if you are kicking the dolphin or flutter kick.

Set No. 3

On this set, you will not only race down the pool against the cord, but you will also race on the way back with the cord pulling you down to your starting end. By having the cord pull you on the way back, this will give you a "faster-than-race pace." Make sure you hold your technique together on both lengths of the pool.

8 × 50 at .20 seconds rest with the cord; fast each way

1 × 300 swim without the cord; easy

THE PROS KNOW

Be sure to shop around for the gear you want; many small companies make unique and fun products you may not find in big retail stores. Check your phone book for your local swim shop or surf the web to make sure you get the right equipment at the right price. Appendix B lists some online suppliers to get you started.

Tethers

A tether is a great training tool if you have a partner to swim with. A tether can be hooked to the wall or lane rope at one end and attached to your waist at the other end. With the tether, you will be swimming in place. This is a great opportunity to partner up with another swimmer and take turns watching each other swim. While one person is on the tether, the other can be watching from underwater. You can give feedback to each other on technique to help perfect your stroke. These cost between $40 and $60 for basic cords and up to $200 for a fancier poolside installation version.

More Optional Equipment (the Dry Kind)

A lot of swim centers and most gyms with pools have some equipment you might find useful. These are also items you could pick up at your local sporting-goods stores and train with at home in addition to any other dry-land training you might be doing already. The three kinds of balls covered in the following sections are designed to increase muscular strength and endurance. They are inexpensive, easy to use, and convenient to store at home.

Medicine Ball

Medicine balls come in a variety of sizes and materials, but in general, they look like soccer balls or basketballs and can weigh anywhere from 2 pounds to as much as 15 pounds and heavier. If you get the kind that bounces (which we prefer), they can be used for a variety of lifts and stretches, including core training (in which you will throw the medicine ball at a (preferably masonry) wall and catch it at your sides on its rebound). There are dozens of guides and resources available on medicine ball training, and you may find this device useful to supplement your training.

Physio Ball

A physio ball looks like a large bouncing ball that you used to get from the quarter machines at grocery stores when you were little. These balls, though, can be extremely useful for a variety of home and even gym exercises.

When it comes to core work, these inflated balls are a top choice for practicing stability and training secondary muscle groups. They make doing crunches comfortable on the lower back yet extremely challenging on the abdominals. Further, you can also use a ball such as this to place your feet on while doing push-ups for added tension on the core. Like medicine balls, there are a huge variety of things you can do with this tool.

BOSU Ball

The BOSU (an acronym for "Both Sides Utilized") ball isn't really a ball at all; rather, it's just half of one. It's similar to the physio ball in that it's made of inflated rubber, but rather than being a complete circle, the BOSU has a flat bottom and is designed to allow users to develop balance. Doing things like body-weight squats and one-leg step-ups can be quite challenging with this tool and provide a great workout. An added benefit is that it's relatively compact, so when not in use, it can be put in a closet or slid under a bed for easy storage.

The Least You Need to Know

- Being creative with your training keeps things fresh and allows you to challenge your muscles in new ways, such as adding fins to a swim set and emphasizing a strong kick.

- Paddles are great for adding strength to the upper body but require extra attention to technique for safety.

- Using technology such as underwater MP3 players and underwater video can keep you motivated and provide you with unique feedback during your training.

- Resistance-giving accessories such as chutes, cords, and tethers can help burn more calories and build more strength.

- Medicine, physio, and BOSU balls are optional accessories you can use at home to keep fit when you can't make it to the pool.

Strength Training for Swimmers

In This Chapter

- Why swimmers should strength train
- Upper- and lower-body exercises you can do outside the gym
- Upper- and lower-body exercises for the gym
- The value of super sets
- How many sets should you do?

Most people associate strength training with free weights or machines to be a body-building-type activity. People look at gyms and think of dirty floors; rusty weights; and big, bulked-up people sweating, grunting, and swearing when they're lifting a lot of weight. But we've come a long way since the "golden era" of bodybuilding, and with gyms being adorned more often now with upbeat music, bright lights, daycare, and cardio equipment, the mystique has softened a bit. Bodybuilders can do their thing, and those who have differing goals can do theirs, too.

Even with the image issue changing, though, people get hung up a bit on lifting weights for a variety of reasons. Some people also just don't think that it will help them if they're only looking to swim faster. But believe us, weight training can definitely assist your goals in the pool as well as help you build a leaner, healthier body. While your training will be a bit different than you see others doing in the gym, it's definitely something you should take an open-minded approach toward if you want to take your fitness routine to the next level.

Will I Get Bulky?

Before we get too far into this discussion, let's address a concern many women have about strength training—that lifting weights will cause them to get "bulky" and develop large muscles, giving them a masculine appearance. We're here to help crush that fear right now: lifting weights will not make a woman look manly. It just doesn't happen.

Countless women are missing out on the health benefits of lifting weights due to this misguided fear. Building muscle is definitely the goal behind lifting progressively heavier and more challenging weights, but it's not an easy task. If putting on muscle were easy, you wouldn't hear nearly as many men complaining about wanting to be bigger or being unable to put on muscular size. Adding lean tissue (muscle) to the body is a complex process that involves the body's hormones (largely testosterone, which women have very little of), nutrition (adequate calories and essential nutrients), and proper training. And it's unfortunately a much slower process than many would prefer.

As such, women stand to gain a lot of health benefits by heading to the gym and pumping some iron. Doing so will result in adding some lean tissue and reducing body fat levels. The end result will be toned, beautiful muscles to be proud of—not unwanted bulk.

SINK OR SWIM

Exercise to improve the quality of your life. More than two thirds of Americans are classified as overweight or obese. Keep training to ensure a happier, healthier you!

How Strength Training Differs for Swimmers

The general public doesn't get a lot of opportunities to see a wide variety of training other than two very specific types: the late-night infomercial type, which promises you a new body in 60 days or your money back (or not), or the mainstream ESPN style. The latter is generally something along the lines of a few clips spliced together of professional football players doing some Olympic-lift squats, deadlifts, or cleans. Those are great exercises, but they tend to lend the idea that being a great athlete involves those exercises. On the other hand, there are the bodybuilders-turned-movie stars who come on screen larger than life with big, bulging muscles that tend to make people think that to be strong you have to be big. That's just not true.

The things you may see football players, baseball players, or even bobsled athletes do are all great methods of training—for them. You're a swimmer; your training should be different because the goal of your sport is different. As such, if you're training like those athletes, you're probably not doing yourself justice.

Unlike football and baseball, your realm of competition or even training doesn't revolve around a few seconds of action immediately followed by a break. That isn't to say those sports aren't difficult, but they're simply different than what you are doing. For example, you may be trying to see how fast you can swim the 1,650-yard freestyle event. Doing the same leg training, for instance, that someone does when trying to run 100 meters in under 10 seconds probably isn't in your best interest.

So the question becomes, "What should you do?" Well, the first step is to understand the goal of entering the gym as a swimmer. First and foremost, your health is obviously the most important thing. Second is doing activities that will make you the most effective swimmer possible. This is the key difference in dry-land swim training as compared to dry-land sports. Your sport now is very continuous and active, so we're looking to mimic those types of efforts. We do this by developing functional strength, which is a new level of strength that you can take and adapt into your in-water endeavors. Being strong is great, but if you can't use that strength, it won't do you much good. So let's get a better understanding of what you're trying to develop.

Functional Strength

Guys who can bench press 400 pounds or more are pretty impressive. Guys who have arms that stretch a tape measure over 20 inches look like real-life superheroes. But they probably aren't very good swimmers. Why? They aren't trying to be. They have very specific goals, and as such, they train with those goals in mind—just as you should. When we refer to types of strength, we are most concerned with developing what we call "functional strength," which means strength that assists in the actions you're conducting in the water while swimming. As an example, it may be fun to practice being able to do exercises you only see on the World's Strongest Man competitions, but most of those techniques probably aren't of much value to a swimmer. Contrast that to specifically working the deltoid muscles in your shoulders—a very important muscle group, given that every stroke is based around them—and now we're finding something useful.

The interesting thing about dry-land weight training for swimmers is that there are really not a lot of exercises that exactly correlate to what you do in the water. The best we can do is get close and translate that strength to the water. It's an equation of sorts, if you look at it from a mathematical perspective.

Let's say you walk into the gym and can bench press 100 pounds on your first day. If you focus and train hard, eat right, and stick with it, you'll naturally increase your ability to bench press more weight. Maybe after a couple months you can now bench press 150 pounds, which is a 50 percent increase. Great job! But the downside is that you can't expect you'll suddenly be 50 percent faster in the water when you swim, because there's not that large of a functional transition with the new strength you've developed. Combined with proper technique, your new strength can indeed help you get faster and more efficient in the pool—but it's important to keep in mind there's certainly no direct correlation.

To try to develop more functional strength rather than just sheer size and bulk, we suggest doing things with a higher number of repetitions than you may see most people doing in the weight room. Even a sprint 50 is longer in duration than a lot of individual plays you may be used to in other sports, so we're looking to give you a functional change to how your muscles respond.

FUN FACTS

Muscle burns three to four times more calories at rest than body fat does. So not only will replacing fat with muscle make you look and feel better, but muscle will help keep fat away even during periods of nonactivity, when you're just sitting around or even sleeping!

Swim Before or After Lifting?

A question that comes up a lot is whether or not lifting should be done before swimming or if swimming should come before lifting. The confusion usually stems from the basic knowledge that one way or the other, one of them is going to suffer because you'll be a bit more tired. Even if you do one in the morning and one in the evening, the body can't completely recover in the interim—so you'll be slightly sluggish or will tire more quickly.

In general, the answer is to put your highest priority first. If you're reading this book, we'll assume you want to be the best, most athletic and fit swimmer you can be. As such, whenever possible, swim first. A lot of people only have the opportunity to train in one portion during the day, and many people swim at their local gyms. With hectic schedules, no one expects you to fit in two trips in the same day to the same place. So if that's you and that sounds like your schedule, get your swim in first and then hit the weight floor. Even as athletes and coaches realize that strength training is becoming more and more important for swimmers, it is still, above all else, a technique-based sport. If you get in the water and are dragging because you just did some difficult squats or some other exercise, or if you can't quite maintain your technique because your arms are so tired they hurt with every stroke, you're not doing yourself any favors. Your technique will suffer, and that's just not what we're after. So whenever possible, swim first and lift second.

Now if you find yourself in the predicament of being able to swim with a team but their training time comes after the only time you're able to get to the gym, you'll just have to do what you can. In this situation, it may be possible to have days off from training with your swim team. If you can weight train on those days, then that would be a way of making the best of the situation. But if you can only weight train on the same days you swim, and you only have time to lift weights before swimming, then just make sure you aren't pushing yourself to limits so far beyond that it will profoundly affect your ability to maintain your technique in the water. Make the best of it, but listen to your body.

Weight-Free Exercise on Dry Land

We've done a lot of talking about the gym, but that doesn't mean you actually need a gym to train on dry land. There are plenty of things you can do in your own home or in your own backyard that can help increase your level of fitness. We'll cover some basic, simple exercises you can do without the need to travel anywhere off your own property. That said, we're only able to give you a brief look at the types of training available. The numbers of resources on strength training are vast, so feel free to continue your education beyond this book.

THE PROS KNOW

Stay active to increase your quality of work. Studies show that those who exercise regularly are significantly more productive at work, so make exercise a priority—it pays off later!

Upper Body

Having a lean and muscular upper body is great for your swimming, but it's also great for your peace of mind. When you look good, you feel good, and these exercises will most certainly help build useful and aesthetic muscles and strength in your arms, shoulders, and all of your major upper-body muscle groups.

Exercise: Dips

How to Do It: Use the side of a couch or a steady chair positioned against a wall. Facing away from the object, place your hands with your palms down on the end of the couch or chair with your fingers pointing forward. Extend your legs out so they are straight, and straighten your arms so that you are supporting your body weight. Make sure you are forward enough that when you bend at the elbow you are clear of the chair/couch. For the actual exercise, lower yourself until the backs of your arms (the triceps) are level, pause briefly, and return to your starting position.

Exercise: Raised Push-Ups

How to Do It: Place your feet up on a bench or couch when doing your push-ups to increase the balance needed to perform the exercise as well as the proportion of your body weight you'll be moving.

Exercise: Triceps Push-Ups

How to Do It: Most people think of a push-up simply as placing the arms outside shoulder width and repeating a down/up process. Certainly, it is seen as a chest exercise. But we can put a little twist on it and turn it into a great triceps exercise. Assume your normal push-up position, but place your hands slightly lower than usual and in line with the shoulders or even slightly farther in toward your middle. Keep the elbows next to your body, and slowly lower yourself to just above the floor.

Lower Body

For some people, their legs are only seen when wearing shorts in the summertime. For swimmers, you're showing them off every day at the pool. With these exercises you'll not only increase the efficiency and power of your kick, but you will also craft legs you'll be proud of!

Exercise: Bodyweight Squats

How to Do It: Place your feet just outside your shoulders, and place your arms either straight out in front of you or bend at the elbows and place your hands behind your head. With your feet remaining stationary, lower yourself until your upper leg is flat. Pause there, then return to your standing position. Make sure when doing this that your back stays straight and your lower leg doesn't lean; keep your shins in a straight up-and-down position.

Exercise: Step-Ups

How to Do It: For this exercise, find a steady, flat bench or flat chair you can set up against a wall to ensure it won't tip over. Once that is in place, simply place your hands on your hips and place a foot up on the raised flat object and step up. Raise yourself up until the leg you're stepping with is extended, but don't place your opposite foot on the object. Once above the platform, return to your starting position and repeat by alternating legs.

In the Gym

Training in the gym can be daunting if you don't know a lot about using weights, so we're going to cover some very basic, easy-to-learn exercises to start. Almost all of these exercises are done with dumbbells, which we believe are more beneficial due to the increased range of motion. Additionally, because all you really need is a bench or chair and a set of dumbbells for the majority of these training ideas, you may find that many of these can be done at home with minimal investment required.

SINK OR SWIM

When you're in the gym, let common sense rule and don't train with your ego. It doesn't matter how much weight you're lifting compared to the next person. You're in the gym, moving weights around with a purpose; let that guide you, not what anyone else nearby is doing!

Upper Body

Because swimming offers such a variety of manners in which to exercise—four strokes, three kicks, and a seemingly infinite number of drills—you're constantly working different muscles. As such, it's great to give them a different sort of stimulus when you're training outside of the pool. If you're interested in doing so, mixing in some weighted, gym-centric exercises can give your muscles yet another different type of resistance that will help you move faster through the water.

Exercise: Seated Dumbbell Raises

How to Do It: Take a pair of dumbbells and sit in a chair with a flat back, or on a bench (and ensure you focus on keeping your back straight). One arm at a time, alternate keeping your arm almost completely straight—save for a slight bend at the elbow—and raise the dumbbell to the side until it's level with the shoulder. Slowly lower it to the starting position, and alternate with the other arm.

Exercise: Dumbbell Shoulder Press

How to Do It: Take a dumbbell in each hand and sit in a flat-backed chair. Raise the dumbbells straight overhead until just before your arms would lock out completely. Slowly lower to the starting position and repeat. For the safety of your shoulders and elbows, don't extend your arms completely and don't touch the dumbbells together above you.

Exercise: Shoulder Shrugs

How to Do It: With a dumbbell in each hand, ensure you are standing with proper posture. Keeping your hands at your sides, shrug your shoulders as high as possible. Pause at the top, and slowly return to your starting position. Many people think it is proper to roll the shoulders in this exercise, but that can be dangerous. Focus on only going up and down with the exercise.

Exercise: Dumbbell Bench Press

How to Do It: With a dumbbell in each hand, lean back on a flat bench and raise the dumbbells above you so that they are horizontal. With each arm, slowly lower them down and out until the backs of your upper arms are parallel with the floor. At this point, push them up until your arms are almost straight, ensuring you don't hit the dumbbells together.

Exercise: Dumbbell Flyes

How to Do It: If you haven't done this exercise before, ensure you start with very light weights. Take a dumbbell in each hand and raise them above you while you are lying on a flat bench. Position the dumbbells so that the length of the weight is the same as your body (your knuckles will be facing each other). Keeping your arms nearly straight, slowly lower your arms out to the sides. You'll feel your chest really stretch with this exercise. When your arms are just about level with your body, pause briefly before raising your arms back to the starting position above you.

THE PROS KNOW

Using free weights activates more muscles in the body than machines. By using dumbbells and barbells, you use stabilizing muscles that aren't needed when using machines and that overall are more effective.

Exercise: One-Arm Dumbbell Rows

How to Do It: Place a dumbbell to the right of a flat bunch. Place your left knee and left hand on the bench with your right leg slightly back and slightly bent. With your right arm, take the dumbbell in your hand and draw it back to the side of your ribs. Slowly lower it until your arm is extended with just a slight bend, and draw it up once more. Repeat for a set, then switch positions to do the same thing with your left arm. Be sure when doing this that your back stays flat and is not allowed to become rounded.

Exercise: One-Arm Triceps Extensions

How to Do It: Take a dumbbell in one hand and raise it straight above you, keeping it in line with your shoulder. Bending only at the elbow and not allowing the lower part of your arm to move out, bring the dumbbell slowly behind your head— extending back up to complete the repetition. Alternate arms.

SINK OR SWIM

Although most people associate the biceps with big, muscular arms, make sure you don't neglect your triceps. The triceps actually make up two thirds of the muscle in the upper arm.

Lower Body

Adding weights to your lower-body training routine can really help you get more power out of your kick. Exercises such as the weighted Barbell Squat are similar to the pushing motion of the breaststroke kick, for instance. By increasing your strength in these core areas of the body, you'll improve your ability to kick more powerfully for longer durations.

Exercise: Weighted Walk

How to Do It: This exercise is actually hard to categorize because the main muscle groups being worked actually depend on how much weight you choose to use.

Take a pair of dumbbells, one in each hand, and walk the distance of a preset path (your gym may have a court or studio that is perfect). At the end of the path, turn and return to where you started. The goal is to see how far you can go with the added weight. This will work your shoulders, forearms, and legs specifically. If you have trouble holding on to the weights, you can use weight-lifting straps to help a bit.

The main benefit of this exercise is that it causes your body to perform under a constant level of stress. When you're swimming, as you get tired, you naturally apply less force to the water. But with this exercise, because the weight stays the same, your body can't willingly exert less energy.

Exercise: Dumbbell Lunges

How to Do It: Stand up straight with a dumbbell in each hand. Take a step forward with one leg, and bend at the knees until your forward leg's quadriceps are just about flat. You will know your step was the proper distance when your shin stays straight up and down and your knee does not extend over the foot. After lunging down, stand up and repeat with the opposite leg. You can do these in the same position by returning to your starting point, or if you have the room, you may do these continuously (called walking lunges).

Exercise: Dumbbell Roman Deadlifts

How to Do It: With a dumbbell in each hand, stand up straight with your knees only slightly bent. With the dumbbells in front of your legs, keep them close to the legs as you slowly bend forward. The dumbbells will slowly move down in front of the legs as you proceed, and your back should stay straight. When the dumbbells are just above your feet, pause and return to your starting position.

Exercise: Barbell Squats

How to Do It: With a weighted barbell positioned comfortably across your upper back, stand with your feet just outside your shoulders. For comfort if you're not flexible, you may want to angle your feet out just a bit. Once positioned properly, slowly squat, being sure to keep your knees over your feet and your back straight. Once your quadriceps are parallel to the floor, drive your body back up by pushing evenly into the ground with your feet. Be sure you don't lean forward during the exercise, and don't drop too far below parallel as it puts undue stress on the knees.

Super Setting

Now that you know several exercises you can do, we'll explain a technique we like to see swimmers use called "super setting." You can also look at this as a continuous motion–type of training, but giving it a term is an easy way to help remember it.

The key behind super setting is to take your body beyond the limits of a single exercise. A problem with regular strength training is that you have a limited number of repetitions you can perform with that particular exercise/weight. But that doesn't mean your muscles are entirely exhausted. For example, if you are doing 50-pound barbell curls and you can do 10 repetitions and fail trying to do the 11th, your body has exhausted its ability at that moment to do more curls of 50 pounds. That doesn't mean you couldn't squeeze out a few more repetitions with, say, a 30-pound barbell. And that's what we're after: stressing the muscles to stay functional. You can do this with a single muscle group, or you can spread it out among different muscle groups to give your body an overall push beyond its comfort zone.

> **THE PROS KNOW**
>
> Make sure you stay hydrated; not only is it good for countless functions of the body, but it may even help you lose weight. Staying hydrated naturally helps alleviate hunger because drinking water makes you feel fuller. Depending on your exercise load, drink at least a half-gallon or more daily. Unless you're training for long periods, stick with water over sports drinks.

Single-Group Super Setting

You can target a specific muscle group with super sets by sticking to a similar exercise or continuing with the same exercise. Using the example of curls again to target the biceps muscles, you can drop the weight of the barbell to continue getting more repetitions. Similarly, you may go from using a 50-pound barbell to 15- or 20-pound dumbbells and alternate arm curls as your super set.

For legs, you might like trying regular barbell squats in a power rack—and once you can't safely perform any more squats, go straight over to a pre-prepared hack squat machine and try getting a few repetitions with that. You will, of course, have to play around with the weights you're using to find what works best.

Multiple-Muscle Super Setting

Because when we swim we involve so many muscle groups, and on the premise of trying to adapt as much as possible on land to our water efforts, this is a really effective and fun method of training for swimmers. Multiple-muscle super sets are great for building functional strength, but they're also a unique type of cardiovascular training. Because you go from one fresh muscle to another after the first tires, you're maintaining a higher heart rate that you've developed from the first exercise. You can do this for two exercises, three, or more depending on how much you want to test yourself and how long you can hold up.

The basics behind this type of training are to do an exercise until you can no longer do any proper reps, then immediately start working a muscle that is opposite of the first until you can no longer do any proper reps of that exercise.

A great example involves the quadriceps and hamstrings. You can go from lying leg curls, where you are face-down on a bench and curling your hamstrings from an extended position up toward your rear, and progress right into leg extensions, which will work your quadriceps. Other great combinations for this type of training include:

- Chest and back
- Anterior and posterior deltoid
- Biceps and triceps
- Abdominals and lumbar

As you can see, this works well with all muscle groups (big and small). Additionally, if you're really focusing on the cardiovascular aspect or if you have limited days you are able to train in the gym, you can super set from one body part to another, such as bench press followed by hamstring curls. But if you do that, be sure on your second go-around that you alternate which you do first (so each has a turn at getting initial maximal effort behind it).

The Right Number of Sets

"How many sets should I do?" Every coach, trainer, and relatively athletic-looking person has been asked this question by energetic people new to training looking for all the tips and tricks they can get their hands on. There is no one right answer, but we can give you a good place to start and help you work the rest out from there.

If you've never lifted weights before, you'll very likely get sore from just about any level of weight training for the first couple weeks. You just can't prevent it; it's such a new stimulus that your muscles are going to react rather harshly. This doesn't last very long, though, and in short order you'll be able to pick up the *volume* of training.

DEFINITION

Volume refers to the total amount of training you're doing. Increasing volume means adding more sets or repetitions to your weight-training routine.

To start, try just two exercises with three sets per exercise per body part. That will make six total sets. Over the next couple weeks, add three sets, and for every three sets add one new exercise. Do this until you reach 12 to 15 total sets, depending on how well you recover from training. To give you a visual, it would look something like this:

Week 1:   Barbell squats—three sets

Leg extensions—three sets

Week 3:   Barbell squats—three sets

Leg extensions—three sets

Hamstring curls—three sets

Week 5:   Barbell squats—three sets

Leg extensions—three sets

Hamstring curls—three sets

Roman deadlifts—three sets

The information in this chapter is general advice that you can adjust to your own needs. The key to everything is to start slowly; make sure you don't overtrain yourself. You don't want to get discouraged and you don't want to end up so sore you lose your desire to continue working out. If you find that a suggested exercise or number of reps or sets is too much at first, reduce it to your preference. Do what's comfortable. Challenge yourself, but don't risk injuring yourself—mentally or physically. You're in control of your body and to make the positive changes you're after, you must enjoy yourself, so gradually add to your workload, have fun, and watch the mirror as your body makes some amazing changes.

The Least You Need to Know

- Weight training can encourage additional muscle size and strength to accompany training in the water, which can promote increased efficiency, speed, and technique improvements.

- Like with any form of exercise, always warm up properly before weight training to make sure you're ready to train hard and injury-free.

- Prioritize your training. If improving in the water is your focus, then whenever possible, swim before strength training to capitalize on having fresh muscles in the pool.

- Motivation is a key factor in sticking with any exercise program, so start slowly and only add volume or advanced techniques like "super sets" when your body is ready.

- What's right for someone else may not be right for you, so don't try using heavy weights or high tension on any exercise you aren't comfortable with, and don't copy someone else's technique in the gym if you don't understand it.

What Else to Know

Obviously, this book isn't *just* about how to swim efficiently and quickly but also about how to achieve results, whether that's pertaining to the skill of swimming or simply getting in shape. And because all of your day isn't going to be spent at the beach, at the pool, or at the gym, it's important we cover how to handle all the "in-between" stuff, so that you can go from locker room to board room if you want to. From the best methods to combat chlorine-damaged hair to the best way to fuel up for your next training session, we have you covered in this part. And to top it all off, we'll lead you in the right direction to find yourself a great Masters swim team (if that's where your passion takes you!).

Aches, Pains, and the Ravages of Chlorine

In This Chapter

- Swimming-related injuries
- Causes of shoulder and neck pain
- Preventing lower-body pain
- Training when you're injured
- How to prevent swimming injuries
- Treatment for common ailments

Nothing derails a normal training routine more quickly than an injury. However, when people think of sports-related injuries, swimming generally isn't the first thing that comes to mind. Nothing in life is entirely risk-free, though, and that includes swimming. If something has affected you physically, whether it happened in the pool or out, it's easy to get discouraged. But fear not: being injured isn't the end of the world. When you're suffering from an ailment, there are usually some changes you can make to your program that will keep you active and quite possibly speed your recovery along and get you back to being as good as new—or perhaps even better than before!

Understanding Injuries Related to Swimming

Swimming isn't a sport where lots of stuff flies around. If a baseball, football, or soccer ball somehow hits you, it's going to be a fluke. There also aren't any hockey sticks that might strike you by accident, and you're not running along any tennis courts or tracks where you may accidentally slip and sprain your ankle. No, fortunately for us aquatic types, swimming is a pretty safe activity. The risk-to-reward analysis is *hugely* in the favor of reward. But that isn't to say that at some point in your swimming career you won't find a nagging pain somewhere along the body.

There are, of course, rare occurrences that you should be aware of on a pool deck. Obviously it's going to be slippery, so be careful when poolside where you step and heed all the signs that advise you not to run. Perhaps most important, never dive into a pool or any body of water without knowing the depth. If you aren't positive the water in front of you is very deep, don't jump or dive in!

SINK OR SWIM

In general, swimming injuries can be tracked down to improper technique being used by the athlete. The advantage to this is that it can be fixed quickly and easily. The downside is that if you continue with bad habits for too long, they can exacerbate themselves and increase the pain you're enduring. If you ever find yourself uncomfortable while swimming—with pain being the cause—stop and examine your stroke immediately.

Shoulder and Neck Pain

The most common injury associated with extensive swimming is shoulder pain, followed by neck issues. The neck plays an extremely important role in swimming because any small movement in any direction can change your spine—and thus your entire body's positioning.

Shoulder pain and neck discomfort can be brought on possibly by a couple different things, but improper technique is the most common. This is solved by making adjustments in your stroke. By practicing the form taught in this book, you should be pain free—but just in case you start feeling any annoyances, go through this list of potential form problems:

- **Are you entering your hand nearly in line with your shoulder on each stroke?** Whatever you do in the water, think of how it would feel on land. You need to ensure you're entering in line with your shoulder. Try that while just standing up on dry land. Entering forward in the proper body alignment is very easy and comfortable. If you move too far away from that particular position, it may not be painful but would feel awkward. If you add resistance, such as water, you can now more easily see why this can cause an injury over thousands of swimming strokes.

- **When you're breathing, are you turning with just your head instead of rotating the body?** If you just sat in your chair all day at home and turned your head, your neck would get pretty sore. Now when you add resistance and gravity to the mix, it becomes even more difficult. If you're having neck pain while you're in the pool, it's likely because you're recreating this same situation.

  The neck is comprised of relatively small and weak muscles. If you use them on their own, they tire quickly. When you're swimming freestyle, you need to make sure you're turning the head as a byproduct of rotating your upper body. Not only is that safer for your neck muscles, but it's also proper technique. In the butterfly, you may find trouble with your neck if you're whipping your head back too far when you go to take a breath. Remember to only lift your head up far enough so that your mouth clears the surface of the water and you are able to take in air. The breaststroke is similar in that you don't want to pull your head back. Keep it in line with your body, and don't rock it back and forth.

- **Are you pulling too far underneath your body in freestyle?** You might notice a trend with our checklist of potential problems here: they tend to relate, at least initially, to freestyle swimming. If you noticed that, you're absolutely right. The reason is that freestyle is the main stroke people swim and therefore the most likely to cause problems that need a quick fix.

  In this case, you know that you should be keeping your elbow high near the surface of the water and keeping your arm straight below that point. You know where to enter your hand (just outside the shoulder line) with each stroke, and you know how to kick properly to keep yourself afloat. Even when doing all of that, though, you could still be running into a slight issue as you're finishing your pull. By "underneath" we don't mean too deep in the water. If you have long arms and are pulling deep water, that's fantastic. What we're referring to by "underneath" is whether or not you're crossing too far over your body when pulling. Once you catch the water with your hand, pull it down the length of your body. Do this down your side, not under your stomach.

  Imagine having a dumbbell weight in your hand. If you raise it straight up above you in line with your shoulder and then straight down to your hip, it is a pretty simple and painless action. But if you leave that line and have to stabilize the weight under your chest, stomach, or hips, you're using different muscles of the shoulder and putting them in positions they aren't used to—and that may cause injury. Focus on maintaining a proper pull pattern with each stroke, and you will be—literally and figuratively—in great shape!

• **Are you bobbing your head up and down while swimming?** When you tense your neck muscles, you can end up with a significant amount of discomfort—not just in those muscles but also in the form of headaches. "Bobbing" your head in the water—as in you're causing a lot of disturbance in the water with an up-and-down motion rather than forward—can be solved with a couple of alterations.

First, ensure you are kicking. It's very easy to let the legs lag behind. When this happens, you lose a great stabilizer for your stroke. Focus on a steady kick no matter how fast you're swimming, because it is one of those universal pieces of technique that is always relevant. Whereas your stroke rate and pattern may change, you should always be kicking when you're swimming.

Second, be smooth when you enter your hand into the water. As we talked about in Chapter 4, you want to be very fluid when you break the surface of the water. If you slap the water and cause propulsive effort to go down, which sends you up rather than back—which sends you forward—you can end up looking more like a buoy instead of a swimmer. And incidentally, you can end up with a sore neck.

• **When kicking with a kickboard, are your hips dropping low in the water?** Most people don't associate kicking with shoulder pain. In general, they are right. With a kickboard, though, things are slightly different and the shoulders do get brought into the equation. Picture yourself on the surface of the water, floating completely flat. Now put a kickboard in your hand and kick. If you're on the surface still, things are just great. But as your hips sink into the water, the pivot point becomes the shoulders. Because the board is going to float unless you try really hard to sink it, it will keep your upper body floating with it. If your hips sink, it puts pressure on the joints and ultimately can wind up creating shoulder problems for you.

For the most part, because a kickboard doesn't make up a huge portion of a workout, even kicking with a board improperly won't cause lasting shoulder pain. While you may have some discomfort, it shouldn't stick with you once you discontinue kicking. It is instead largely a contributor to increasing pain in the neck or shoulders that had been created elsewhere. But if you do find yourself using a kickboard a great deal, it can be the cause of pain all on its own. To solve this, simply ensure you are kicking properly and that you are keeping your head in line with your shoulders.

If you are kicking too leisurely or with improper technique, there won't be adequate propulsion to keep your body afloat. And if you are leaning your head back too far, your spine will bend and send your torso and hips—and thus your legs—downward.

Another very real possibility of annoying shoulder pain could have nothing to do with your technique. You may be swimming exactly how you have been taught with impeccable technique that would make an Olympic-level coach flush with pride. Still, you might have something bothering you between your neck and your arms. What could it be?

There's a chance you're just doing too much or that you're just doing too much too soon. The shoulder is made up of relatively small muscles and an intricate structure around the joints. If you're not giving these muscles adequate time to adapt to your newfound level of activity, they can become overwhelmed and lead to painful movements. In this particular instance, you can generally fix the problem by resting for a few days and then reducing your volume—but it is best to avoid this problem in the first place.

THE PROS KNOW

It's easy to get excited about increasing your volume and efforts in the pool. It's fun, and the results are often quite noticeable in a short amount of time. But even though you may be ready to go mentally, make sure you are equally prepared physically before ramping up your program.

Lower-Body Pain

Because the upper body has a lot of motion while swimming, it tends to be the general area where you may experience discomfort—but that isn't a steadfast rule. It's possible that you may develop soreness or an injury in the groin and/or knees. But don't worry … these too can be easily manageable by going through the following list and pinpointing your problem. Let's take a look at a few of the common problems, how to fix them if you are currently dealing with one, and how to avoid them altogether:

- **Are you warming up enough?** If you're enduring some pain caused by kicking breaststroke, make sure that going forward you increase your warm-up length. Most groin injuries are caused by putting too much pressure on those muscles when they aren't prepared for it. Do a good deal of freestyle swimming first as well as some flutter kicking on your back. Then move into some gentle kicking with a kickboard. This allows you to stay afloat while building into your kick, so take advantage of that and start slowly and gently.

- **What direction are you kicking?** When it comes to proper technique in breaststroke kicking, most importantly make sure you're kicking straight backward and not wildly out to the sides. Proper form is essential to safe swimming. Using another analogy that will allow you to think of yourself on land, think about how simple it is to squat when you simply bend at the knees and stand right back up by driving your heels down. Now if you were to put your knees out wider and feet even farther and push at downward angles instead, you will have both a truly unique but also inefficient kick. Even worse, the latter could cause injury in your lower limbs. Also, when it comes to kicking in the right direction, any adjustment to that causes unnatural pressure on the knees, which can result in discomfort. Always know where you're kicking!

- **Have you stretched properly?** Kicking through water is not much like anything you do on land, so your body has very little experience with the motions you're now using. Because of this, it isn't uncommon for new swimmers or swimmers who are new to a higher volume of swimming to experience some discomfort in the hips or the ankles.

If you have previously been a runner, you likely are aware of the importance of stretching to ensure your legs have a full range of motion available. But if you haven't been stretching, you could just be putting yourself into positions that are so new you cramp up or get sore relatively quickly. In this sense, it's easier to fix a flaw in flexibility than a flaw in technique. If you just feel tightness throughout your legs when you kick, take time to stretch after every workout. In short order, you will be much more flexible and kicking will feel a lot easier. (Review Chapter 10 for stretching basics.)

Training When Injured

Unlike running or other sports where you're limited to one method of performing—on your feet—you have several advantages in the pool. An injury for a swimmer doesn't mean he or she has to stay sedentary and slowly lose his or her hard-earned level of fitness. Depending on the type of injury you're dealing with, you can make simple adjustments that will allow you to stay in the pool. Here are some tips:

- If you're dealing with any leg pain, create a temporary program that emphasizes your pull, then tell yourself that you really needed to put a little extra focus on that anyway—so your injury is almost a blessing in disguise. Don't overlook the potential of a pull buoy. They are great tools and perfect for occasions you'd rather not, or can't, use your legs.

- If you're dealing with an upper-body issue, focus on leg-centric training. If it's comfortable to use a kickboard, do so. If you can streamline, kick on your stomach or back. At this point, if a really tight streamline is painful, you can give yourself a little leeway and loosen it up a bit.

Now once you're limited to particular training, create your workouts around a central theme of either endurance or sprinting.

THE PROS KNOW

According to Megan Jendrick, two-time United States Olympic gold and silver medalist, injuries don't have to be setbacks that cause you to lose your level of fitness. Megan has had a number of unfortunate injuries throughout her career, but she has found that doing the things she still can in the water—just on an altered program—not only keeps her in shape, but the change of pace actually helps her improve her technique and thus her workouts once she's fully recovered. The bottom line? Never get discouraged!

Preventing Injury

The best way to prevent swimming injuries is simply to swim with proper technique. Additionally, there are a few things you can do to ensure your time spent in the pool is done so in a fun and healthy manner.

Make sure you always warm up before getting into hard training. Take your time. Work on your technique and gently glide through the water, pulling and kicking easily. Depending on your experience, your warm-up may need to last several hundred yards or even a couple thousand yards. This will also vary by the day and what you're looking to do. Specifically, any time you want to train for power during your pool session, you should take extra care to warm up. Muscles that are cold are especially prone to injury.

Also ensure you take the time to stretch after every workout. Tight muscles can lead to discomfort and injury with use, so properly stretching them after working out can be very helpful to your recovery and fitness.

Last, take basic precautions. Don't swim alone in open water, don't swim when the conditions warrant caution, don't mix alcohol and exercise, and never dive into shallow water or water in which you're unsure of the depth or temperature. (Review Chapter 3 for basic water safety precautions.)

Treating Common Swimmer Ailments

Some of the following ailments are swimming specific while others are simply athlete specific. The important part is to have knowledge of how to handle them so when they occur, you can manage them quickly and get right back to doing what you love: swimming!

Cramps

Cramps are generally associated with swimming for one of three reasons, all of which are preventable with a little precaution:

- **Dehydration/fluid imbalance.** If your body is dehydrated, then the muscles do not contract as they should and can cause cramping. If you're an ultra-endurance athlete of sorts or are overworking your normal limits, then it's possible you're also imbalanced in electrolytes (which is where a sports drink–type beverage would come in handy) or potassium. In either case, make sure you're staying hydrated throughout the day. Try to build up to, then maintain, drinking a gallon of water daily. Swimmers don't realize how much they sweat because they are in water, and become susceptible to dehydration.

- **Overusing a muscle.** If you're simply using a muscle too much, you will likely experience cramping. That is one of the ways the body tells you to back off! Make sure you're slowly working into your routine rather than jumping into a huge volume of exercise. When you build your program slowly, not only will you be more mentally prepared—which means you're more likely to enjoy it and stick with it—but your body will also have time to adapt and do so comfortably.

- **Overflexing a muscle.** Cramps caused by too much flexing of a muscle are usually relegated to the lower body. There is so much talk about the importance of proper technique when kicking that sometimes people overdo it and tighten up. This can happen in your hips if you're thrusting your breaststroke kick too far out to the sides and in your calves if you're pointing your toes too much. You do want to have your toes pointing to the wall behind you when kicking freestyle, but you want this to be a reaction of flexible ankles and proper kicking technique, not because it is forced. Relax your legs and think about going through the proper form in a smooth motion, and you should be able to avoid discomfort.

All in all, cramping is a byproduct of muscles that are not happy about what they're going through. Stay hydrated by drinking plenty of fluids, build into your program, stay relaxed in the water, and make sure you stretch after every workout to develop a nice level of flexibility. Your muscles will thank you!

You probably heard the warning growing up that you should wait at least 30 minutes after eating before you go swimming. This has been supposed "sage wisdom" since swimming was created, but there's little truth to it. For some people, it's comfortable to swim right after eating. Open-water swimmers even eat little bits *while* they're racing! For others, a half-hour isn't enough time to digest and get in the water. There's no set time limit on when you should get back in the water after eating; it's up to each person. Do what's comfortable for you and you'll be just fine.

Swimmer's Ear

Swimmer's ear is caused by an inflammation of the ear canal that's brought on by various causes, two of which can include water getting trapped in the ear or by swimming in polluted water. This can set off an infection inside the ear, and symptoms include various degrees of pain.

DEFINITION

Swimmer's ear is an infection of the ear canal often brought on by extensive water exposure, caused by water trapped in the ear canal and a growth of bacteria.

If you're developing some discomfort, take extra precaution to make sure your ears dry out after your swim. If you feel water inside your ear canals, make sure you shake it out. You can also try ear drops, available over the counter, which are usually an alcohol base that you can put in to help dry out your ear canal. The best way to avoid swimmer's ear is to prevent it, so with a little care you can make sure you remain pain-free.

Dry Skin

Chlorine is a chemical that has been used for a century to keep water clean. Unfortunately, a byproduct is dry skin when exposed for prolonged periods. To top it off, when you shower after a swim, you're also shedding the remainder of the oils that are on your body, further drying your skin and opening your pores (which allows even additional chlorine damage to manifest itself). But don't worry: you can use a lotion or aloe vera gel to help soothe the skin, and they tend to be very effective at relieving the dry and rough sensations.

Chlorine "Burn"

When the chlorine levels are too high in a pool or if the water hasn't been properly maintained, the chemicals react with the relatively sensitive skin on the face and can leave behind a burning sensation. This "chlorine burn" usually shows up beneath the eyes (areas that can't be covered by your goggles) and can look very much like a sunburn. Most people don't like to use a regular body lotion on their face, and because of the nature of this type of dryness, it can be advisable to use something that is of a thicker consistency and will last longer while soothing the burn. You can try one of the many moisturizers that are specifically made for damaged skin on the face, or you can get a bit more creative: if you don't mind sharing a product originally meant for cows, many swimmers have found success using a product called Bag Balm to take care of any redness they may experience after swimming. Of course, if you prefer something more traditional, hydrocortisone is also an option.

Chlorine-Damaged Hair

This is more of a worry for women than for men, but it's still a concern that warrants a bit of attention. In the same way that chlorine strips away moisture from your skin, it also does so to your hair. You can help keep this to a minimum by wetting your hair with fresh water prior to entering the pool, which prevents the chlorine from absorbing into dry or oily hair, and by rinsing your hair well as soon as you leave the pool. Also, make sure you use conditioner immediately after your swim so your hair gets essential moisture back as quickly as possible.

There are shampoo and conditioner formulas out there that are specifically made for swimmers' hair by brands such as ACQUA and UltraSwim. Because everyone's hair differs, and because everyone has different preferences on how their hair should feel, try various brands until you find the one that works best for you.

For as long as most people can remember, they've heard the legend that chlorine can and will turn your hair green! Each summer, this issue creeps up—and the fear of lettuce-colored hair has actually kept more than a few people (generally girls) out of the water. So the question is: Does chlorine really turn your hair green?

The answer is no. Chlorine does not turn your hair green. If it did, logic would reign that those who spent the most time in pools would have the greenest hair. To date, though, no one who has ever competed in the Olympic Games in swimming has had naturally green hair. Chlorine is actually a whitening agent, so if anything, it would lighten hair (which many blonde swimmers have actually noticed) and certainly not turn it green.

So where did this myth come from? It all started because there have been people who have left the pool only to find out later their hair has taken on a shade of green. But it's not the chlorine that did it—it's actually copper. Copper enters pool water in a variety of ways, but unlike water (which evaporates), copper just continues to build up. So the amount slowly grows and grows, and it can interact with chemicals in the hair that give you that glowing greenish hue. If the pool you are swimming in is properly maintained, this shouldn't be much of a worry. Make sure you wash your hair out, and you'll be good to go. Just don't blame chlorine if your hair does go green!

The Least You Need to Know

- If something begins to hurt, first look at your technique and determine if it is easily corrected, or if it is more serious.

- Being injured doesn't mean you have to stop training, but it will require adjustments to ensure you're not aggravating an injury while staying fit.

- Keep your muscles healthy and happy by stretching properly and often and staying hydrated by drinking fluids before, during, and after training.

- Shower soon after swimming to remove chlorine from your skin and hair and to prevent cumulative damage from the exposure brought on by your time in the water.

Fueling Your Vessel

In This Chapter

- Proper performance nutrition
- Fueling your body before and after you work out or compete
- Dispelling some common food myths
- Achieving lasting weight loss

Your level and quality of nutrition is equally as important as the training you do. Eating the proper foods to fuel your body will improve your workouts and help you recover more quickly so that you can return to the pool, ready to give it your all. Improving your skills in anything is a result of the focus you put into it, and unfortunately for a lot of people, proper eating habits cost them a great deal in the realm of athletics and fitness. The human body just can't handle being run down day after day in the pursuit of improvement; it has to have the proper fuel to produce results.

Understanding Performance Nutrition

Nutrition is a relatively simple concept. There are a few things that your body needs and that you should really focus on giving it, but there are almost an infinite number of options to reach that goal. On television and in magazines, you see innumerable "secrets" and "special diets" that athletes and celebrities supposedly follow. You just can't go through a store's checkout without reading about some sort of amazing breakthrough. After a very short time, this can all seem pretty daunting, and fast food ends up looking like the simplest—even if not the best—option. Fortunately, the simple truth is that proper performance nutrition is very easy to achieve.

Carbohydrates

Carbohydrates are your main source of fuel. They are also likely the most misunderstood category of food! Once the Atkins Diet hit the mainstream, people all over decided to shun "carbs." It suddenly somehow seemed logical that you could eat as many hamburger patties from McDonalds as possible, but you couldn't eat the bun. Or an apple. Because they both have "carbs." Luckily over the years the hysteria has calmed significantly and people have started breaking down the facts to more properly ascertain their nutritional needs.

Carbohydrates aren't evil, but they can be abused, so to speak. The easiest way to view carbohydrates is by separating them into two categories. We have our "simple" and our "complex" carbs. Simple carbs are the type you find in candy and other sweet treats. They make you feel energetic for a short while, but they spike your blood sugar and can promote fat storage later on. Complex carbs, on the other hand, are slow burning and provide you with lasting energy without a massive spike in blood sugar. As the saying goes, "Slow and steady wins the race." These types of carbs also rate lower on the Glycemic Index (GI), which is the measure of effect foods have on blood glucose levels.

Here are some facts on the Glycemic Index from www.glycemicindex.com:

- Low GI diets help people lose and manage weight.

- Low GI diets increase the body's sensitivity to insulin.

- Low GI carbs improve diabetes management.

- Low GI carbs reduce the risk of heart disease.

- Low GI carbs improve blood cholesterol levels.

- Low GI carbs can help you manage the symptoms of Polycystic Ovarian Syndrome (PCOS).

- Low GI carbs reduce hunger and keep you fuller for longer.

- Low GI carbs prolong physical endurance.

- High GI carbs help refuel carbohydrate stores after exercise.

One of the most common sources of carbohydrates, especially early in the morning, is breakfast cereal. It's not just for kids anymore! Quite a few cereals provide quality carbohydrates while also being fortified with essential vitamins and minerals. These are great, tasty choices to make in the morning, but you do need to be discerning with your selections. Look at the ingredients panel on the side or back of the box. Ingredients in foods are listed by the amounts they're included. So if sugar is the first ingredient, put it back on the shelf. Look for something with whole wheat.

Protein

Proteins are comprised of amino acids, which are the building blocks of your body. Amino acids facilitate muscle and tissue growth as well as physical recovery from exertion and are metabolized directly in muscles to provide energy. Having a steady supply of amino acids in the body also helps prevent *catabolism*, which is the breakdown of muscle for energy.

DEFINITION

Derived from the word "cannibalism," **catabolism** is the breakdown of complex tissue, such as muscle, into simple forms so that it may be used as energy.

Amino acids are broken down into two types: essential and nonessential. Nonessential aminos are those that the body can synthesize itself, while essential aminos must be consumed through dietary measures.

Just as the hysteria surrounding carbohydrates changed the way millions of people around the world ate for many years, there has been a large misconception about protein as well. A common belief is that eating too much protein is hard on the liver and kidneys. In actuality, there have been very little documented risks presented by high-protein diets in healthy adults. Issues arise only when an individual has pre-existing liver or kidney issues. And in those cases, protein isn't the only thing that needs to be carefully monitored. If you have a genetic predisposition to particular diseases or if you're unsure, check with your doctor before making any dietary changes.

Fats

Dietary fat has been given a bad name over the years because it shares a name with the same stuff that people have, but don't want, around their waists. Fortunately, that's about where their similarities end. Fat is a very necessary part of your diet. And in fact, eating the right kinds of dietary fat can help you get rid of unwanted body fat!

Like carbohydrates, all fats are not created equal. There are saturated fats and trans fats, which should be avoided, and unsaturated fats, which can be quite beneficial. Of the unsaturated variety, there are monounsaturated fats and polyunsaturated fats. When you eat these types of fats over the saturated kind, you can actually reduce your risk of heart disease by improving your cholesterol levels.

So what kinds of foods have the fats you're after? To understand why you'll be making particular choices, think of fats as a long-term energy source. If foods could be related to swimming, fats are the long-distance swimmers. Nuts, olive oil, and a huge variety of fish—which provide Omega-3 fats—are all great choices. They are heart-healthy and tasty options that can improve your overall well-being and aid in restructuring your physique!

Hydration

It's extremely important to maintain a proper level of hydration, not just for a high level of activity but also for optimal health. Water is the best option; save sports drinks for long-duration exercise sessions. We suggest that you drink between a half gallon to one full gallon of water each day, based on your activity level. It may seem like a lot, but if you just keep a water bottle with you throughout the day and sip as you go, you will find it's easier than you thought. On days you're extremely active, don't be afraid to drink a little more than usual.

THE PROS KNOW

Swimmers, being surrounded by water, are often unaware of how much they sweat, which means it's hard to calculate how much water your body is losing. And if you wait until you're thirsty before drinking, it's possible you're already slightly dehydrated. Being dehydrated can reduce your athletic abilities as well as bring on headaches, fatigue, dizziness, and in some cases extreme heat-related illness. So play it safe and drink up! On the flip side, if you're feeling a bit waterlogged by *too much* water, scale it down. With all things health related, listen to your body.

Day-to-Day Nutritional Basics

Now that you have a little background on the basics of what you're eating, it's time to put together something more substantial that you can put into play immediately. Nutrition is the backbone of any athletic endeavor as well as absolutely mandatory for peak health, so it's important not to gloss over its importance in your life. While we're focusing mostly on performance nutrition, these principles apply to standard good-health practices as well.

The first key in changing the way you eat is to plan on doing so gradually. You don't want to make profound changes all at once, because it can put a near-immediate stall on progress. The body is amazingly adaptive and does its best to maintain balance. When you're eating a certain way for a period of time and a similar number of calories each day, the body does its best to adjust your metabolism to that amount of food. When a sudden drop occurs and is held over time, the body goes into defense mode and severely limits the amount of body fat it will burn for fuel. When this happens, it becomes much easier to store fat—and when you're left with so little calories, there's nothing there to cut anymore and progress screeches to a halt.

Gradual changes are the way to successful and lasting changes in your body composition. Don't immediately focus on counting calories and macronutrient ratios; just slowly start changing the foods you're eating. If you normally skip breakfast, start eating it. If you normally have a donut, make it a whole-wheat bagel. Make incremental changes and only further it when you're ready. Doing too much at once makes it far too easy to just say, "This is too much—I'm done" and return to previous, less-healthy habits.

Refer to the following table to load up on quality proteins and healthy fats while making your carbohydrate choices from the lower end of the Glycemic Index.

Example Food	Why It's Good for You
Oatmeal/steel-cut oats	Slow-burning carbohydrate for sustained energy
Eggs	High in protein; no carbohydrates
Nuts	Quality fats, no carbohydrates; provides a small amount of protein
Whole-wheat bagels	Slow-burning carbohydrate for sustained energy
Lean meat/chicken	High in protein with expansive amino acid profiles
Fish	High in protein with healthy Omega-3 fats
Fruits and vegetables	Nutrient dense with high-quality mineral compositions and no added sugars or chemicals
Cottage cheese	Low-carb, high-protein snack
Yogurt	Great source of protein, vitamins, and calcium

The following table shows the GI rating of some foods. A low GI rating is defined as a number lower than 55.

Food	GI Rating
Apple, raw	40
Banana	59
Broccoli	10
Brown rice	50
Oat bran	50
Oatmeal	51
Peanuts	13
Fresh pineapple	66
Crisp rice cereal	82
Skim milk	27
Strawberries	40
Sweet corn	62
Watermelon	80
White bread	71
White rice	85
Whole-wheat bread	49

Fueling Your Efforts

All foods certainly aren't created equal. Whenever you're ready to get active, whether that's a long run, a swim, or just preparing for the day at hand, you want to make sure you have physically prepared your body for the work ahead.

Eating Before Your Workout or Race

Swim meets are often long and when coupled with a big slate of events can become pretty arduous. You want to make sure your body is fueled with long-lasting nutrition to help you not just get through the day but also perform in peak shape. The same is said of long workouts in the pool and gym. You wouldn't go on a long road trip in your car or on your motorcycle without fueling up your vehicle beforehand and ensuring you knew of plenty of fuel stations along the way, so treat your body with that same respect. Like an important business trip, it's always better to over-pack materials that you don't end up using than it is to arrive, go through the motions, and find out you need something you neglected to bring along.

Whether it's just another training day or a day ahead that is full of competition, you will want to start your day with a full slate of nutrients. There's no specific meal plan that fits everyone, so we aren't going to give you a specific outline that's difficult to follow. Instead, we're going to offer suggestions that will allow you to create meals you actually want to eat. And because it's the most important meal of the day, we'll start with breakfast.

When you wake up, you may have gone eight (or more or fewer) hours without any kind of nutrition. Your body is craving food and is quite ready to break down muscle for energy if you don't give it what it wants. Especially on competition day, you will want to give it quality protein, carbohydrates, and fats.

Here's one sample breakfast:

> Eggs (protein)
>
> Cereal with whole grains (carbohydrates)
>
> Whole-wheat toast with natural peanut or almond butter (carbohydrates and fats)

It's as simple as that. You can of course mix this up to what works (and tastes) best for you by adding things such as yogurt, granola, turkey bacon, and so on.

 SINK OR SWIM

When eating breakfast, make sure you're not stuffing yourself. That can create problems later in the day, when you're in need of replenishment for your muscles if you're still too full to eat again or are experiencing some stomach discomfort brought on by too much food and then exercise.

If you work out in the morning, wait until you're comfortable and hit the pool or the gym and enjoy. Contrary to the old adage of waiting a certain amount of time before swimming, there's no set time before you're magically ready to train. Just wait until you feel good, and go for it.

If you train later in the day, the same principle applies with emphasis more on protein and carbohydrates for energy.

Here are some sample pre-workout meals:

> Whole-wheat pasta with chicken
>
> Cottage cheese mixed with pineapple
>
> Turkey sandwich made with whole-wheat bread, American cheese, and sliced tomato

As you can see, eating well before exercise isn't a difficult endeavor. While it's more involved than stopping at your favorite fast-food restaurant on the way to the pool, it isn't hard to find foods you like that your body will also benefit from.

Eating After Your Workout or Race

When you've been training hard, your body quickly runs out of energy stores. The main goal immediately after a workout or a race is to replenish those stores as quickly as possible. To do this, we can employ a different variety of foods than you consumed before you started training.

Going into training, you consumed necessary nutrients that were slow-burning. This was so you wouldn't "crash" physically during your workout and would have sustained energy during whatever activity you were about to do. Now that your goal is to refuel, you want foods full of amino acids and carbohydrates that can be digested, absorbed, and put to use quickly by the body to replace what you've used up. Back to the car analogy, you're filling up your tank after you've burned a lot of fuel traveling.

Thanks to modern advances, an extremely popular method of post-workout recovery nutrition is consuming a protein and carbohydrate drink mix. These are scientifically formulated and often made with extremely high-quality ingredients. If you would like to try a protein powder mix, look for one made with whey protein isolate, which is the purest and fastest form of protein you can put into your body after a workout. Then look for it to include fast-acting carbohydrates such as dextrose and little to no fat. Fat slows down the digestion process, which will add time to how quickly your muscles get their much needed nutrition. Depending on your size, take between 20 to 40 grams with some fast-digesting carbohydrates, and you're good to go until you can get a full meal in.

If you're not a fan of supplements or just can't find a protein drink you like, there are certainly alternatives. You can also try yogurt drinks, which have become quite popular over the last couple years. They aren't as quickly digested, but they have a nice ratio of protein to carbohydrates. Another wonderful choice is low-fat chocolate milk for the same reasons.

SINK OR SWIM

Unlike liquids, which are in a simple form and digest quickly, protein or carbo-hydrate bars take too long to break down and get put to use by the body. Because of that, we suggest avoiding those types of supplements too soon after a workout.

An hour or 90 minutes after your immediate post-workout meal, make sure you get in a full meal rich in lean protein and slow-digesting carbohydrates. Lean beef and a potato, or chicken and brown rice, will cover all the nutritional bases and help you reach the path toward optimal recovery. Add vegetables to these meals, because they are a wonderful source of vitamins and minerals.

Dispelling Food Myths

As with most any topic, there have certainly been a litany of urban legends that have developed over the years pertaining to food. You can ask 10 people what they know about a particular food and you'll get a new answer every time. Some will say it's great, while others will say it's bad for you. Fortunately, science makes it simple for us to determine what foods really benefit our bodies and which don't. Still, myths persist, so we're going to tackle a few you may be struggling with.

Nuts Are Fattening

People have avoided peanuts, walnuts, almonds, and various other nuts for many years because they see how high the calorie content is. The serving size is decently small, and the calories are more than a can of Coca-Cola—so clearly, they should be avoided.

But truth be told, the fats in nuts are actually very good for you. They are packed with unsaturated (good) fats, which can even help lower LDL (bad) cholesterol. Nuts are so good for you, in fact, that unless you're allergic to them, they should most definitely be part of your diet. They don't have to be eaten every day, but having a serving or two a couple times a week is just smart.

> **THE PROS KNOW**
>
> Total calories consumed certainly need to be watched in order to lose unwanted body fat, but cutting out all foods that are high in calories isn't necessarily the way to do it. Nuts, for instance, pack a great dose of healthy nutrients. Use them to replace other less-beneficial foods that are currently in your daily diet.

Alcohol Is Bad

Drinking in excess is definitely a bad idea, especially for someone trying to get into shape or lose body fat. But for healthy adults, not all alcohol is bad for you (contrary to popular belief). This isn't to say that going out to grab a six-pack of beer is a wise idea, but depending on the kind of alcohol you enjoy, it may not be all bad.

Red wine, for instance, is high in antioxidants (which have proven to be heart healthy). So if you'd like a drink every once in a while, you may actually be doing your body some good. Just remember that moderation is key. On the flip side, if you don't drink alcohol, don't start for any potential health benefits; red and purple grape juices can also provide many of these same types of benefits.

Too Much Protein Is Bad

Many people believe that high amounts of protein can be detrimental to your liver and kidneys. In the past, some research has shown a detriment on kidney function with the consumption of high amounts of protein. But what is left out is that these studies have been done on people who already have issues with normal kidney function that were not brought on by the consumption of protein.

No reliable studies have been done that show regular consumption of protein in amounts as high as one gram per pound of body weight has any negative health effects. The important thing is to ensure you're getting your protein from a variety of lean sources and not simply from red meats that are high in saturated fat. The reason is to protect your cardiovascular system and cholesterol.

Liquid "Celebrity Diets" Are Successful

The body is a complex system that can do incredible things, many of which researchers and scientists are still learning more about every day. But on the basic level, we all know that the body was made to process and digest solid foods. Because of this basic function, going on liquid diets is not a good idea. In doing so, you become vulnerable very quickly to malnutrition.

"But that celebrity on television drank only Special X juice and lost 10 pounds in 10 days!" you may be saying. And you're probably right—to an extent.

When you're working out and making efforts to live a fit and healthy lifestyle, you want it to last. Going on a liquid diet may very well cause you to lose a few pounds very quickly, but it's not healthy and certainly isn't permanent. Many of these "celebrity diets" are cleansers that cause the body to get rid of just about everything, including significant amounts of water. In the short term, you will cause the numbers on the scale to be smaller, but you could be doing irreparable harm to your body.

FUN FACTS

Cinnamon is highly beneficial for diabetic patients. Research has shown that consuming as little as one-half teaspoon of cinnamon daily can reduce blood sugar levels and lower cholesterol.

Brown Sugar Is Better Than White Sugar

For years, people have had the misconception that brown sugar is better for your body than white sugar. It probably follows the ideology that because wheat bread is better for you than white bread and brown rice is better for you than white rice, anything with a color closer to grain must always be healthier than its brighter alternative. Unfortunately, this just isn't so. Brown sugar is actually largely made up of regular white sugar. It simply has molasses added to it.

Now to be fair, molasses does add a few minerals to the nutritional makeup of sugar, but trying to get your daily dose of calcium or iron from it would be a serious mistake. There just isn't enough of any mineral to make it wise to eat any type of sugar for health reasons. This includes naturally sourced sugars like maple syrup and honey.

Brown Eggs Are Better Than White Eggs

Brown eggs generally cost more than white eggs; therefore, they must be more nutritious, right? That, at least, is a relatively common assumption that is just a myth. The color of an egg's shell doesn't affect the nutritional value of what's inside. In fact, the shell color only tells you that the egg came from a different, less-common breed of hen.

You'll find a variety of egg options in the supermarket aisle, such as omega-3 enhanced eggs, free-range eggs, and cage-free eggs. The latter two have been shown to be of the same nutritional value as regular eggs, but omega-3 enhanced eggs have been shown to have significantly more healthy omega-3 fatty acids than standard eggs. Depending on your diet, this may or may not be a great way to increase the amounts of healthy fats you're taking in each day.

And while we're on the subject, it's often theorized that egg yolks are unhealthy. Unless you have high cholesterol, this shouldn't be a worry to you. Egg yolks contain much of the healthy components of eggs and should be enjoyed!

All Brown Products Are Made with Grain

This one is a bit of a summary of our examples using sugar and eggs. As America becomes more health conscious, people gravitate toward the words "whole grain." This is a great idea. But don't forget, marketers know this. People who are new to shopping for healthier products often just see a package of brown noodles, for example, and pick it up for purchase assuming it's made with whole wheat. It may not be. Always check the ingredients on the packaging, because it shouldn't be a shock to know that companies often color foods for a variety of reasons—not the least of which is to make their product look healthier than it really is.

How Lasting Weight Loss Is Achieved

People don't pick up swimming, running, or tennis just because they love the activity. Sure, that's part of it—but there is usually an accompanying goal that maintains a high priority. For a lot of people, they say it's "weight loss." While the theory is good, the premise is a bit unsound.

If you're looking to lose a few pounds, you need to put everything into perspective. You need to understand what it will take to lose it and what it will take to keep it off. People look at a scale, see a number they don't like, and hurry to find the quickest way to bring it down a few pounds. But that shouldn't be your goal. Actually, the numbers really mean very little.

Your body weight is a compilation of your bones, organs, water, and body fat. But it also accounts for your muscle, and too many people forget that. No one would tell a professional bodybuilder that he or she needed to lose weight despite the fact he or she might be 250 pounds. The reason is because when that person is competing, he or she is in the single digits with body fat. His or her weight is compromised largely of muscle, not fat. And that should be your goal: lose body fat. Don't worry about weight.

If you're trying to get in better shape and live a healthier life, putting the scale away for a while or even throwing it away isn't such a bad idea. Look in the mirror to see whether you're getting the results you want; don't let a number decide for you. As you swim more and more, you'll notice your muscles becoming longer and leaner. You will drop body fat, and you'll notice your clothes fitting better. People might compliment you on your physique. You'll feel great about yourself. But you may not have lost a pound. And the bottom line is, it doesn't matter—because you look and feel *great!*

FUN FACTS

Women were first seen in the Olympics for swimming in 1912. Australian Sarah Durack was the world's first female swimming champion.

The Least You Need to Know

- Proper performance nutrition comes from a balanced and appropriate diet that includes slow-digesting carbohydrates, quality proteins, and healthy fats.

- Hydration is another essential key to performance. Thirst is not an adequate gauge of whether you have been taking in enough fluids, so be sure to drink water throughout the day, not just when you're parched!

- The recovery phase of nutrition is very important since muscles only grow and improve at rest. To get your muscles back in training shape fast, eat promptly after a workout.

- Well-rounded nutrition involves consistent eating; never skip breakfast or any meal, because this can slow your metabolism and stop your body composition changes.

Getting Started with a Masters Group

In This Chapter

- The back story of Masters swimming
- Locating a great Masters team
- Workout basics
- Your first day at practice
- Working with your coach
- Swimming in competition

If you've reached a point in your swimming where you want to branch out a bit, or you're just interested in swimming regularly with a consistent group of people, you may want to join a team. For the 18-and-older set, there is a large, wonderful organization called United States Masters Swimming (USMS) that might be just what you're looking for. They supply knowledgeable staff, friendly teammates, and opportunities to train on a regular schedule with like-minded people. Sounds pretty good!

Masters Swimming in Brief

Masters swimming in the United States started officially in 1970 and is currently overseen by its national governing body called, appropriately, United States Masters Swimming (www.usms.org). The program is aimed at competitive and non-competitive swimmers age 18 or older. Over the years, Masters swimming official membership has grown to more than 50,000. The membership is made up of people from all walks of life, from college students to retirees, from former age-group all-stars to elderly individuals who have previously never touched chlorinated water.

DEFINITION

Masters swimming is a level of organized swimming competition dedicated to the aquatic interests of swimmers age 18 and up. Governed by United States Masters Swimming (USMS), the group is focused on the health benefits achievable through swimming. For the competitive athlete, USMS plans, promotes, and sanctions pool and open-water races.

For the competitive minded, Masters swimming offers opportunities at all levels, from local community meets up through annual national championships as well as world championship competitions. For individuals who have no desire to race, Masters swimming offers the opportunity to learn skills and improve personal fitness in a friendly environment with educated coaches and a supportive group of teammates.

Finding the Right Masters Group for You

There are more than 500 clubs that currently operate within United States Masters Swimming on a daily basis. There's likely one very close to you, and depending on your location, you may even have several options. Not all teams are created equal, of course, so you will want to do a little homework:

- Look at their training schedule. Does this fit your schedule and work around your employment and family life? In addition to that, how many workout options do they have?

- Make sure that their monthly dues fit your budget, which can range anywhere from $40 to $100 a month. Take into account the distance you travel, meets you will compete in, and equipment costs.

- Take a look at the pools where they train. Are they near you? Do you enjoy the atmosphere? Make sure you'll be swimming somewhere you're comfortable traveling to.

- Talk to the coaches. You'll be seeing a lot of them, so get to know them, their styles, and personalities—and make sure you understand each other's goals.

Swim coach and competitor Lisa Dahl gives the following advice for getting the most out of Masters swimming:

> For swimmers to get the most out of their Masters swimming experience will depend on why they are swimming in the first place. The reason they are swimming will greatly determine what team they join and how to get the most out of it. For instance, if a very social person wanting to swim to hang out with people joins a competitive team that does nothing social and only competes, he may not feel he is getting the most out of it. If a tri-athlete wants to improve her freestyle and gets a coach determined to make her swim the other competitive strokes, that athlete may not feel she is in the right program. Remember, the most important aspect to Masters swimming is doing what you want, when you want, and no one gets to tell you otherwise. You get to choose! No parents or coaches get to tell you what to do; it's all up to you.

Some Basic How-Tos

If most people were to sit around a pool deck for a day and listen to swimmers engaging in normal, everyday chatter, some might think they're speaking in an entirely different language. Sets, intervals, and the variety of names for different training tools are largely foreign to the non-swimmer. Now that you're part of the family, however, it's time to get you caught up quickly on the things you'll hear at a workout so you'll understand them and be able to join in. Next thing you know, you'll be throwing out swim terms like a pro.

How to Read a Workout

Swimming workouts are broken into sets. A set is a compilation of swims grouped together for a specific purpose on a sendoff. Often, these follow a specific pattern or share a particular theme, but they don't have to share the same length for each swim or use the same stroke the entire time.

You may have asked, "What's a sendoff?" A sendoff is the time interval for each swim during the set. All of that may sound complicated, but once you see it on paper, it's very simple. We'll break it down with an actual example:

4 (times swum) × 50 (distance) freestyle (stroke) at 1:00 (interval)

This means you're going to be doing four separate 50-yard (or meter) swims, using your freestyle stroke, on an interval of 1 minute. Every minute, you'll need to be back where you started and ready to go again. If you finish the swim in 50 seconds, you'll get 10 seconds rest in between.

How to Read a Pace Clock

Now that you know how to read a set, you might be curious as to how you're supposed to know exactly when to take off for each swim. Don't worry—you're not expected to keep count in your head or strain your eyes to find a wall clock.

Several decades ago, a legendary coach from Australia named Forbes Carlile created what is called the "pace clock," which is an extremely large, generally wheeled clock that is placed on the deck on the sides of the pool. Instead of noting the hours like a regular clock, it rotates clockwise in one-minute turns and has large digits for every five seconds. This way, if you have a set on 45 seconds or another interval that isn't rounded off to the minute, you don't have any problems keeping track.

Of course, the pace clock wouldn't be a uniquely swimming thing if it didn't also have some of its own terminology. "On the top" is something you're likely to hear your coach say. When he or she says this, it means to begin the next swim or set when the clock's hand reaches 60, which is the number positioned on the top side and in the center. Likewise, you may hear "On the bottom," which means to leave the wall when the clock's hand hits 30.

> **THE PROS KNOW**
>
> Masters relays are very different than USA Swimming competition relays. In Masters swimming, there are mixed-gender relay events that are organized by *cumulative* age!

First Day of Practice

Breathe, relax, and smile. Think happy thoughts. Your first day at swim practice should be an exciting experience, not one filled with worry. Masters swimmers are an enthusiastic bunch and are all there to have fun. A huge difference in the makeup of age-group teams compared to Masters teams is that in age-group swimming, there are unfortunately a few swimmers who are there because their parents make them go. When people don't want to train, they can bring down their training partners. In Masters swimming, you have groups full of people who are there for no other reason than because they love to swim. Doctors, lawyers, custodians, the unemployed—it doesn't matter. People from all walks of life come together to swim for the sake of swimming, and they're happy to be there. They're happy you're there, too.

Get to the pool comfortably before practice starts to introduce yourself to your coach and your new teammates, and find out how the lanes are divided in the practice group. When you find out the best lane for you, set your things down at the end of the lane (making sure they won't be in anyone's way as practice goes on) and get ready to go!

What to Bring to Practice

The packing list for swim practice is pretty basic and can easily fit in specially made mesh bags you can find at any swim shop. These are aptly nicknamed "toy bags" and beat backpacks and duffel bags for carrying your gear because they don't hold water and dry quickly.

Here's a checklist for what you should bring to practice:

- ❑ Suit
- ❑ Towel
- ❑ Cap (if you choose to wear one)
- ❑ Goggles
- ❑ Hand paddles
- ❑ Pull buoy
- ❑ Fins

Focusing on the Workouts

It's not uncommon for a swimmer of any level who is new to a team to want to go out there and show everyone what he or she knows. Here's some good advice: don't do that. Instead, pace yourself and get into the rhythm of your new training group.

Workouts are divided into patterns, and your coach will generally tell you what your effort level should be. Make sure you follow that. Remember that if a part of your workout calls for 75 percent effort, no matter what that translates into speed-wise for you, you should concentrate on hitting that mark. The reason for this is because depending on your effort level, you're working different systems of the body (anaerobic compared to aerobic). There are sets you will do that focus on endurance (such as lower effort for long distances) while others will focus on speed (full-on effort for short distances). To become a well-rounded swimmer, it's prudent to follow these. Racing the entire workout won't do you much good, and neither will loafing an entire workout just because it's easy.

Workouts are conducted with a wide variety of skill levels; always swim to your own abilities, and don't try to race through something just to catch up to someone else.

If you find yourself needing a break or for any reason not being able to complete a swim while others are still going, never stop in the middle of the lane. This is where your fellow swimmers are going to be turning, and they need that space on the wall to keep going. If you don't want to get out of the pool while you're resting or waiting to get started again, move as close to the lane line as possible. If someone else is also there, move behind them. The general rule is: don't crowd the wall. (See Chapter 3 for basic tips on pool etiquette.)

SINK OR SWIM

In the United States, swim workouts are conducted in counterclockwise motion, so always start to the right of the lane and never cross the black line on the bottom. If you do, you risk colliding with another swimmer—and especially on occasions where hand paddles are being used, this can be very painful.

Getting Your Coach to Coach You

Masters swimming is a passion. Even if you tried really hard, odds are you wouldn't be able to not enjoy yourself at Masters practices and meets. The sense that everyone is there because it's something they love to do is undeniable—and that includes your coach.

Sometimes you'll find coaches who are former swimmers. Other times, you'll find out your coach is a current swimmer and works as a coach for the team as a side job, and the occasional really big team has dedicated full-time coaches. But even then, you have to remember that your coach is a person like anyone else who has myriad things going on in his or her life. They have jobs, maybe a second (or third) job as well, their families, their friends, and maybe even some pets. On top of that, they have a couple dozen swimmers in a pool at the same time taking their advice. What does all this mean? Simply put, your coach is a busy person. Don't think that if he or she doesn't give you a stroke tip at every practice that he or she doesn't care. Your coach does. Believe us, coaching swimmers is not the path toward riches. If they are even on deck, it's because they care.

Let your coach know you're open to advice. A lot of swimmers aren't; some are just there for the opportunity to exercise and couldn't care less about improving their technique. Keep in mind, too, that if that's you, there's nothing wrong with that. What counts is that you're in the water and are becoming healthier with every stroke.

That said—if you do want some extra advice, it's okay to ask for it. Don't hound your coach, but occasionally asking him or her to look at something with your stroke is perfectly fine. This is also where knowing your own strokes comes in handy, because if something feels off, you can ask specifically for help. Asking, "Hey, Coach, could you watch my recovery/head position/breaststroke kick/pullout/and so on?" won't ever be responded to negatively.

Branching Out into Competition

The vast majority of swimmers in the world never compete. That isn't what swimming is all about. But if you're the type who does want to test yourself against others, there are plenty of options once you have your stroke down and your endurance up. Unlike a marathon, for example, where you have one race option (you know, more than 26 miles of sheer fun), in swim meets you're given the option to swim in dozens of events. When you add in relays—where you swim with teammates and friends—your options expand even further.

USA Swimming Meets

The governing body of organized swimming competition in the United States is USA Swimming (USAS), a nonprofit organization tied to the U.S. Olympic Committee that oversees competition from age-group levels up through the American Olympic team. The registered membership of USAS exceeds 300,000 and is continuing to grow.

There is no age limit on competing in USA Swimming competitions, and meets run nearly all year long over a variety of courses. Short-course yards season typically runs from September through March, while long-course meters season runs from April to August. Most teams do take a couple weeks to a month off during the year as a break from training and competition, though. This will vary by team.

You can find a team local to you through USA Swimming (www.usaswimming.org). To compete in their competitions, you need to be registered with the governing body.

FUN FACTS

The world's very first Olympic gold medalist was just 18 years old. Hungarian Alfred Hajos-Guttmann won the 100-meter and 1,200-meter freestyles in Athens, Greece, in 1896.

Masters Meets

Options for competing in organized Masters swimming begin at age 18. While USA Swimming maintains the general standards for world records, Masters swimming instead has its own records—which are set against other nations' Masters organizations—and they are also broken down by age group. Masters age-groups are broken down as follows: 18–24, 25–29, 30–34, 35–39, 40–44, 45–49, 50–54, 55–59, 60–64, 65–69, 70–74, 75–79, 80–84, 85–89, 90–94, 95–99, and 100-104.

Masters meets also offer a wide array of new events that you won't find in age-group meets. Things such as the 50s of specialty strokes and the 100 Individual Medley are phased out of USA Swimming meets after a certain age, but in Masters, they are open to all! Further, Masters meets include mixed relays—men and women on the same team—as well as relays that are broken down by combined age. In early 2010, a relay was swum in the United States with a combined age of 361 (90, 90, 90, and 91!). Unlike age-group swimming, Masters events are also swum combined with men and women in the same heats.

There are not nearly as many Masters teams as there are USAS teams, and the overall membership is smaller—about 50,000—but clubs can still be found all around the country. Masters teams are broken down into "zones" based on their geographic location and are then further broken down into Local Masters Swim Committees (LMSC) groups. You can find the appropriate LMSC for your area at www.usms. org. Each LMSC has its own meets, and there is sure to be something going on that will fit your schedule and desire to compete. Like USAS, you need to be a registered Masters swimmer to compete in sanctioned Masters meets.

Finding the Right Competition for You

The general rule with competition is that it's always better to start small and build into bigger events than it is to take on the world all at once. If you enter something too big that you aren't sure you can finish or a meet with too many events, you may experience a premature burnout or get down on yourself mentally if you don't perform up to your own expectations. In contrast, if you start small and only swim a couple events at your first meet, after you swim as well as you know you can, you will want to train harder so you can come back and swim more.

Swim meets are magical (or not) gatherings of athletes and fitness enthusiasts who congregate to challenge themselves in an official format. They're crowded, busy, and noisy—and for the first timer, sometimes intimidating. Fortunately, they're actually a lot of fun—and with these tips, they'll feel like a second home even if it's your first-ever event.

Meets generally run in one of two formats. They are either set up for a single day, where every event is swum, or in a multiple-day format where events are spread out (and, depending on the events you enter, may require you to come back on separate days). Lots of Masters meets are one-day events while age-group meets are commonly divided over a weekend. Swimming is becoming more and more popular as a competitive event, so it usually works out to a swimmer's advantage to break things up when he or she wants to swim a lot of different races.

Competition Basics

If you're swimming for a club team, your coach will be happy to help you decide which meet events would be best for you. If you're swimming mostly on your own but want to enter a competition, there are a few things to think about when signing up. First, look at the schedule of events. How are they spaced out? To give yourself the opportunity to rest enough so you can race at full throttle in each event, it is generally not recommended that you sign up for events that are back-to-back. If your two favorite events come one right after the other, this may mean you have to sacrifice swimming one of them—but it will help you perform better overall.

General Meet Format

Show up for the meet before the scheduled start of competition. Depending on how far into the meet your first race is, you will want to ensure you have enough time to get into the competition pool and get a feel for it. Many facilities have an entirely separate pool for warm-up and cool-down, but it is always good to get a feel for the pool in which you will be racing. Get an idea of the water temperature so it doesn't shock you when you dive in, and get used to the feel of the wall when you turn. These little things will make you more comfortable during your big race, and that familiarity will help ensure you put together your best swim possible.

When you arrive, meet warm-up will be going on. It will likely be crowded, but don't worry—it's a type of organized chaos. Generally, there are no differences in the lanes when warm-ups begin, so find one that is less crowded than the others and is moving at a pace you're comfortable with. Then hop in.

As the warm-up progresses, you'll hear toward its end that certain lanes are going to become "Sprint Lanes." This means those lanes are going to get cleared out and swimmers are going to be able to practice a start from the blocks and use the open space to try out some speed for a length. In these lanes, you don't turn when you reach the wall. Instead, you hop out and either get in a non-pace lane to swim or walk the pool deck back to the blocks and start again.

Reading a Heat Sheet

Heat sheets are the culmination of entries compiled into brackets to determine who swims and when. These are generally available for purchase by spectators—or if you want one as a keepsake—as well as posted on the wall near the pool for everyone to look over. Heat sheets are divided up by event and in the order the meet will progress. *Heats* are generally swum slowest to fastest, so you will get the opportunity to race people of your same speed (ensuring you have some quality competition).

DEFINITION

Heat sheets are printed sheets at swim meets in which swimmers find the events in which they entered, the order the meet will run, and in which heat and lane they will compete. In a swimming meet, athletes are divided into races by event and entry time, swimming against others of similar ability in individual **heats**. As many heats are conducted as necessary until all swimmers entered in the event have raced and achieved an official time.

Here is an example of your average heat sheet:

Event 2 Men's 100-Yard Freestyle

Heat 4

1 Johnson, Tom 24 1:01.00

2 Smith, Joe 25 1:00.90

3 Your Name 26 1:00.01

4 Anderson, Don 27 1:00.10

5 Thompson, Lee 28 1:00.55

6 Barker, Aaron 29 1:00.99

Looking at this heat sheet, this means you're in lane 3 of heat 4, entered with a time of 1:00.01.

It's suggested you arrive behind the blocks a few heats before you're due to swim so you'll have time to take off any warm-ups you're wearing and adjust your cap and goggles.

What to Bring to Meets

A common sight on a pool deck are a ton of backpacks, duffel bags, grocery sacks, and all kinds of things in between to hold an athlete's belongings. While you don't need to make it look like you're moving into your dorm room all over again, there are some things that you will want to take along with you to make your swim meet experience so much more pleasant. They won't take up a lot of room and won't be hard to handle, and you will be glad you have it all with you.

Suits and Equipment

We recommend you bring at least two suits to your swim meets. Warm up in one before the meet begins and 20 to 30 minutes before your first race, towel off, and change into a fresh, dry suit. This suit doesn't need to be new, of course, but many swimmers like being in a suit that isn't wet when they dive in for competition. This can help slightly with drag because your suit will take a few yards of swimming before becoming entirely water-logged, but it also puts you in a mental state for racing.

If you do want to change suits before your race, one suggestion is to have a suit that is one or two sizes smaller than your training suit. When you're training, you are in the water for hours at a time and want a comfortable suit for the duration of your exercise. When you're racing, a smaller suit can help with compression of your body while holding less water (and thus creating less drag) and generally is still comfortable for a short duration (such as a swim meet).

In addition to your suit, goggles, and cap (if you choose to wear one), you may want to warm up with some of the same equipment you use during training. Unfortunately, this generally isn't allowed due to the number of people in the pool. Lanes can get very crowded, and novice swimmers are sometimes unsure of etiquette generally afforded to such busy times—so things such as hand paddles could end up injuring someone.

Nutritional and Hydration Needs

Never underestimate the amount of food and water that you will want to bring to a swim meet. The general rule is that you want to over-prepare rather than under-prepare, because if you're hungry or dehydrated, it will hamper your performance. And because the point of competition is to see how fast you can go, there's no reason to be lax on something so critical.

Just to be safe, pack two bottles full of ice water. If you prefer, you could bring one with water and another with a sports drink of your choice. Pools are notoriously hot and humid, and quite often drinking fountains provide water that's warm—so you'll want to have your own cold drinks. One thing you can do to help ensure your ice stays frozen as long as possible is to fill up a bottle halfway and freeze it the night before. Then before you leave for the meet, fill it the rest of the way with your drink of choice.

When it comes to food, now isn't the time to bring last night's lasagna leftovers. You want things that are light but filling and packed with quality carbohydrates. Refer to Chapter 17 for some great examples.

The Least You Need to Know

- A list of Masters teams and potential events in which you can join can be found at www.usms.org.
- To ensure you will be able to participate in any set your coach gives you, always bring all of your equipment to workouts. Be prepared with a spare suit and goggles just in case yours rips or breaks.
- To ensure you're gaining the skills desired, focus on swimming the workout exactly as given to you by your coach and never race a portion of a workout that calls for a lesser effort.
- Be open with your coach and let him or her know your goals so, whenever possible, sets or events can be tailored to your specific objectives.

Glossary

aerobic   Literally "requiring oxygen," in fitness the term refers to activities that increase the need for oxygen in the body.

age-group swimming   Swimming competition for athletes 18 years of age and younger.

anaerobic   Literally, "absence of oxygen," in fitness the term refers to exercises that place the body in an oxygen-deprived state.

backstroke   Basic swimming stroke with the swimmer on his or her back, kicking with elongated legs and moving the arms in a windmill-like motion.

block   The starting platform.

breakout   The portion of a swim where a swimmer's body breaks the surface of the water and he or she begins a stroke; it occurs after starts as well as turns.

breaststroke   Known as the original swimming stroke; swimmers scull with the arms and kick the legs in a froglike motion.

build   Refers to the increase in speed and effort over the course of a swim.

bulkhead   A platform that extends into the water and is usually used to separate portions of a pool.

butterfly   Newest swimming stroke, with the swimmer moving arms simultaneously over the top of the water while kicking in a whipping fashion with the legs together.

catabolism   The process of the body breaking down complex tissue to be used as fuel.

catch-up   A drill used in freestyle or backstroke swimming where one hand remains in place, extended, until the other hand reaches the same point.

circle swimming Swimming in a counterclockwise direction; always remaining to the right of the line on the bottom of the pool; in some countries, swimming in a clockwise direction.

coach An individual who teaches techniques and safety pertaining to swimming.

crawl *See* freestyle.

descend Refers to the interval on which a swim is performed; to increase speed/effort as a set goes on to reduce the amount of time each swim takes to complete.

distance per stroke (DPS) The effort of reducing the number of strokes taken per length.

dolphin kick Swimming kick where the legs remain together and move in a whip-like manner, maintaining only a slight bend at the knees.

DPS *See* distance per stroke.

drag The resistance of the water against the swimmer's body. *See also* drag suit.

drag suit Usually a second, baggy suit worn to increase water resistance against the swimmer.

drill A focused swim exercising a particular technique to improve overall efficiency and/or speed.

drive point The area of the body that is the catalyst for propelled motion.

dry land Term used by swimmers that refers to training outside the pool.

FINA **Fédération Internationale de Natation,** the worldwide governing body of the sport of swimming.

flags Flags strung across the pool five yards/meters from each end of a pool; used by backstroke swimmers to know where they are in the pool and when to begin the execution of turning motions.

freestyle Most commonly swum stroke; swimmers propel themselves with alternating arm motions that enter in front of the swimmer and exit by the hips while maintaining a kick in which the legs are extended behind.

heat In a swimming meet, athletes are divided into races by event and entry time, swimming against others of similar ability in individual heats. As many heats are conducted as necessary until all swimmers entered in the event have raced and achieved an official time.

heat sheets   Printed sheets at swim meets in which swimmers find the events in which they entered, the order the meet will run, and in which heat and lane they will compete.

individual medley (IM)   A consecutive swim in which an athlete uses all four swimming strokes, swum in the order of butterfly, backstroke, breaststroke, and freestyle.

interval   A specified amount of time to complete a swim and begin the next, judged by a swimmer using a pace clock.

lane lines   Dividers between lanes, usually made up of round plastic blocks or rope and buoys.

long course   Refers to a 50-meter long, Olympic-size pool.

Masters swimming   A level of organized swimming competition divided into age groups, beginning at age 18; in the United States, Masters is run and governed by United States Masters Swimming (USMS).

meet   Competition format where athletes race one another in a variety of distances and stroke events.

monofin   A training tool in which a swimmer places both feet into a single, solid piece of material that is shaped into a fin; used to significantly increase speed and muscular resistance.

negative split   Swimming the second half of a swim faster than the first half.

open turn   A method of turning done predominantly when swimming the butterfly and the breaststroke. It involves both hands touching the wall simultaneously, and the swimmer bringing the knees up toward the chest, placing the feet on the wall, and pushing off in a streamline position to return to swimming.

overreaching   The act of reaching beyond the optimal entry point for efficiency in a stroke.

pace clock   A clock visible by athletes in a pool used to keep track of how long individual swims take as well as to track rest periods.

pull buoy   A buoyant training tool that swimmers place between their legs to assist in the flotation of the lower body; often used to train new swimmers and to focus on upper-body-oriented technique work.

pull-out   The motion a breaststroke swimmer uses to transition from streamline position to the actual swimming stroke; involves pulling the arms the length of the body and recovering underneath the stomach and face while using one breaststroke kick.

recovery   The phase of a stroke in which the pulling portion has been completed and the hands are returning to their starting position.

relay   A team of four athletes swimming together as part of a single race. The term can refer to freestyle relays, where all athletes swim freestyle over an equal distance; or a medley relay, where each athlete swims a different stroke in the order of backstroke, breaststroke, butterfly, and freestyle.

resistance training   Any type of training that causes a muscle to contract against a force or object with the goal of increasing muscular endurance, size, or strength.

sculling   An in-and-out sweeping motion of the hands.

set   A compilation of swims grouped together for a specific purpose, usually done on a send-off.

short course   Refers to a 25-yard or 25-meter pool.

split   Refers to the time a portion of a longer swim takes to complete, or the halfway time of a given distance.

sprint   A maximum-effort swim, aiming for as much speed as a swimmer can create.

streamline   The most efficient body position in swimming, where an athlete has his or her arms and legs fully extended with the biceps pressed against the head and one hand overlapping the other.

super setting   Two or more sets/exercises performed one right after the other.

swimmer's ear   An infection of the ear canal often brought on by extensive water exposure, caused by water trapped in the ear canal and a growth of bacteria.

taper   To decrease training volume and total intensity over a period of time with the goal of peaking for a competition by being well rested and ready to swim fast.

touch pad   The device used to register a duration of time, measured from the start of a race until touched by a swimmer.

transition   In swimming, the process of switching from one stroke or technique to another. The individual medley involves three transitions: butterfly to backstroke, backstroke to breaststroke, and breaststroke to freestyle.

turnover   The speed in which a swimmer takes his or her strokes.

United States Masters Swimming   *See* Masters swimming.

USA Swimming   The governing body of swimming in the United States.

vertical kicking   Kicking to stay afloat when the body is vertical in the water.

volume   The amount of total training; increasing volume refers to adding more sets or repetitions to a weight training routine.

warm down   The process of swimming easily to reduce heart rate after a strenuous swim or event.

warm up   The process of slowly increasing energy expenditure to ensure the joints and muscles are prepared for strenuous activity.

Zoomers   Fins with a shorter length, produced by Finis, designed to gradually increase kicking resistance and improve swimming speed.

Online Resources

Advice and Tips

www.getwetgetfit.com   Extensive online resource for swimming tips, nutrition advice, product reviews, and more.

Community and Charity Swimming

www.swim.com   This extensive website features online forums for swimmers new and old to connect and share conversation. Additionally, swim.com offers a tool to find local pools in your area.

www.swimacrossamerica.org   Run by Swim Across America, Inc., this website maintains a list of organizations' events that are dedicated to raising awareness and funds for cancer research, prevention, and treatment.

www.swimfoundation.org   The online arm of the USA Swimming Foundation and home of the Make a Splash campaign, a national child-focused water safety initiative created by the USA Swimming Foundation, focusing on a goal of teaching every child in America how to swim.

www.swimmingworldmagazine.com   Online home of *Swimming World Magazine*, a site dedicated to covering news and events from around the aquatic world, from diving to swimming to water polo. Covers age-group, high school, Masters, and Olympic-level swimming.

www.swimnetwork.com   The official news site on the Internet for USA Swimming. The site includes news and updates about upcoming events, photos, archived race footage, and live coverage of dozens of swimming competitions around the United States every year.

www.swimnews.com   Internet site for *Swimnews Magazine* and worldwide swimming news site. Includes stories from around the globe as well as the most updated source of the top-ranked swimming times of the year.

Find Competitive Events

usopenwaterswimming.org/   Website that maintains a hugely extensive database of open-water swimming contests in the United States and abroad.

www.active.com/swimming   An online site that offers a variety of information, from training tips to message boards to local event listings near your area.

www.fina.org   FINA is the worldwide governing body for aquatic sports; their website includes information about sports ranging from diving to synchronized swimming to pool swimming, open-water swimming, and water polo. The site also includes information regarding events, history, and statistics.

www.swimbikerun.org   Online resource for learning about triathlons and finding events near you.

Find a Local Masters Swimming Team

www.usms.org   United States Masters Swimming is the overseeing authority for Masters swimming in the United States. Their website includes ways of finding your local Masters club, upcoming event information, tips, a record database, and more.

Find a Local USA Swimming Club

www.usswim.org   As governing body for competitive swimming in the United States, this website is a mecca of information about the sport in America. It includes features ranging from training tips to local swim club information to biographies of the United States National Team.

Health Products

www.acquabody.com   Online retailer of active lifestyle body care products specially formulated for chlorine-soaked and sunburned skin.

www.healthenterprises.com   This online vendor sells a variety of products intended to help swimmers train more comfortably, offering products ranging from SwimFit earplugs to help prevent swimmer's ear to AfterSwim relief for water-clogged ears.

Swim Lessons

www.swimlessons.com   The biggest online resource for finding swim lessons. This website offers a database that includes the option of finding instruction ranging from an individual coach or even local swim schools.

Swimsuits, Caps, Goggles, and Other Gear

www.finisinc.com   The online store of Finis, manufacturer of swimming goods that include unique items such as the front-facing snorkel, monofin, and Zoomers fins.

www.hanspaddles.com   Created by Hall of Fame coach Dick Hannula, this website features and sells Coach Hannula's original holed paddles.

www.kastawayswimwear.com   Internet vendor that offers products ranging from the basics, such as customized swim caps, all the way up to advanced technology, such as the Vasa Trainer Ergometer.

www.kiefer.com   The online destination for Kiefer, a brand of its own and retailer of a variety of the most popular brands in swimming; the brand was started by 1936 Olympic champion Adolph Kiefer.

www.swimproshop.com   This online vendor is a quality source for a variety of swimming and water sport accessories and apparel for swimming, water polo, and other water activities.

www.swimtether.com   Online retailer of a stationary swimming installation that allows swimmers to utilize small pools and uniquely shaped bodies of water.

www.tyr.com   Web landing for the apparel company TYR, creator of a wide array of swimming suits and accessories as well as one of the world's most popular manufacturers of triathlon gear and open-water wetsuits.

Contributor Bios

Even though your journey with swimming may just be beginning, we wanted to make sure that you learned from some of the best, most educated professionals in the sport. We reached out and contacted champions of past and present to contribute some of their own advice to help you obtain and retain skills quickly. These are athletes who have competed at the highest level of the sport and, cumulatively, have over 100 years of swimming experience. They were gracious enough to lend their advice to help you avoid some beginner's mistakes that they themselves had to go through, as well as share some tips and tricks they discovered along the way.

The following contributors are some of the minds behind the technique advice and "The Pros Know" sidebars you've read throughout this book. Without them, this book wouldn't be the great resource that it is. Several of these athletes are still competitive while others are working in the coaching community; others are some of the faces and voices you see calling the action when you see swimming on television!

Megan Jendrick

In 2000, Megan won two Olympic gold medals at the Sydney Olympics, winning the individual 100-meter breaststroke and by swimming the breaststroke leg of the women's 400-meter medley relay. In 2008 at the Beijing Games, Megan took home a silver medal as part of the 400-meter medley relay. Over the course of her career, Megan has set 27 American and world records and won 10 U.S. National Championships, 10 U.S. Open titles, 3 World University Games gold medals, and 2 World Championship silver medals. She is also a 3-time Masters world record holder and 10-time Masters national record holder.

Chloe Sutton

Chloe Sutton is America's first-ever open-water Olympian, having competed in the inaugural marathon swim at the 2008 Olympic Games in Beijing. Chloe has competed in the World Championships as both an open-water and pool swimmer and is a multiple national champion in both sports as well. She has won Pan American Games gold as well as gold and silver in open-water World Cup events.

Scott Goldblatt

Scott Goldblatt was a member of the 2000 Sydney and 2004 Athens Olympic teams for the United States. In 2000, he swam as part of the men's 4 × 200-meter freestyle relay, winning the silver medal. Four years later in Athens as part of that same relay, Goldblatt captured gold. Additionally, in international competition, Scott has won bronze and silver medals at World Championship events as well as gold and silver at the World University Games. During his collegiate career, Scott swam for the University of Texas and accumulated 14 All-American awards and was part of four NCAA Championship–winning relay teams.

Adam Mania

At the 2004 Summer Olympics in Athens, Adam competed for Poland. He also swam at the University of Wisconsin-Madison and became Big 10 Conference champion in the 400-yard freestyle relay. Adam was a 13-time All-American and has won two U.S. National Championships. Today, Adam has switched his nationality and now competes for the United States of America.

Mel Stewart

In 1992, Mel won two Olympic gold medals at the Barcelona Games, winning the 200-meter butterfly as well as taking part in the victorious men's 4 × 100-meter medley relay. At that same Olympics, Mel also took part in the 4 × 200-meter freestyle relay and helped Team USA capture bronze. Mel is also a 14-time U.S. National Champion, a World Championships gold and silver medalist, and a 4-time Pan Pacific Championships gold medalist.

Tommy Hannan

Tommy competed in the 1999 World University Games, winning a gold medal, and during the 2000 Sydney Olympics he helped lead Team USA to gold as part of the 4 × 100-meter medley relay. Later, while swimming at the University of Texas, Tommy also was part of three NCAA championship teams. After retiring from competitive swimming, Tommy went on to coach at the Division I level as an assistant coach at the University of Washington.

Index

Numbers

A

B

F

W-X-Y-Z

CHECK OUT THESE BEST-SELLERS

More than 450 titles available at booksellers and online retailers everywhere!

978-1-59257-115-4

978-1-59257-900-6

978-1-59257-855-9

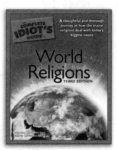

978-1-59257-222-9

978-1-59257-957-0

978-1-59257-785-9

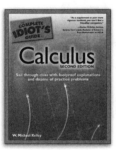

978-1-59257-471-1

978-1-59257-483-4

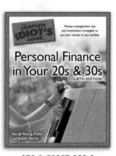

978-1-59257-883-2

978-1-59257-966-2

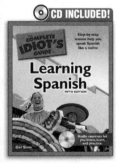

978-1-59257-908-2

978-1-59257-786-6

978-1-59257-954-9

978-1-59257-437-7

978-1-59257-888-7

ALPHA   idiotsguides.com

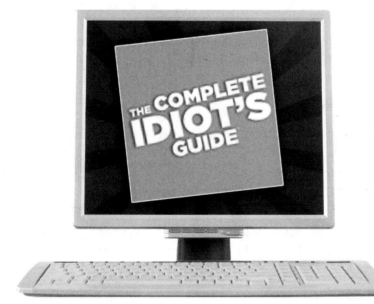